GARDNER'S *guide to*

television
scriptwriting
the writer's road map

Marilyn Webber

GARTH GARDNER COMPANY

GGC publishing

Washington DC, USA · London, UK

Art Director: Nic Banks
Editor: Bonney Ford
Cover Illustration: Nic Banks
Project Director: Garth Gardner, Ph.D.

Editorial inquiries concerning this book should be addressed to the editor at
GGC, Inc., 2545 Sandbourne Lane, Herndon VA 20171

This publication is designed to provide accurate and authoritative information in
regard to the subject matter covered. It is sold with the understanding that the
publisher is not engaged in rendering professional services. If professional advice
or other expert assistance is required, the services of a competent professional
person should be sought.

"Gardner's Guide" is a trademark of Garth Gardner Company, Inc.

Library of Congress Cataloging-in-Publication Data

Webber, Marilyn.
    Gardner's guide to television scriptwriting : the writer's road map / Marilyn
Webber.
       p. cm.
    Includes index.
    ISBN 1-58965-004-2 (pbk.)
       1. Television authorship. I. Title.

PN1992.7 .W38 2002
808.2'25—dc21

2002013042

Printed in Canada

Table of Contents

Acknowledgments

I could not begin this book without acknowledging Garth Gardner, my publisher who believed in these books; and Bonney Ford, my editor, who also looked upon the Writer's Road Map series as a labor of love.

In addition, I would like to thank Rick Copp and David Goodman, friends and colleagues, who hired me for my first prime-time freelance assignment. Also, a special thanks also goes out to my dear friend, Linda Steiner, at Warner Bros. who hired me for my first one hour drama assignment.

As always, to all my teachers, both past and future, I send my heartfelt gratitude for making my journey of learning an interesting one. To all my students, both past and future, I also say, "Thanks," for compelling me to continue stretching as both a writer and a teacher.

Last, but certainly not least, to every television writer, director, producer, editor, cinematographer, actor, musician, etc. whose work has inspired my passion for television writing and whose names are too numerous to list here, bless you. To each of you, I owe a lifetime of gratitude.

Author! Author!
About the Author

Marilyn Webber's work has garnered nominations for both an ACADEMY AWARD and a HUMANITAS. In addition, she has won an NAACP AWARD, an NEA AWARD: For The Advancement of Learning in Broadcasting, an AMERICAN ASSOCIATION LIBRARY AWARD: For Most Notable Children's Video. Her short film was WINNER OF THE INDIANA FILM FESTIVAL.

Earning her M.F.A. at The American Film Institute, she has worked as a professional writer in Los Angeles for the past eight years. She began her career in children's programming, writing Saturday morning cartoons and animation teleplays before switching to one hour dramas and action/adventure for both day time and prime time TV.

Miss Webber has freelanced for networks such as ABC and CBS, and for studios such as; Universal, Disney, and UPN. Her feature film, "Murder Seen" was recently produced by Saban Entertainment, and her screenplays have been optioned by numerous producers including those at Hearst Entertainment, Saban Entertainment, and Paramount Pictures.

In addition, her romantic comedy, *Killing Harry*, won BEST SCREENPLAY at the Texas Film Festival while recently her two hour teleplay, *A.K.A.*, won "BEST TV PILOT" in the ScriptapaloozaTV Contest. Several other of her screenplays have placed as finalists in The Writer's Foundation AMERICA'S BEST CONTEST.

A member of the Writer's Guild of America, she has also been a judge for the Cable Ace Awards in the category of dramatic writing. In addition, Miss Webber has taught creative writing extension courses through Johns Hopkins University IAAY program. Occasionally, she consults as script analyst for several A-lists writers.

Currently, she is producing and writing an animated feature for Omniway Solutions. In addition, she has recently finished a television pilot and feature film. She continues her nonfiction book series for Garth Gardner Company Publishing.

Introduction

Are you a confirmed couch potato who secretly yearns to write your own TV series or snag a job as a staff writer on a hit television show? If your answer is yes, this book is for you! Whether you're a novice writer or a writer looking for a new medium to stretch your literary muscles, everything you need to know to turn your script idea into a teleplay is right here. *Writing One Hour Teleplays: The Writer's Road Map* will guide you through various exercises, helping you turn your story ideas into a TV series pilot script and/or a TV spec script for an existing series. In addition, this book will guide you in developing and pitching your TV series and/or episode ideas for a current series once you have completed your two one hour scripts. These two scripts will be your calling card.

Writing for television is not only a thrill, but it can be very lucrative as well. Not only do you get paid for the initial script, but every time your episode airs past the original run, you get a check called a (which is residual generally about half of your original pay for the script, and continues to decrease by half to a WGA set percentage). In addition, you get paid foreign residuals when your episode(s) appears overseas. These checks appear like free gifts because the work has long been done. Besides accumulating wealth and fame, there is one other added bonus: the next time your parent, spouse, or significant other complains about the TV time you're logging, you can defend all your viewing as research.

With more and more opportunities available for writers every year in television, why not give writing for TV a try? Television writers are actually respected; they even get to become producers of the series for which they write. Ergo, they have more say in how their script is produced, directed, cast, and edited. Screenwriters are often cut out of the process as soon as their script is sold, and don't see their "baby" again until it appears on screen. By then, it's usually been rewritten by numerous writers to the point that it may be unrecognizable to the original writer. This can be a very heart-breaking experience. In television, however, as a freelance writer, you work closely with the producers who are the top writers of the show. If you impress them, you can end up with a coveted staff job. That means you'll write for that one particular show, and you're on your way to making the big bucks! Each consecutive year, you'll advance up the literary ladder, moving from a staff position to a story editor, then co-producer, producer, and finally to executive producer where you have the greatest control over your work (and also a huge paycheck per episode - think six figures and more on network TV).

All the networks and cable channels have more and more need for products. Each network and many of the cable channels develop almost two dozen episodes per series. That's a lot of scripts required. Now while most are written by staff writers, it is customary for these series to freelance at least two of its episodes per year, and that is where a new writer can get his/her foot into the door. All you need is two one-hour sample teleplays that prove your writing talents.

Through simple analogy, *Writing One Hour Teleplays: The Writer's Road Map* includes everything you need to know to write a one hour TV spec or pilot. It depicts: distinctions between television genres, the basic four act structure, TV plot gimmicks, character types and motivations, scene construction, dialogue devices, themes, prose, and rewrite checklists. It also discusses the do's and don'ts in writing sample teleplays as well as showing how to create a television series and pilot script, and/or sample scripts that the reader (and hopefully future audience) will find appealing.

Once you've completed your one hour scripts, *Writing One Hour Teleplays: The Writer's Road Map* will give helpful hints about how to get your scripts read by agents and producers, as well as how to pitch your series idea to the appropriate people.

Regardless of what your writing goals are, *Writing One Hour Teleplays: The Writer's Road Map*, will zoom you onto the road of TV writing in an easy manner. So stop talking about that great idea and start putting it down on paper. By the time you finish Chapter One, you'll be on your way to a thrilling new career. Being a couch potato can actually pay off - at least in the wonderful world of television.

Chapter One
TV Tunnels

The basic genres of television include drama, romantic comedy, action/adventure, science-fiction, mystery, and fantasy. These categories can be divided into numerous other one hour genres, with new TV genres created all the time in hybrid forms. Some of the most popular genres include: family drama, cop drama/action, courtroom drama, mystery, medical drama, romance comedy/drama, daytime/ nighttime soap opera, teen, western/ pioneer, science-fiction, political, war, horror, and fantasy. Each genre is a tunnel in which the style of writing is exclusive to that particular TV series. Genres do cross over into other genres. For example, you'll have some kind of action in many of these genres, but that doesn't necessarily make it an action tunnel. Likewise, all genres will include some type of drama. Grasp what tone dominates the series, and ask what is the main story of each episode about? What is the audience tuning in each week to see? The answers to these questions will help you categorize the show's genre if it isn't already obvious to you.

A major trend favors combining genre tunnels to create new hybrids. Ten years ago, *Law & Order* offered a fresh new genre by combining the cop drama with the courtroom drama. The first half of the hour would be told from the detectives' point of view while the second half of the hour would be from the district attorneys' POV. *Buffy The*

Vampire Slayer brought us the horror dramedy (comedy/drama) and *Smallville* constructed a teen fantasy drama. Mixing and matching tunnels helps to create a series that's fresh and different, yet familiar too.

Let's take a closer look at these popular TV tunnels:

1 Family Drama

This tunnel never goes out of style. It generally focuses on the characters in one family, although the family can be a group of friends that serve as a family group. The story's main plot lines are most often character plots. That is, the story derives from the traits and needs of the series' characters and their relationships to each other. It is an emotional story line. The audience watches each week to see what happens to the characters and to witness issues that are relevant to their own families. This type of tunnel often has a moral or lesson plotted within its structure (as we will discuss in the next chapter). Sometimes, this tunnel debates various sides of a moral and/or ethical issue, using its characters to present different points of view on the subject.

Series such as *7th Heaven, Judging Amy*, and *Once & Again* represent this genre. *Judging Amy* breathes new life into the family drama by focusing one of its main plots on a juvenile court case and the other main plot on a family storyline, creating a hybrid of family and courtroom drama. *Once & Again* portrays two families overcoming the devastation of divorce and finding hope in new relationships as they strive to become one family. *Thirty Something* examines the joys and tribulations of marriage and single life through a group of seven friends.

2 Cop Drama/Action

This tunnel divides into two categories: cop drama or cop action. It examines the lives and the job of cops and detectives in a particular city. It can be an ensemble of characters, or a show focusing on a particular pair of cops. It almost always opens with the characters arriving on the crime scene or with the actual crime in progress, and from here the story spins. This is the crime the cops will solve or not solve by the end of the episode. The audience watches because they are fascinated by crime stories as well as by the intricate and complicated lives of those honorable and sometimes not so honorable men and women in blue. The A-story (main plot line) will always be about solving the crime while the B-story (subplot) will generally involve the character story about one of the detectives or cops. A third plot line will usually involve a second crime to solve by the supporting characters of the series. Often you'll see current true-life crime fictionalized in this tunnel.

Series like *Homicide*, *NYPD Blue*, and *Hill Street Blues* illustrate this tunnel through an ensemble cast. Shows such as *Cagney & Lacey*, *Nash Bridges*, and *Miami Vice* present the crime dramas about police partners.

3 Courtroom Drama

Generally in the opening, the audience is introduced to a character in desperate need of a lawyer. The A-Story is always about the case, and the A-story's climax is almost always going to end with the verdict. Within this tunnel, we get to watch the cleverness of the lawyers solving and unraveling their cases. Sometimes, the lawyers' beliefs and ethics will clash with a case and/or client they or their associate must represent which makes for great drama. Other times, the lawyers play detectives, uncovering clues which may prove or disprove their client's innocence, like in *Matlock*. The audience tunes into these series to see if justice is served. These shows often point out flaws in the current justice system as well as present ethical and/or moral issues in debate in today's society. For this reason, these series are more cerebral than some of the other TV tunnels.

The *Practice* and *Family Law* bring us into the world of lawyers and their relationships while *J.A.G.* mixes and matches the courtroom drama with the action/adventure tunnel to form a unique show (and new hybrid genre) about the lives of the naval judge advocate generals. Likewise, *L.A. Law* mixed and matched tunnels to form an exciting courtroom nighttime soap opera.

4 Mystery

Mysteries can be divided into those series which offer a lone private investigator, a team of private investigators, and the non-professional mystery solver. These whodunits are a fun way to pass time and allow the audience to play amateur detective from his/her couch while munching on pizza. We, as viewers, tune in to follow the clues and solve the mystery (who committed the crime and how they pulled it off) before the detective does. These series almost always open with a crime which spins the A-story (main plot). In the fourth act, the criminal and his/her motive is revealed.

While most of these series are set within the world of the private investigator(s), they don't have to be. *Murder She Wrote* and *Diagnosis For Murder* weave mysteries that are solved by a novel writer and a doctor respectively. *Magnum P.I.* and *Nero Wolfe* also are examples of this TV tunnel and take us into the world of the private investigator. *Crossing Jordan* and *C.S.I.* cleverly and informatively brings us into a whole new world as it introduces audiences to forensic detectives.

5 Medical Drama

This is always a favorite tunnel because writers can extract so much dramatic conflict from the medical arena. Disease, accidents, violence - this tunnel has everything. These dramas often open with a person(s) needing medical attention and from there, the doctors spring into the storylines. Through the subplots, the medical staff's relationships with friends, lovers, spouses, and children, are revealed. The A-story will wrap up with the patient either dying, being cured, or remaining status quo while the doctor will have survived another tough day of playing God. These shows can bring an audience information about current health issues and allow us into that life-or-death scenario without ever having to leave our livingroom. This tunnel reminds us of the fragility of life, and therefore, can help the audience see what is really important in life.

St. Elsewhere brilliantly depicts the lives of the patients, doctors, nurses, and even orderlies in the Boston County Hospital of St. Eligius. *ER* brings us into the exciting and often gruesome world of emergency room doctors and nurses while *Strong Medicine* focuses heavily on the health issues concerning women.

Shows like *Emergency* and *The Third Watch* take us onto the streets and to the patient, allowing us to ride along with the paramedics and experience the adrenaline as the paramedics face the ever amazing challenges that we humans get ourselves into. Since they take us outside the hospital, they are more likely to contain more action in the plot than usually found in the medical drama arena, and thus are categorized as medical action dramas.

6 Romance Comedy/Drama

Or dramedy, as they are sometimes called, is a fairly even mixing of comedy and drama in a series. These series usually have a cast of quirky characters, two of which are destined to be together. This romantic element allows an audience to root for two characters who we know belong together, but on the show often appear to hate each other (or they like each other, but are too afraid to admit it). Sometimes, they realize they like each other, but one or both are unavailable due to other relationships they are in.

In this tunnel, the audience watches to see these two main characters get together. Every week, the two either battle it out, protesting their true feelings for each other in the course of whatever else is going on in their lives and/or mope about the fact that they can't be together. This tunnel provides us with laughs and dramatic tension as well as with romance. Most often the characters do not get together until the last episode of the series, because, if they do, then the viewers have no more reason to watch the show. Once the characters get together, the audience wants them to live happily ever after. So getting the couple together only to break them up makes the audience feel cheated. The viewer wants the tease, the courtship, that first kiss, but they don't want to see them together until the final episode. There are exceptions, but it is tricky to get the two characters together and then play out their relationship weekly because the story's suspense is dissipated.

TV series such as *Northern Exposure* depict two main characters destined for each other, but who put up quite a fight before they finally get together. *Ed* falls into this category as well. *Moonlighting* was a brilliantly written mystery romance comedy-drama set in the world of the private eye. It crossed tunnels to create a snappy show with charged verbal sparring between David Addison and Maddie Hayes. Even though the A-story was about the mystery, I place it in this tunnel because each week viewers tuned in, not to see the crime solved, but to see whether or not David and Maddie would finally get together.

7 Nighttime Soap Opera

The nighttime soap opera really found its audience in the late seventies and early eighties by taking the audience into the world of fascinating characters who were most often powerful and wealthy. In this tunnel, generally, a secret (or several secrets) hangs over one or more of the characters, threatening their doom if revealed. Of course, what really distinguishes the soap opera from a regular family drama or episodic series is the fact that the soap opera must have an arch rival with whom the main character battles weekly. Each week the characters fight against their nemesis and get themselves into tangled messes. Here, the villain can be very interesting because one week s/he can be someone to sympathize with, maybe even root for, and then next week, s/he can become someone the audience loves to hate. Remember J.R. Ewing from *Dallas* and Gregory Sumner from *Knot's Landing*? Both of these nighttime soaps offered us very complex villains to hate and occasionally, to sympathize with.

Series such as *Dallas, Knot's Landing,* and *Falcon Crest* had folks talking all across the season's best cliffhangers: "Who Shot J.R.?" (*Dallas,* 1979-1980 season).

Beverly Hills 90210 reintroduced the popularity of prime-time soaps by creating a teen soap opera which took us into the wealthy world of Beverly Hills teens. Its spinoff, *Melrose Place,* gained popularity after it brought in a villainess, Amanda, played by Heather Locklear.

8 Teen

A current trend of the late nineties, this tunnel puts us into the life of today's angst ridden teen, "angst" being the key word. It focuses on the bonds of friendship, the trials of high school (or college), and the frustration of growing up. This pulls in an audience from two areas: those who are currently teenagers and those who watch to reminisce about their school days. The A-story most likely is a character driven one and will probably depict various issues and hot topics on today's teen scene.

Series such as *Dawson's Creek, My So-Called Life,* and *Felicity* reveal the pain of growing up and coming of age in the 21st Century. *Roswell* combined the teen angst genre with the sci-fi tunnel to create a teen-sci-fi genre.

9 Western/Pioneer

This tunnel depicts the daily hardships of survival in the old west. Often, the audience follows one main family as it deals with some of the same issues facing families of today as well as presenting issues which only our ancestors encountered. Most often, this tunnel depicts good vs. evil (and good almost always wins). Usually, it has a moral to the story. It is a nostalgic tunnel, and the audience watches to see a country emerging in a more innocent time. It's like comfort food. For this reason, we often think of these series as life in a simpler time when most folks were decent and honest, carving their lives out of the wilderness.

Dr. Quinn, Medicine Woman, *Little House On The Prairie*, and *The Ponderosa* all fit this tunnel.

10 Science-Fiction

The sci-fi tunnel can factor in all sorts of interesting elements like the paranormal, space, time travel, aliens…This genre most often is either science-fiction action or science fiction drama, and can be great fun to write or create. The one steadfast rule in the sci-fi drama, however, is to make sure your science-fiction is based on some kind of science. Bad sci-fi ignores the laws of science. Do your research, and make sure you have some type of scientific facts from which to create your fiction.

Quantum Leap offers a time travel series while *Enterprise* brings us a space action series as the first crew of the Enterprise explores the vast regions of space. In its sci-fi tunnel, *The X-Files* uses every element of science-fiction, combining stories about the paranormal, aliens, time travel, space, and even government conspiracy.

11 Political

This tunnel encompasses shows that explore the political arena, and/or various departments within our government, and is the current trend of the millennium. It can be a thriller, action, or drama series with an ensemble cast or a more central hero. If the tunnel is a political action and/or thriller, your teleplay will involve more action sequences than any of the other genres, building the story and culminating in the story's climax with more and bigger action. You must keep hurling obstacles continuously at the characters in this tunnel, causing them to scramble to solve or escape such dangers.

24 is the utmost example of the political action-thriller. Every story line is driven by action. A Fox series, *24* tells the story of counter terrorist agent, Jack Bauer, who has twenty-four hours to stop a political assassin on the eve of the presidential primary in California. The clever hook for this show is that there will be twenty-four episodes (instead of the usual twenty-two) in its one year season because each show is one hour in that twenty-four hour deadline. Thus, every scene is a literal race against time as the show brilliantly captivates the audience's attention by playing out in real time. *Alias* and *La Femme Nikita* are series which also fall into the political action and/or thriller tunnel.

West Wing fits the political drama tunnel by taking the audience into the White House like no series has done before it. It allows the audience to experience the pressures and responsibilities of being the President and/or one of his staff members. With a marvelous ensemble cast and interesting and relevant storylines, this series gives the viewer a look into the everyday workings of democracy.

12 War

This tunnel's episode often is a mission story, and can be either a war action or war drama tunnel. In the war action, each episode will likely be about a new mission the men/ have to carry out. Their success or failure could determine the course of the war or the success of another vital mission. Every episode is about survival. In the war drama tunnel, the storylines generally focus around an ensemble cast. As an audience, we watch to understand what it must have been like for these men and women in uniform to serve our country under such extraordinary circumstances. This tunnel examines the complex moral and ethical questions war raises.

Combat! first took us into the war arena on a weekly basis. *Baa, Baa, Black Sheep* allowed us to experience the lives of WWII marine squadron pilots. *China Beach* showed us what it was like to serve in a mobile medical hospital during the Vietnam war, combining the war drama with the medical drama.

13 Horror

This tunnel provides thrills and chills as the main character is stalked by creepy villains. It examines the dark side of humanity and/or creatures, extracting stories from famous fables, legends, and folklore where the themes of good vs evil are explored. Each episode generally ends in a climactic battle between the hero and the creature du jour.

Buffy The Vampire Slayer mixes the horror tunnel with the comedy/drama tunnel to create a wild new genre. It's spinoff, *Angel,* likewise mixed drama and horror to find its tunnel boundaries. *Charmed* cleverly mixed the family drama with horror tunnel to create a story about three sisters, who just happen to be witches, and who must also follow their destiny of ridding evil from the world (or at least from their lives).

14 Fantasy

This tunnel has an element of magic, mythical, and wishful desire to it. It creates pure escapism for the audience, and can be combined with many of the previous tunnels discussed to create an original series. They are often feel good shows, and so usually have good ratings.

Twice In A Lifetime allows the characters to relive their lives and do it right this time, while *Touched By An Angel* reveals the lost souls of different guest characters each week who are helped by our main characters, angels sent by God to help the character find his/her way again.

Smallville blends the teen-angst drama with a touch of fantasy as it tells the story of Clark Kent; only this time we see Superman as a teen growing up in Smallville, Kansas. Unable to understand his unique powers, he must keep them a secret which adds up to major angst, and brings a fresh twist to an old comic book character.

Tunnel Vision

As a writer, decide which genre best fits your writing style and holds your interest. If you're brilliant at writing action, then perhaps you want to create sample scripts for political thrillers or cop action tunnels that allow you to showoff this talent. It's also important to familiarize yourself with the various TV series currently on the air. What is the popular trend? Certainly, teen, cops and sci-fi in the 1990's. In the new millennium, courtroom dramas and political action appear to be on the rise.

Whichever tunnel you choose, you'll want to write *both* sample scripts in that genre. Producers will want to read at least two sample scripts from the *same* genre as their series to see if you have an understanding of the genre. Also choose two series which have been on the air at least a year, and one that is currently "hot," that is, one which is splashed across the magazines and entertainment shows. You want to write for a show that has good ratings and critical acclaim, a show that is respected among the industry. Don't associate yourself with some show that may not return to television the following season because then your spec teleplay won't be current - it'll be dead and you can't show it.

Unfortunately, you can never truly be secure in writing a spec script. A critically acclaimed series can still be canceled, and even if it is successful, elements may change on the series which makes your spec obsolete. Case in point: when *NYPD Blue* premiered, I immediately knew this is the series for which to write a spec. It's hot; it's current; it's got critical acclaim. It will definitely be nominated for the Emmy and it will by around for years. And fortunately, I was correct in all those assumptions. So in earnest, I studied the show, tracked the episodes week by week, then developed my story and wrote a spec script. Just as my agent was ready to send it out, David Caruso (who played Detective John Kelley) decided to leave the show. Poof! Four months work down the drain in an instant. You just never know.

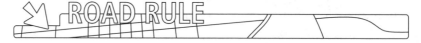

Road Rule #1: Whatever genre you choose, remain within its tunnel boundaries.

You must have tunnel vision when it comes to genre. Don't mark yourself as an amateur by writing a action episode for a family drama. That's not to say that sometimes a show might break out of its tunnel, but when this happens, you can bet it's one of the show's producers breaking the mold, not someone trying to get their first freelance assignment.

NOTE: For the exercise below, choose TV series presently in production, popular with either critics or the audience, and the genre you are interested in writing. Pick a series you are passionate about as you will be viewing and reviewing the same episodes throughout the course of this book. **Don't, however, choose the series for which you eventually want to write.** For legal reasons, producers can't and won't read sample scripts written for their own show. They don't want to be accused of stealing ideas submitted to them so choose a series *similar* to the one for which you would like to write, one which will show off your skills as a writer, and the genre in which you wish to work.

Exercise 1. List the two TV series for which you would like to write your two sample episodes. If you are writing your own original pilot script, choose just one series for which to write a sample spec.

NOTE: Those creating your own original series will develop a pilot teleplay for your series and a spec teleplay from an existing series that's in the same genre of your pilot script. You want to have a script which illustrates that you can also write for someone else's characters and TV world as well as your own.

Exercise 2.A. Record and view three episodes for each of the two series you've chosen to write your sample teleplays (make sure both series are of the same genre). That's a total of six hours. Record each of the three in consecutive order if possible.

Exercise 2.B. Record and watch three episodes for the one series you've chosen to write your sample spec teleplay (for a total of three hours).

Make sure it is of the same genre/tunnel as the original pilot script you are creating. Record the three episodes in consecutive order if possible.

Now, it's time to start constructing your story.

Chapter Two
The Premise

The premise of your script is what you as a writer want to say to the audience, and what your character will learn in the course of the story. In some series, your premise can be as simple as a moral or lesson as often found on the TV show, *7th Heaven*. The premise can also be just an idea that you as a writer want to prove to an audience, such as, "love conquers all", or "the needs of the many outweigh the needs of the few".

Regardless of what you want to convey, never state your premise in the form of a question. It must be a declaration and one worth proving, so use strong action verbs when forming it. In television, often you'll find that the premise of the episode is *implied* rather than *stated*, but either way is acceptable. It just depends on the rules of that particular TV series.

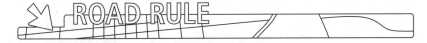

Road Rule #2: Your premise will be that flashing light in the distance that keeps you on course as you plot your script, and/or series.

Some television series even have a series's premise, meaning that there is an underlying premise which permeates throughout the entire series. For example, in *The X-Files*, the series premise is, "The truth is out there." This premise is stated in the credits. A premise that dominates many of the show's stories is, at least from the villains' point of view is "The needs of the many outweigh the needs of the few."

Most crime shows imply the premise "Crime doesn't pay" or "Justice triumphs." Only occasionally do these series allow the criminal to win, and in such cases, it is usually to imply that a law needs to be changed or updated so that more injustices won't occur. Shows such as *NYPD Blue* and *Law & Order* depict cops and lawyers defeating the criminal each week (at least most of the time) thus proving the premise that justice triumphs. *The Practice* series premise which reverberates through most of its episodes is "For the justice system to work, you must defend the guilty as fervently as the innocent." This premise often provides most of the main characters inner conflict as they sometimes sacrifice their own personal happiness and peace of mind for the greater good of the justice system. In *Buffy the Vampire Slayer*, the premise that prevails in almost every episode is, "Good triumphs over evil."

Sometimes, a character will state the premise somewhere in the episode, but whether it is spoken aloud or just implied, your premise must always be *embodied* in a character who will complete it at the end of the episode, or at the end of the story's arc which might occur over several episodes. A *series* premise, however, will not be answered until the last episode, otherwise, there's no place left for the series to go.

In *West Wing:* "The Fall's Gonna Kill You", the premise "lies destroy" is implied through several characters. Each character's career is threatened as s/he becomes part of the president's lie. Now the central question put forth in the following episodes is, "Will this lie destroy them all?"

In *Law & Order:* "Ritual" the premise is the "end justifies the means". This premise is embodied in the father, Mr. Martin, who in panic and desperation, accidentally kills a man who was going to perform a abhorrent operation on his preteen daughter. While he does accept a plea and will do jail time, the sympathy is with this father and his actions to protect his daughter at any cost.

Can you have a subpremise within the main premise? Absolutely, just make sure it enhances the main premise. For example:

In *Enterprise:* "Fight or Flight," the premise is, "You must believe in yourself. A subpremise is that, "To thrive in a new environment, you must adapt." These are the lessons Hoshi learns as these premises play out in the climax of the story's episode.

In *24:* "4:00a.m.-5:00a.m.", the premise is, "Sometimes you must sacrifice personal happiness for the greater good." "The needs of the many outweigh the needs of the few," is a subpremise.

In the beginning of the series arc (growth of a story) as Jack searches to stop the assassin, he cannot comfort or help his wife with their daughter's disappearance. Thus he must sacrifice the well-being of his own family for his job. Likewise, Senator Palmer's family sacrifices their own personal happiness in an effort to ensure the Senator a place in the White House. Both Jack and Senator Palmer pursue their respective careers in the belief (and subpremise of the series) that, "The needs of the many outweigh the needs of the few."

In *Gilmore Girls:* "Double Date," the premise is, "Lying gets you into trouble." This premise above is played out in the story like this:

Act One: Lane gets Rory to set up a double date with Todd.

Act Two: The girls decide not to tell Rory's mom about Lane's date as Lane is not allowed to date boys her parents haven't met and approved of; they'll just say they are meeting Rory's boyfriend at the movies.

Act Three: Lane and Rory meet the boys for a secret double date in the opening of the act and at the end of the act, Lane's mom discovers her daughter's deception.

Act Four: Mrs. Kim orders Lane home, and Lorelai reprimands Rory for not telling her the whole truth. Rory promises never to lie to her mom again and Lane is grounded, proving the premise.

NOTE: Those writing two samples for existing series, always follow the "A" exercises when given, and those writing an original pilot and one spec script for an existing series, always follow the "B" exercises when given.

Exercise 3A. From the six episodes you recorded, write down the premise of each. What is the writer saying to the audience? Was it spoken in the episode? If so, by whom?

Exercise 3B. From the three episodes you recorded, write down the premise of each. List if it was stated by a character in the episode, and if so, by whom.

(Hint: Since the premise is always embodied in a character, generally the character the story is focusing on, by examining what this character has learned during the course of the episode, the premise can be found.)

These exercises will help you start building your own list of premises. If you start keeping a journal of every television episode (and films too) you watch during the course of a year and write down what the writer conveyed to the audience (what the premise was) you will have an invaluable list of premises from which to build future story ideas. It's also a great way to see how the same premise can be executed in very different stories and in very different genres.

Exercise 4. Look over the premises you've listed along with those in this book. Pick one of these premises that you can build your story idea around. You may choose a subpremise as well.

Chapter Three
Universal Appeal

One of the first things executives or agents want to know is does your story have universal appeal? What is the idea that an audience can identify with? Is this idea something an audience has experienced or would like to experience? What jeopardy plagues the characters so the audience can relate to their plight? You want the audience to park and get into the car with your characters for that one hour ride. If they don't, it's surf city - that is, the viewer switches channels.

To develop a great central idea with universal appeal, psychologist Abraham Maslowe gave writers a good starting point when he pinpointed the seven basic needs that drive human beings. Choose one main need to build your character and story around, although you may want to use several of these needs throughout your story and/or series, both in the main plot and its subplots.

1 Survival is our most primary instincts. For a writer, it's that life vs death scenario. Our hero fights it out to the end. It can also be a life-threatening illness or accident which strikes a character. Most action/

adventure, medical, thriller, war, horror, and sci-fi series fall into this category. The audience immediately understands the hero's struggle: if the hero fails, s/he is dead (or someone s/he cares about is dead).

Buffy The Vampire Slayer
ER
24

2 Safety & Security: the need to have a safe place to call home. Western/ pioneer, family, cop, political, and courtroom series often construct their plots around this need.

The Ponderosa
Law & Order
West Wing

3 Love & Belonging denotes the need for family or community; for one character to connect to another, thus obviously, this need works well for family and teen dramas along with romance comedy/drama.

Smallville
Judging Amy
Dawson's Creek

4 Esteem & Self Respect are needs which must be earned. In these types of stories, your hero wants to be acknowledged for his/her accomplish-ments.

The lawyers in *The Practice*
Amy in *Judging Amy*
The teachers, principal, and vice principle in *Boston Public*

5 The need to know & understand drives many stories. Cop, science-fiction, courtroom, mystery, and medical series, often illustrate man's need to understand.

Crossing Jordan
The X-Files
C.S.I.

6 The spiritual drive to know there is something out there, a creative force which exists, the need to know that mankind is not alone, and that each life has its own purpose for being. Religious or artistic journeys use this need to appeal to audiences.

Enterprise
Touched By An Angel

Since this need is the most abstract, it can be the most difficult to convey as a writer, but it makes for great inner conflict for your characters. You just have to work harder to externalize your character's need and emotions into actions.

7 Self-actualization is the need to communicate our talents and ideas to others. Series starring an artist or athlete as its main character are likely to use this need to build the story around. In these stories, however, the drive for your hero is not that he desires to be rewarded for his special talent. Your hero dances, sings, or runs for one reason only: because your hero must do so, or s/he will die inwardly. Painting, composing, swimming, teaching, whatever talent you give your protagonist, is his/her heartbeat or life's breath.

The students of Juilliard in *Fame*
Vincent in *Judging Amy*

Exercise 5 Choose one or more of these psychological needs to build your story around. Also list any other of these seven needs which may also be woven into your story's subplots. In addition, if you are creating your own series, also list which psychological need will resonate throughout your series.

Now the real construction begins.

Chapter Four
The Central Idea

Next in constructing your television highway is the central idea. The central idea sums up in a sentence or two who and what your story is about. Around this central idea, you will develop your premise. Depending on the TV tunnel and rules of a particular series, there will be anywhere from 3-8 plot lines to alternate within an episode. Of course, the first two storylines, the A-story and the B-story are your most important ones (the third plot line would be the C-story, the fourth, the D-story, and so on). The A-story and B-story will comprise most of your script's pages, although in an ensemble cast series, the plot lines play out more evenly in regards to how much TV screen each story receives. You will have just 45-47 minutes to tell your story (that's an hour of TV minus the commercials). Thus, you will need somewhere between 56-62 scripted pages on average (we'll discuss this more in chapter 8).

To distinguish between the premise and the central idea, let's take a closer look at our examples:

In *West Wing:* "The Fall's Gonna Kill You," the premise is, "Lies destroy." The central idea is: as the White House Staff debates on how the president will go public with the coverup of his multiple sclerosis, we see the rippling effect this lie has on each character and their realization of its devastation. Babbish interrogates C.J. and then the First Lady while Josh and Leo plan a secret poll. Donna worries about a satellite that's falling from the sky, and Sam, oblivious to the impending doom, prepares a speech concerning the national budget.

In *Gilmore Girls:* "Double Date," the premise is, "Lying gets you into trouble." The central idea is Lane talks Rory into setting her up with Dean's friend, Todd, and the girls sneak out on the unapproved date. Meanwhile, Lorelai reluctantly agrees to double date with Sookie, Jackson, and his cousin, Rune. Soon, both regret aiding their friends as both dates become disasters of *Titanic* proportion.

In *24,* "4:00a.m.-5:00a.m.", the premise is, "Sometimes you have to sacrifice personal happiness for the greater good." The central idea is: Jack follows his only lead on the assassin, a suspect who's just murdered a cop; a lead that might also help him find his daughter, Kim, as his superior is hot on his trail and looking to sideline Jack. Meanwhile, Jack's wife, Teri waits for Janet to recover from surgery so she can ask her where Kim is, and elsewhere, Kim struggles to escape and survive the assassin. Senator Palmer has his own family problems as he worries about whether a reporter's story is true: did his son kill someone?

In *Enterprise:* "Fight or Flight," the central idea is that the Enterprise finally encounters intelligent life - only the aliens are dead. As they attempt to find out what happened, they discover all alien life is not friendly. In the course of the story, Hoshi overcomes her fears and learns to believe in herself when it's up to her to translate and communicate with the aliens. Her success or failure will determine whether the Enterprise crew will live or die.

In *Law & Order:* "Ritual" the premise is, "the end justifies the means," while the central idea is that a father commits manslaughter in order to protect his daughter from having a cultural ritual performed on her. The episode is meant to inform the audience of the inhumane practice of female circumcision.

From these central ideas, the writers of each of the examples above executed their episode's plot lines. For those of you developing your own series, you will have to create the central idea of your series as well. For example:

In *West Wing*, the central idea of the series is that the audience gets an inside look into the powerful and complicated world of politics through the administration of an underdog President and his White House Staff.

In *Gilmore Girls*, every episode will revolve around Lorelai and Rory, a mother and her daughter who are more like best friends than parent-child (the mother seems more like the child in the relationship whereas the daughter is more like the responsible adult). The twosome return to Lorelai's rural hometown in New England to start life anew, and face the usual family situations of life and love in the quirky town of Star's Hollow.

In *24*, the central idea is that counter terrorist agent, Jack Bauer, has just twenty-four hours to stop an assassination attempt on a powerful senator on the eve of the California Presidential Primary. As his family is pulled unwittingly into the danger, will Jack be able to save them all and stop the assassin?

In *Enterprise,* the central idea is the crew of the *Enterprise* sets out to explore space on a ship where the technology is very new and unsure. They will be lead by the enthusiastic Captain Archer, and sometimes a somewhat nervous crew member or two as deep space travel is novel and exciting instead of routine.

An updating of an old series, this series is set one hundred years into our future, which is one hundred years earlier than its original series, *Star Trek.*

In *Law & Order,* the series' central idea is that the viewer sees the process of law and justice, taking a case from the arrival of the cops at the crime scene, through their investigation, then to the district attorneys who will prosecute the case, and ending with the verdict.

In *The X-Files,* the central idea of the series is FBI Agent Fox Mulder investigates crimes with his partner, Dana Scully - that is crimes of the paranormal kind. In the course of these bizarre cases, the two also unravel a top-secret government conspiracy involving aliens.

In *Quantum Leap*, Sam Beckett is a scientist who learns the secret of time travel by leaping from one person to the next, but always within the scope of his own lifetime. The series central idea is that with each leap, he must help the person whose body he leaps into before he can leap into the next body. Each leap, he hopes will take him back to his own life.

The Three Basic Story Plots

Think of the central idea as the fuel which drives your script. To create a central idea, just remember:

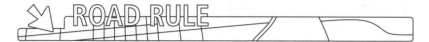

Road Rule #3: All stories come from a variation of the three basic plots the Greeks developed thousands of years ago; man versus nature, man versus man, man versus himself.

1 **Man vs Man:**
In the man vs man plot line, it often is a fight to the finish, but it can also be a non-life threatening competition between two characters. Whatever the characters are vying for, it must be extremely important to each of them. What is at stake is what drives the tension and emotion of the story.

Most action/adventure, thriller, horror, mystery, medical, courtroom, and cop series depict this type of plot for their stories.

In the *Enterprise*, "Fight or Flight," the crew is threatened by two different species. If Hoshi cannot communicate with the aliens, the Enterprise will be attacked and destroyed.

Throughout *The X-Files*, Mulder and Scully end many of the episodes in a life-threatening scenario as does Buffy and her entourage in *Buffy, the Vampire Slayer*.

In *ER*, the main characters sometimes face life and death, just like their patients, as they perform their jobs. In "Be Still My Heart," Lucy and Dr. Carter are stabbed by a schizophrenic patient, and Lucy dies. Most certainly, many of their patients wheeled into the emergency room each week face life and death.

When using the man vs man in a competition, it can be something as simple as a race or something more complex as vying for the girl.

In *Dawson's Creek*, many of the episodes revolved around the competition of Dawson and Pacey who both were vying for Joey's affection.

In *The Practice*, many of the courtroom cases also involved the heated rivalry between the lawyers of the firm and the district attorneys.

2 Man vs Nature:
The man vs nature plot line is generally a life or death situation as well. Here, the character struggles with nature's extremes: a storm, a flood, an earthquake, a volcano, a tornado, a hurricane, an avalanche, blizzard, etc.

In *Dawson's Creek,* "Two Gentlemen of Cape Side" our heroes struggle to survive a storm at sea.

In *Any Day Now,* "One Hour of Drama", Mary Elizabeth and her face to survive a tornado which ravages their neighborhood.

In *ER*'s "The Storm", Dr. Weaver and a new resident risk their lives to help a woman in labor who is trapped in an ambulance as a downed electrical wire snaps about the vehicle.

3 Man vs Himself:
The man vs himself scenario is a character plot line. It simply means that the character is his/her own worst enemy during the course of the story.

This type of storyline was used many times in *Dawson's Creek* with the character of Pacey who, in the beginning of the series, often believed he is not smart or worthy.

In *Enterprise,* "Fight or Flight," Hoshi is her own worst enemy as she allows her fears to damage her self-confidence as a translator.

In the *West Wing's* current story arc which covers numerous episodes, the president's choice to keep his multiple sclerosis a secret during his campaign, is perhaps now means for impeachment.

As you see, it really isn't that difficult to think of a storyline for your teleplay because you aren't coming up with an original plot. So take the pressure off yourself and let the ideas flow. If you have trouble coming up with ideas, "borrow" from the classics, or any favorite episode you remember from the past, just remember:

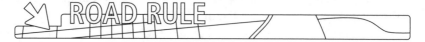

Road Rule #4: A good story idea always derives from character.

Story Road Flags

To help you build upon your central idea more extensively, you'll need to answer the following road flags to formulate the basis of your story.

1   Who is the story about?

2   What does the character want?

3   What or who tries to stop him or her?

4   What will the character achieve in the outcome of the story?

5   What is the universal appeal of your story? That is, what makes the person watching keep watching, and not change the channel?

Let's go back to one of our examples:

In the *Enterprise,* Hoshi feels like a fish out of water, or in this case, like the worm taken from her home planet. Her fears eat away at her self- confidence, especially when the crew boards an alien ship and discovers that the aliens have been murdered. While the Captain debates on what to do next, Hoshi attempts to learn the aliens' language from their ship's computers. When another ship of aliens return to discover what happened to their crew, they suspect the *Enterprise* crew are the murders. As the killers return to the scene of the crime, it's up to Hoshi to translate and communicate to the aliens. If she fails, the *Enterprise* and all its crew will be destroyed.

Flag One: Hoshi, the crew's translator.

Flag Two: To thrive in her new surroundings instead being frightened or uncomfortable aboard the ship.

Flag Three: Herself. In this episode, she is her own worst enemy by not trusting and believing in her talent to translate.
Flag Four: She will save the crew from the aliens and come to believe in herself and that she is of value to the crew.

Flag Five: Survival, the sense of belonging, safety and security.

Now you have rounded out your central idea into a full storyline. In the example above, we can see a beginning (Hoshi feels out of place in her new surroundings) a middle (Hoshi attempts her job, but fails and feels more frustrated and useless) and an end (Hoshi succeeds, saving the ship and her colleagues, realizing she does belong).

Series Road Flags

If you are creating your own series' central idea, you'll need to answer these following road flags:

1   Who is the series about?

2   What does/do the character(s) want?

3   What or who tries to stop him/her/them?

4   What will the character(s) achieve in the outcome of the series?

5   What is the marketability and the universal appeal to your story? That is, what makes the network drooling to buy it?

The Hook

Executives want to hear that something special. Giving your story a hook just means you're taking a story and spinning it in a unique way. This is what makes your story idea high-concept. High concept, simply put, means that you can pitch your story in a couple of sentences and network executives can immediately see the profitability of your idea.

For example, taking a well-known character and creating a fresh new look for him/her. Telling this character's story from a viewpoint we haven't seen before. Who couldn't see the selling potential of showing Superman as a teen, haunted by his special powers and unable to fit in among his peers? It is a brilliant hook that gave the WB Channel a smash hit with *Smallville*.

The hook for *Enterprise* is that it takes place a hundred years before the original *Star Trek* when space exploration is anything but routine and the ship is brand new with a lot of kinks to work out, sometimes creating apprehension among its crew.

When Gene Roddenberry first pitched *Star Trek* to NBC, he pitched it as a *Wagon Train* to the stars. (Building off the popularity of *Wagon Train* which was a big hit of its time.)

For the creators of Thirty-Something, Marshall Herskovitz and Ed Zwick pitched the show as, "you know how in cop shows you see the lives of the cops on the show and then the cop goes home at the end of the day and you see his marriage and family? Well, our show is just about the marriage." That's the hook.

24 created its hook by developing an exciting series around twenty-four episodes, each episode playing out in real time and representing an hour in the life of Jack Bauer, a counter terrorist agent, who must stop an assassin.

Building upon the huge success of the launching of MTV and the popularity of cop shows at the time, the famous NBC memo is probably the shortest hook of all time: "MTV cops". This, of course, became *Miami Vice*. Those two words encapsulated a brilliant hook and helped to develop a smash hit show in the eighties.

The examples above show the hook, that is why a certain show might appeal to viewers. Let's take a hook and combine it with the series road flags to form a pitch (the verbal or written sell of your story). Below is a series I am pitching with Michael Gleason, executive producer of *Remington Steele* and *Diagnosis Murder* to the various networks:

A.K.A. is a family drama with a twist: When Scott Allen inadvertently witnesses a mob hit on a federal agent, he and his family are thrown into the world of the hunted. As they enter the Witness Protection Program, the family is stripped of their identity and forced to live each day as a lie. While they face the normal family problems, they are cloaked with the threat of being discovered. In such crisis, will they become a closer family or will this secret life destroy them? Will the Grimaldi crime family find and execute Scott Allen and his family?

Does this pitch use all the road signs? Let's examine:

Flag One: The Allen family.

Flag Two: To stay alive while also trying to survive the trauma that is now befallen them.

Flag Three: The Grimaldi crime family.

Flag Four: To reclaim their true identities again and get their lives back.

Flag Five: the hook is that the audience can experience the world of the Witness Protection Program and what it would be like if suddenly their lives changed in a single moment. This involves the universal appeal: survival, safety and security, love and belonging.

Chris Carter created the *The X-Files* by putting a spin on *The Night Stalker* from the seventies:

Instead of the newspaper reporter as the lead, the character is an FBI Agent who, due to his passion for the paranormal has been shuffled to a basement office and given the bizarre, low-profile cases. Haunted by a childhood memory, the abduction of his younger sister, he diligently searches for answers to her case as well. As he and his partner, Agent Dana Scully, encounter various paranormal creatures, they pursue the trail of a government conspiracy involving alien contact. Thus, Mulder is not only hunted by paranormal creatures, but also G-men who want to make sure he never finds the truth. The series will be dark, shot in shadows, as week after week Mulder searches for the truth.

Does this pitch use all the road signs? Let's examine:

Flag One: Fox Mulder (and Dana Scully)

Flag Two: To find out the truth about what happened to his sister. Was she abducted by aliens? Is there a government conspiracy?

Flag Three: Paranormal creatures and G-men.

Flag Four: To learn the truth about his sister and about the government's secret group.

Flag Five: the hook is he gets to fight aliens and creepy paranormal beings as he searches through the mystery of his sister's disappearance. This series will use the universal appeal of survival, safety and security, the need for self-respect, and most of all, the need to know and understand.

It's not hard to see why with the central idea above became such a hit series in 1993, and why *The X-Files* became such a phenomenon in pop culture. Despite cast changes, *The X-Files* still succeeded to grab its audience.

Exercise 6. From the six previously recorded TV episodes from exercise two (or three watched episodes if you are writing your own original series) list each of their central ideas. Compare how the central idea and premise merge together to complement each other. Which of the three basic plots did the episodes use? Did they use more than one?

NOTE: Yes, this is a lot of work, but you want to know the existing series from which you plan to develop your script(s), inside and out. The more work you do in the beginning, the easier and more successful your final drafts will be.

Exercise 7. Now choose one of the three types of main plot lines you will use for your first script, regardless of whether writing for an existing series or creating an original series.

Exercise 8. Using the premise you've chosen to write about in your first script, formulate the central idea for it. When you merge your central idea with your premise, make sure the two are compatible. In addition, for those writing an original series, you must also create the central idea of your series and merge it with your series' premise (thus you are doing this exercise twice: once for the story of your pilot episode, and once for the story of your series).

Exercise 9. Build your central idea using the story road flags. Use only four or five sentences to explain your story. As you construct your story, use all five road flags. Make sure your story has universal appeal. For those creating your own series, you must also build the central idea of your series using all five series road flags. Be sure your series has a salable hook.

Chapter Five
Dead End Ahead – The Central Question

The central question of your story is the focus of the plot, and the question which is answered in the course of an episode, a story arc (over several episodes) or a series. It's usually answered in the climax (the big clash or confrontation). The audience must not know the answer to the central question until the end of the episode, story arc, and/or series. On your Road Map, this question is labeled "Central (?) Avenue".

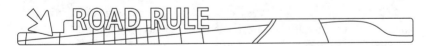

Road Rule #5: Before you construct your plot, know where your road ends. Knowing the ending of your story, will keep you from writing scenes which wander aimlessly in your teleplay, only to be discarded in the rewrite.

In your script, the Central (?) Avenue of the A-story will be answered in the climax of Act Four if the series is a contained one (concluded within the episode) or in a subsequent episode(s) if the series is continuing or episodic (the A-story continues into next week's episode). The number of central questions you have per episode, depends on how many plot lines you have. Each subplot must have its own central question. Whether it is answered in the episode, depends on the format of the series (we'll discuss this more in the following chapters).

In *West Wing:* "The Fall's Gonna Kill You," the premise is, "Lies destroy." Each character's career is threatened as he or she becomes part of the president's lie. Now the central question of the story's arc is put forth in the following episodes: "Will this lie destroy them all?" The central question for this particular episode's A-story is, "How will the American public react to the lie?"

The answer to this question will be played out over several episodes as *West Wing* is a continuing or episodic series.

In *Gilmore Girls:* "Double Date," the central question of the A-story, "Will Lane and Todd get together?" parallels the B-story central question, "Will Sookie and Jackson get together?" The premise ("Lying gets you into trouble") is played out in the C-story central question, "Will the girls get caught in their fib?" And the D-story central question is, "Will Lorelai pass her business exam?" One of the episodic storylines, the E-story plot in this episode, is: "Will Luke finally ask Lorelai out on a date?" The central questions to the A, B, C, and D plots are answered in Act Four, and the premise is proved in the climax of Act Four as Lane and Rory get caught in their fib.

In *24,* "4:00a.m.-5:00a.m.": the central question to the A-story line of the episode is, "Will Pentacost lead Jack to the assassin? Or to Kim, his daughter?" Other central questions in the episode include, "Will Janet survive to lead Teri to Kim?" and "Did Senator Palmer's son, Keith, murder Nicole's rapist?"

In *Enterprise:* "Fight or Flight," the central question of the A-story episode is "What happened to the dead alien crew?" The episode's B-story central question is, "Will Hoshi learn to believe in herself, put away her fears, and adapt to her new life in time to save the Enterprise?"

The above central questions merge together in Act Four, and conclude within the episode as that is this series format.

In *Law & Order:* "Ritual" the central question is, "Who murdered Joseph Mousaad and why?" The B-story central question is, "How can the D.A. best protect Allison?"

Series Central Question

For those of you creating your own series, you will have to think of a central question avenue for your series as well. Your series central question will affect how you plot your weekly stories, so consider it carefully. For those writing for an existing series, this relates to you as well. You might want to use one of the series' central question avenues for your plots.

There are two ways in which a TV series' executes its series' central question: with a continuing central question or a contained central question.

1 Continuing Central Question

This means that the series central question avenue runs the length of the series and isn't answered until the series finale. There's no reason for the audience to continue watching once they know the answer to this question. Thus, the continuing central question acts as a hook to keep the audience watching week after week.

Let's look at a few examples of a continuing central question for a series:

The X-Files: "Will Agent Mulder find the truth?"

Quantum Leap: "Will Sam Beckett's next leap be the leap home?"

Moonlighting: "Will David and Maddie get together?"

Using a continuing central question for your series can give the audience a compelling reason to watch the series every week, but it's not necessary. It all depends on what kind of story you want to tell. You might rather choose for your series a:

2 Contained Central Question

This type means that the same central question is asked each week, which makes the story format easy to plot. For example:

Law & Order: "Will the detectives and D.A. get the criminal?"

The Practice: "Will the defense attorneys win their case?"

Buffy The Vampire Slayer: "Will Buffy kill/defeat the creepy crawler of the week?"

Whatever existing series you have selected to write for, just be sure to incorporate its central question in your own plots when applicable.

Exercise 10. Before you develop your own central question avenues, identify those from the stories in the six or three episodes you watched for exercise two. Is the series a contained or a continuing one?

NOTE: If it's been awhile since you saw them, just watch the last few minutes to refresh your memory. What questions are answered or left open in Act Four?

Exercise 11. Write the central question for the A-story (main plot) and for any other subplots you're creating for your first teleplay. In addition, those creating your own series, write the central question avenue of your series as well. Will your series be contained or continuing?

Chapter Six
TV Bibles

Now that you have your genre, premise, universal appeal, central idea, and central question established for your first script, you need to think about from whose point of view (POV) your story be told. For those of you creating your own series to pitch, you'll also have to decide what time frame you are going to choose. What kind of world will your characters live in? Will your series be historical like *Dr. Quinn, Medicine Woman*, contemporary like *Judging Amy*, or futuristic like *Enterprise*? Does it have a solo character lead (*Alias*) or a duo lead (*The X-Files*) or an ensemble cast (*Boston Public*)? How are you going to narrate the story? Will it be told straight from beginning to end (*The Practice*) or will there be flashbacks (*Any Day Now*)? These are all questions you would answer in your series's bible. For those writing solely for existing shows, keep reading. This has relevance for you as well.

Every series has its own unique set of rules for its TV world and characters. These rules are the restricted lanes of the series's literary highway, and while you won't need to develop a bible to write your sample and/or original pilot script, you will need to understand the function of TV bibles and create information that would occur in such bibles.

For each television series, the creators of that series will write out the rules of their TV world in what is known as a series bible. The TV bible gives the overall view of the series, lists and describes the characters, describes what their relationships are to each other, and establishes the locale of the series. In addition, it contains all the details and plot restrictions of that particular series. In other words, it's the rule book. It is here where the creators capture the style and overall tone of the series. They will also include about half a dozen sample episodes for the series to give network executives an idea of how the series will play out over those first six episodes.

Generally, the TV series' bible consists of 10 to 25 pages and encompasses the following:

1 **Title page listing the title of the show, its genre, and the creators.**

2 **A summary or overview of what the series is about, what arena it is set in, and a brief listing of the main characters and/or villains. (3-5 pages)**

For example, this part of the *Enterprise* TV bible might read like:

The show is set in 2151, and for you non-Trekkies, that's a century before Captain Kirk. In other words, it's a *prequel* to *Star Trek* when space travel for humans is anything but routine. The captain may be gung-ho, but some of his crew can be a little hesitant about all the new technology and uncharted galactic frontier. The ship, the *Enterprise*, makes her maiden voyage which means there'll be a few kinks to work out as the crew travels along. Oh, and did we mention that if one dematerializes in the transport, the crew isn't exactly sure they can rematerialize him/her? Okay, so the ship's gadgets still have some bugs to them, but that makes this exploration in space all the more exciting as this interspecies crew searches for intelligent life.

The crew's roster reads as:

Captain Jonathan Archer, a space pioneer whose enthusiasm for exploration sometimes leads his crew into dangerous territory, but that's okay, because he treats his crew with respect and they'll follow him to the ends of the universe - literally.

T-Pol, is sub commander and a voluptuous Vulcan who doesn't understand humans and most definitely plays by the rule book, but then what else would you expect from those logical Vulcans?

Commander Charles "Trip" Tucker III, chief engineer, is a wisecracking adventurer eager to meet new aliens. He is a kind of overgrown Boy Scout with that impish kind of grin and charm.

Dr. Phlox is a bit of a New Age alien shaman who is very resourceful when it comes to healing. He's fascinated by all things human, especially our food. Somewhat of a philosopher, he's passionate about life and seeks to learn as much as he can about other life forms, in particular, those strange species with whom he's traveling.

Ensign Hoshi Sato, a nervous Japanese translator and linguistics specialist, isn't too confident in her new position aboard the *Enterprise,* but she'll have plenty of opportunities to prove herself.

Malcolm Reed is a security officer who loves his weapons as much as Scotty loves his engine room. So watch out!

Ensign Travis Mayweather, African American, who is the youngest on the crew, however he makes up for his age in experience. You see, he was raised by his parents on a deep space cargo ship and has seen a lot of the aliens.

As for the villains, well, let's just say they are out of this world. The crew must come up against everything from toxic pollen to hostile alien creatures. And that's just in the first few episodes!

3 **A compilation of all major and supporting characters, describing each and every character, including the villain(s), and their backstory. The bible also explains each character's relationship with the other characters on the show (2-8 written pages depending on whether this is a one or two main character series or an ensemble series.)**

This would be a further extension of your character list, only this would be a more in depth look at who each character is and how they relate to the other characters in the series. You don't want to be too long and verbose here, but you do want to include a more extensive view into each character's personality and their relationships with other characters in the series. Think paragraphs on each, not pages.

4 **It also lists all the rules of the series' particular TV world where the characters live and breathe. (1-4 pages)**

These are the boundaries by which the characters live. Generally, the more unique and interesting the rules, the more viewers you will capture.

Let's take a look at some of the rules of the TV world for *Quantum Leap*:

A. Sam Beckett's next leap will never be the leap home until the series' finale (with few exceptions). Each week he will leap into some new time and place and body.

NOTE: For a clever writer, there are always ways of breaking the rules if your story absolutely dictates it. In the rule above, the writers broke their rule of Sam never leaping home until the finale episode by having Sam leap into his childhood.

B.   The leap always has to be within the time span of Sam's life. Thus, he can't leap back to the Jurassic Period and hang out with the dinosaurs, or to the assassination of Lincoln because neither period occurs within the frame of his own life span.

C.   Sam Beckett is aided by his friend, Al, who appears in the form of a hologram. No one can see or hear Al except for Sam (well, sometimes little children, handicapped characters, or animals can, but only rarely and these are exception not the rule).

D.   Before Sam can leap into the next body, hopefully, his own, he must change the course of the person's life he's leaped into, for the better.

5   If applicable, explains how the particular TV world came into being. (1-3 pages)

In *Smallville*, the pilot episode depicts how a meteor crashed into the rural community of Smallville, Kansas, and how shards of the meteor still have varying affects on the townsfolk today. It also reveals how Lex Luther lost his hair and how Clark, as a toddler, found his parents after his ship landed in the meteor crash. All this info would be defined in the TV bible.

6   The set-up of what the show will be about each week which will include any plot rules applicable to the particular format of the series.

Let's go back to our example, *Quantum Leap*:

Each week the show opens with Sam Beckett in a comic and/or dangerous predicament as he leaps into the next body. As soon as Sam is able, he tries to catch a glimpse of who he looks like in the mirror which reflects the true physical image of the body Sam has leapt into. The story will revolve around Sam and Al trying to figure out why Sam has leaped into this particular person's life, who he is there to help (usually the person he's leapt into) and how he is to change this person's life for the better. Once he has accomplished this mission, he will automatically leap to the next person. Every show ends with a teaser of where and who Sam leaps into the following week to entice the audience to tune in the following week. As Sam takes in his new surroundings, he'll utter his famous line, "Oh, boy."

For *Law & Order*, every week will be about a particular crime and case. The teaser will open with a crime in progress or being discovered. The detectives arrive on scene, make a snappy comment, and we go to commercials. The detectives follow one lead after another, following the clues through acts one and two until they turn the suspect over to the district attorneys who then try to prosecute the case in acts three and four. Most of the time justice wins, but not always.

In *24*, each episode will play out in real time, that is whatever happens to our characters happens minute by minute in the course of one hour.

7 **A half dozen brief paragraphs of sample episodes for the series.**

This is where those 4-5 sentence story pitches you worked up for your central ideas in Chapter Four would go.

8 **The tone of the show which might include the style of dialogue for the show if it is unique. You can sprinkle a couple of lines of dialogue here for effect - just make sure they're very good lines. (1 page)**

For example, in *Moonlighting* TV bible, the creator would mention that the characters dialogue will overlap, and be rapid fire.

Television Writing Fines

These fines are what will leap off the page and shout, "amateur!" to the professional reader, because when producers and/or executives read spec scripts, there are certain things they watch out for. Make sure you follow the road rules below because you are beginning your television writing career, and believe me, you can't afford to be fined.

One of the most important factors producers watch for is to see if you truly know their show and their characters. In other words, they want to know if you've done your homework so:

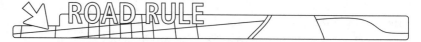

Road Rule #6: Don't break the rules of the series's TV world!

Whichever show you select to write for, make sure you stick within the rules of its TV world so you present yourself as a professional. You don't want to write an episode of *Diagnosis Murder* where the good doctor doesn't figure out who the killer is and the murderer gets away with his crime, because you would be breaking the rules of this show's TV world. Later, when you are established with a particular show and want to pitch a story that does break their rules because your story is sheer genius in its originality, by all means do so. Just don't attempt it when you're starting out because it can backfire on you.

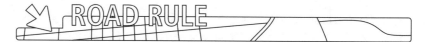

Road Rule #7: Limit crowd scenes unless the series often incorporates such scenes.

Any script that presents difficulty or greater costs to producers will be "ticketed" for a huge fine (that is, you can forget selling your spec pilot script or getting a freelance assignment). As a television writer, you have to be aware of the financial ramifications of producing what you write, especially if you aren't writing for one of the Big Four (ABC, CBS, NBC, and FOX). Cable channels don't have tons of money to pour into original shows so don't knock yourself out of the market by writing an original series or spec teleplay that demands hundreds of extras every week.

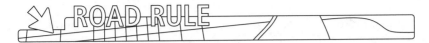

Road Rule #8: Don't add numerous new locations and/or new sets unless that is a rule of the TV world for which you are writing.

Sets for the TV series are established in the pilot episode and those episodes that follow. They are reused for time and cost efficiency. So use these sets and locations when you write your sample teleplay. Adding new locations and new sets in a series is costly. So is writing a story in which a set is remodeled and/or destroyed. In addition, by using established sets and locations, your script will look and read like the show for which you're writing.

For example, if you are writing an *ER* episode, stay within the *ER* and hospital area. While *ER* does occasionally go outside their arena (going to a train crash site or saving a boy in a flooded drain tunnel) these are special episodes written by established writers and producers. Producers don't want to know if you can write an *atypical* episode; they want to know if you can give them a dynamite story that takes place in the emergency room and hospital because that's the arena of their TV world.

If you wanted to write an *ER* episode, you'd want to keep most of your scenes in the emergency rooms, the waiting area, the corridors, and the front desk. The lounge or operating room sets could also utilized. Outside the *ER*, there is the diner set and the set area where the ambulances drop off patients and the doctors shoot hoops. There's also a heliport/roof set, and on occasion, various rooms in the private homes of the doctors are shown.

Study the show for which you want to write your sample script. Know the series' sets and locations so you can develop a story that incorporates as many of these as possible. You are not forced to use these places. Don't feel your creativity is being thwarted by these rules. You just want to prove you know the show and respect its financial limitations. If you need to add a new location or two, do so. Just don't create an episode which requires a dozen new locations and sets.

For those creating your own series, don't develop one which requires a cast of twenty characters traveling to exotic locales every week. You don't want to break any of these Road Rules for your series and suffer TV fines either. You want to keep your series idea as appealing as possible to network or studio executives. This means keeping costs low while coming up with a saleable series.

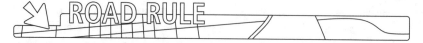

Road Rule #9: Don't kill off a series regular in your story!

Even if you have a super story on how Joey Potter is tragically killed, don't write it. Katie Holmes and the producers probably aren't ready for her to leave Dawson's Creek, and when they are, they'll be the ones writing that teary-eyed farewell episode.

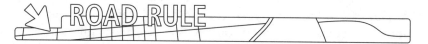

Road Rule #10: Follow the standard industry script format!

Use a format of 52 lines per page with the 52 lines appearing between the top and bottom holes of your three-hole punched paper (brads in top and bottom holes only). That falls in the range of a .170-.172" in line height using the industry's standard font "Courier New". Don't try to jazz up your teleplay by using some funky font. You'll only look like an amateur who's trying to pull attention away from his story.

Thus, regardless of whether writing an original pilot and/or a sample script for an existing series, you don't want to be "ticketed". You want your scripts to appear as professional as possible. Down the road, you will have greater flexibility once you have a track record with producers. For now, conform as much as possible in your own original way.

NOTE: Again, for those writing two sample scripts from two existing series, follow the A exercises. For those writing one sample teleplay from an existing series and one original pilot, follow the B exercises.

Exercise 12A. From the six episodes you recorded, write down all the rules in each of the two series that the characters follow in their TV world. List as many as you can observe.

Exercise 12B. List all the rules you observe in the three episodes of the series you recorded. Next list the rules for the TV series you are creating.

NOTE: Once you get a freelance assignment on a particular show with your sample scripts, you will have access to that TV series' bible so you can get to know their show even more.

Exercise 13. In each of the six or three episodes you recorded, go back through the episodes and see how many TV Fines, if any, occurred in these episodes. If they did break several rules, check out the writing credit. Odds are the writer was the executive producer who can afford such TV fines.

Exercise 14. Next, create a log of the locations and sets used in the six or three episodes you recorded. In addition, for those creating their own series, list the obvious sets and locales your series will be using.

Exercise 15. From the two or one series you've viewed, write the show's set-up. How is the story or plot played out each week? Repeat this exercise with your own original series if you are creating one. Just list brief overviews for now.

Chapter Seven
Graphing

The best way to learn the structure of a one hour series is by graphing numerous episodes of that series. By graphing, I mean writing down the structure of an episode, scene by scene. You do this by first recording the episode, then by making a list of its scenes as you view it. This way you can pause the recorded version while making your notes. Write down the location of the scene, the time of day in which it occurs, which characters are in the scene, what is the point of the scene, any important information listed in the scene that's relevant to major plots, and any line of dialogue that sums up the scene.

In addition, make a note of the real time the scene occurs in the episode. For example, when does the sixth scene occur? Four minutes into the episode? Two minutes? Or maybe even eight minutes into the episode? This will help you determine the approximate page that scene would fall on, as well as be a guide when you're trying to structure story sequences in later chapters.

Below, I have included the graphs of three one hour episodes which have already aired on television. These are the graphs we will be discussing in the subsequent chapters. These are my notes, and sometimes include my own shorthand. I chose these particular episodes for several reasons:

1   They are accessible for study in reruns

2   They represent various TV tunnels

3   They follow the Writer's TV Road Map Structure

4   The episode is from a successful series

5   They were produced by various networks and/or studios

NOTE: If you get a chance to record these three graphed episodes when they rerun, do so. You can also probably find a fan of the series who probably has every episode of a particular series taped. It isn't necessary to have seen the episodes to follow the examples, so if you can't view them, don't worry about it.

On average, there will be somewhere between 6-10 scenes or scene sequences per act in each one hour episode. Thus, in the graphs below, each scene is listed numerically and in order as it appears in the episode by four sets of tens. List the very last scene of each act on a multiple of ten as I have done in the examples below. (We'll discuss this plotting scheme more in the following chapters.)

Graph Of *West Wing*

"The Fall's Gonna Kill You"

Central Question of the story's arc: "Will this lie destroy them all?"

Central A-story Question: "How will the American public react to the lie?"

Central B-story: "How much trouble is C.J. in; will this lie ruin her career?"

Central C-story Question: "How much trouble is Abbey in; will this lie destroy the First Lady's career as a doctor?"

Central D-story: "Will Donna find anyone who cares about the satellite crashing to earth?" (The comic relief subplot)

Central E-story Question: "Will Sam change the line in his speech?"

Central F-story Question: "Will Leo give funding for the Justice Department to keep suing the big tobacco company?"

ACT ONE

(1) TEASER: Office of White House Counsel: 5:30a.m. C.J. Cregg waits, then Babbish asks if anyone saw her coming down to his office.

(2) They enter his office, and begin arguing, she's worried and defensive, he's trying to find out when she learned the President had Multiple Sclerosis. She admits she's lied about the president's health to the public on many occasions. (3 minutes into episode)

CREDITS (5 minutes)

(3) Mr. Connelly waiting to see Josh Lyman. Donna Moss learns a satellite is hurling to earth, worried where it will crash.

(4) Leo McGarry's Office: Toby Ziegler, Leo, Josh: Toby wants to see some polling on what people will think about an official who lied about his health before an election. Get Joey Lucas to do a poll secretively. Toby does not want to tell Sam about the president's coverup until after Sam writes a speech he's working on. The group disperses.

(5) Toby and Josh in hall, Toby warns Josh to be careful with Joey. Josh and Donna walk and talk as Donna informs him about the crashing satellite. (6) Josh's Office: Mr. Connelly meets with Josh, money is gone for the tobacco case, they need more from the Justice Department if they are going to win against the big cigarette companies. Connelly determined to take companies down because they perpetrated a fraud on Americans by lying that nicotine wasn't addicting. The fraud line hits home to Josh, that is what the president has done by not being honest with the American people about his illness.

(7) -writer did not use-

(8) -writer did not use-

(9) -writer did not use-

(10) GREEN LIGHT: C.J. reviews her press release about the president's health with Babbish. His secretary hands C.J. a note, and Babbish asks what's it say? C.J. replies that the sky is falling.

(13.5 minutes into the episode) Commercial Break:

ACT TWO (return 17 minutes into the episode)

(11) Conference Room: Sam Seaborn works with a group on speech, he is called out.

(12) Corridor: Sam walks with two people on the way to his office.

(13) Sam's Office: the threesome discuss the projected report on money they will have to spend, the national budget. It's good news for what they want to do.

(14) Babbish office: Babbish still with C.J., grills her on the day the president collapsed. She's sarcastic. He wants her to get out of the habit of giving too much of an answer, answering more than what is asked.

(15) Dining area: Sam finds Josh and gives him news about the national budget, that slower economic growth is expected, and that the Chicago people want a certain line put in the speech. Sam refuses to do so.

(16) Donna with Charlie, she's worried about the falling satellite, Charlie Young jokes about it, then gets beeped and rushes out, leaving Donna more worried.

(17) -writer did not use-

(18) The First Lady, Abigail (Abbey) Bartlet, returns from out of town. Gets out of car with her group and goes inside the White House.

(19) Secretary gives her a list of the First Lady's appointments as they walk through White House.

(20) MIDPOINT/U-TURN: Oval Office: the president and first lady argue; she's upset she wasn't told he was going public, he tells her he was forced to due to his intern reading a medical form she signed for their daughter, Zoey's college entrance. On the form, she did not mark MS under illnesses within the family. He tells her she will have to speak to the White House Council.

(25 minutes into the episode) - Commercial Break

ACT THREE (begins 29 minutes into the episode)

(21) Corridor: Leo and Josh discuss that the First Lady is back.

(22) Leo's Office: Josh asks Leo for thirty million for tobacco lawsuit. Leo tells him they will lose anyway and to staff it out for an analysis report, then get back to him later. Josh is on his way to the airport to meet Joey, their poll analyst.

(23) Ext. Shot of D.C. (30 minutes into episode)

(24) Sam meets with Jane Gentry and Richard Will, they argue to put in the line that their opponents want to help the rich pay for bigger jets and swimming pools. Sam says he is not going to put that in the speech.(33 min.)

(25) Airport: Joey meets with Josh, she has a new deaf interpreter, Josh asks him to leave them alone. They sit at a table and she reads his lips and passes notes as he tells her about the president's illness. They need a secretive poll to gauge how the public will take the news. She agrees to do it, using a governor who has a serious illness. (36 minutes into the episode)

(26) -writer did not use-

(27) -writer did not use-

(28)-writer did not use-

(29) -writer did not use-

(30) ROAD OF NO RETURN: Babbish's Office: First Lady enters, she chit chats nervously, then answers his questions awkwardly and elusive. She accuses him of using this to build his career, what a coup to defend the president. He says his career is just fine as it is, he's not looking forward to this, and he wasn't the one who lied. Fact is, in a week, they are going public with the information, and she better be ready to answer the tough questions because what's about to happen next is going to be huge!

(40 minutes into the episode) - Commercial break

ACT FOUR (return 44 minutes into the episode)

(31) Airport: Joey with Josh; he tells her they will be going public in a week, try a model poll that will get them the answers they need, and they need the results within ninety-six hours. She says she will do it. Says she will make it a governor of an industrial state with a degenerate illness. Josh warns her that by knowing this secret, she too will suffer repercussions. She understands, and asks how the president is doing. Josh says he's okay. She leaves and he destroys the note on the napkin by pushing down into his drink. (46 minutes into the episode)

(32) Corridor: Donna with Charlie; she's still upset about the satellite; he tells her it could have plutonium on it. Now she's more worried, and no one seems to be taking this seriously. First Lady joins them as Charlie exits. Donna and Abbey briefly chat; each one misinterpreting the conversation; one speaking about the satellite hurling towards earth, the other about the horrible lie about to explode. (47 minutes)

(33) C.J.'s Office: First Lady knocks and enters. Abbey apologizes about the lie, wanted to be with her when the president told C.J. C.J. is upset she didn't know, both are worried and afraid of what is to come. C.J. admits having seen Abbey give the president an injection during the campaign, and that she never really asked for more information, she always just asked if there was anything else she "needed" to know. (50 minutes)

(34) Leo's Office: Josh enters, tells him Joey's plan. He's worried what will happen, they too perpetrated a fraud on the public. He's scared they all will go down with the president. Leo says the public won't compare them with "big tobacco". Josh is not so sure. Leo excuses himself, the president is waiting. (51 minutes into the episode)

(35) Oval Office: President and Leo, president is upset at Leo; why did Leo tell Abbey about the form, that it was her mistake that's making them go public? Leo defends himself, the president knows it would have eventually come out, couldn't keep it from her. Leo tells president that Joey is doing a poll for them, and soon they should have some kind of statistics which will help them decide how to break it to the public and what to be prepared for. President tells Leo to get Sam; it's time to tell him. (53 minutes)

(36) Toby's Office: Sam and Toby; Sam informs Toby he may have offended the staff of American's for Tax Justice Caucus. Toby says it's okay, he trusts Sam to write and give the speech as it should be. Leo tells Sam the president wants to speak with him.

(37) -writer did not use-

(38) -writer did not use-

(39) -writer did not use-

(40) CLIFFHANGER: Outside the White House: C.J. and Josh walk along the street; she's had a horrible day obviously. He asks her opinion about the poll. She starts laughing, uses the Butch Cassidy & The Sundance Kid analogy; the president's been lying and Josh and Leo are worrying about the poll, and that they may look bad. "It's the fall that's gonna kill ya," she retorts, upset. Josh talks about the crashing satellite and how Donna is worried because she doesn't realize that satellites fall to earth weekly and have yet to land in a populated area, mostly they land in the ocean. So Josh guesses that they are due for a hit. This doesn't make C.J. feel any better. (56 minutes into the episode) - Commercial Break - End Credits (58 minutes)

Graph of *Gilmore Girls*

"Double Date"

Central A-Story Question: "Will Lane and Todd hit it off?"

Central B-Story Question: "Will Sookie and Jackson find romance?"

Central C-Story Question: "Will Rory and Lane get caught in their fib?"

Central D-Story Question: "Will Lorelai ace her business exam?"

Central E-Story Question: "Will Luke finally ask Lorelai out on a date?"

ACT ONE

(1) TEASER: Alarm rings: Rory and Lorelai in kitchen doing their morning routine; only speak one word as they leave.

(2 minutes into episode) - Credits - Commercial break

ACT ONE (returns 5 minutes into the episode)

(2) Gilmore Den: Rory and Lane listen to CD's and discuss boys; Lane wants Rory to ask her boyfriend Dean, to set Lane up with his friend, Todd. Rory hesitates, but agrees because Lane really wants to go on a date with Todd. Lorelai keeps interrupting, using their music as an

excuse; she is trying to study for a business exam. Finally, Lorelai plops down with them, giving up studying.

(3) Ext. the Inn. (9 minutes)

(4) Lorelai studying, her assistant, Michel, says they are overbooked, Lorelai solves the problem.

(5) Inn, the kitchen: Sookie, her best friend and the inn's cook, acts awkward with Jackson who brings the vegetables for the Inn. Lorelai watches their exchange confused. Jackson leaves and Sookie admits she asked Jackson out, but they never set a specific time and now it's awkward. Lorelai encourages Sookie to call and ask him now. Sookie leaves a message on his cell phone. (13 min)

(6) -writer did not use-

(7) -writer did not use-

(8) -writer did not use-

(9) -writer did not use-

(10) GREEN LIGHT: Rory reading on bench in town square park. Dean joins her, Rory asks him about setting Todd up, just be casual, they can double date. Dean reluctantly agrees.

(16 minutes into the episode) - Commercial break

ACT TWO (returns 19.5 minutes into the episode)

(11) Inn Lobby, morning: Lorelai studying, but gives up as Michel keeps badgering her; Sookie rushes up to the front desk, excited. Jackson called to say yes to a date on Friday night, only thing is, his cousin is in town and Sookie promised to get Lorelai to come along and they will make it a double date. Lorelai very reluctantly agreed. (21.5 minutes)

(12) -writer did not use-

(13) -writer did not use-

(14) Lorelai bedroom, evening: she helps Sookie put on makeup for the big date; she's very nervous.

(15) Rory's bedroom: she helps Lane get ready. Rory and Lane discuss whether or not they should tell Lorelai that Lane does not have permission to go out with Todd, they decide to leave that info out. (24 minutes)

(16) -writer did not use-

(17) Gilmore den: Lorelai waits on Sookie as Rory and Lane hurry down the stairs, tell her they are going to catch a movie with Dean. They rush out as doorbell rings: It's Jackson with his cousin Rune. He sees Lorelai and freaks out. Jackson says to excuse them for a moment.

(18) On porch: Rune is upset as he is very short and Lorelai is very tall, he wants to go home.

(19) Lorelai and Sookie exchange a look as of course they hear the whispered argument and the insults by Rune on the porch.

(20) U-TURN/MIDPOINT: Jackson makes Rune go even though he immediately dislikes Lorelai. Lorelai is not thrilled to be going either, but does so for her friend. They start out. It's going to be a long, torturous night.

(27 minutes into the episode) - Commercial break

ACT THREE (returns 31 minutes into the episode)

(21) Classy Restaurant, still evening: It's awkward, Rune is rude, Sookie rambles, only talks to Lorelai; Lorelai tries to include Jackson who is becoming disappointed in the date. Lorelai orders a martini and tells the waiter to keep them coming. (33 minutes)

(22) In line for the movie: Rory hopes Lane is having a good time while Lane tries to make conversation with Todd, but soon realizes they have nothing in common, and that he's not very smart.

(23) -writer did not use-

(24) -writer did not use-

(25) Sookie continues to ignore Jackson, and Rune won't respond to the conversation either; Lorelai makes Sookie follow her to the lady's room.

(26) Near lady's room: Lorelai asks Sookie what is the matter with her, why is she rambling to her and ignoring her date? Sookie is nervous and the restaurant is not right, she feels ridiculous; Lorelai says they can salvage the evening; they'll go to Luke's diner and keep it casual. Sookie agrees.

(27) The teens watch the movie. Lane is determined to find something in common with Todd, but it's hopeless. (38 minutes into the episode)

(28) -writer did not use-

(29) -writer did not use-

(30) ROAD OF NO RETURN: Luke's Diner: The foursome enters, Lorelai goes to order their food at the counter and begs Luke to stay and keep talking to her. Tells him about her awful date - Rune. Rune wants to leave and go bowling, begs Jackson to come with him. Jackson starts to leave, but Sookie asks him to stay, they haven't really started their date yet. Jackson agrees and Rune storms off. Lorelai and Luke watch Sookie and Jackson as they get to know each other. Both would like to be dating someone; to feel the excitement of courtship. They start playing cards when Lane's mom sees Lorelai and hurries inside, demanding to know where the girls are? Lane is supposed to be watching a video at Rory's. Lorelai says the girls are at the movie with Dean. Lane's mom furious and rushes out after her daughter. Lorelai follows after her. Luke was just about to ask Lorelai out, so he's disappointed.

(43 minutes into episode) - Commercial Break

ACT FOUR (returns 46 minutes into the episode)

(31) Still evening. Movie ends and the girls exit with their dates. Todd wants to go for ice cream, but Lane is ready to go home. Suddenly, her mom yells, and orders her home. Lane hurries off with her mom in big trouble. Lorelai and Rory start home.

(32) Walking: Lorelai is upset Rory lied, Rory apologizes, didn't want to, but she knew Lorelai wouldn't let them go if Lane's mom, Mrs. Kim, hadn't approved the date. Lorelai says can't trust Rory if Rory acts this way, Rory promises not to lie again.

(33) -writer did not use-

(34) Days later, Outside Lane's upstairs bedroom window: Rory climbs up in tree to roof to talk to Lane who is grounded. Lane says she doesn't like Todd anymore, misses hanging out with Rory. Grounded for a long time. Hears mom, and shuts window as Rory climbs down.

(35) Mrs. Kim argues with customer, he broke a lamp, he buys it. Lorelai comes to talk to her about Lane, that Lane is a good kid, they argue, Lorelai apologizes, promises that the girls won't lie to her again and that she can trust her to let Lane come over to Rory's. Lorelai says that maybe if her parents had listened more and not been so strict it would have made her teenage years easier and she might have made less mistakes. Mrs. Kim and Lorelai come to an understanding. Lorelai leaves. (53 minutes)

(36) -writer did not use-

(37) Luke's diner: Lorelai and Rory enter, Lorelai excited because she aced her test. Rory proud of her. Lorelai tells Rory that Sookie and Jackson are on their third date, totally ga-ga for each other. Cell phone rings.

(38) Kim yard: Lane's standing in the yard on her cell phone, her mom let her go in the front yard for fifteen minutes.

(39) Luke's diner: Rory goes outside to talk on phone to Lane. (54 minutes)(40) Luke's diner: Luke comes to table to take Lorelai's order. Luke attempts to ask her out, then chickens out, but then finally says he had fun playing cards and they should do it again sometime. She says sure. Rory hurries back in and gives cell phone back; says going to go talk to Lane, be back in ten minutes to eat. Lorelai looks over wistfully at Luke.

(55.5 minutes into the episode) - End credits

Graph of *Twenty-Four*

"4:00a.m.-5:00a.m."

Central Series Arc Questions: "Will Jack find and stop the assassin from killing Senator Palmer?" and "Will Jack and Teri get their daughter back to them safely?"

Central A-story Question: "Will the suspect lead Jack to the assassin? To Kim?"

Central B-Story Question: "Will Kimberly escape her kidnappers?"

Central C-Story Question: "Will Janet survive surgery?"

Central D-Story Question: "Did Palmer's son, Keith, murder Nicole's rapist?"

ACT ONE: (begins 02:23; after clips showing the previous episode)

(1) TEASER: Emergency Room: doctor's look at spine X-rays of Janet

(2) St. Mark's Hospital: Hospital Corridor wheel Janet on Gurney, prepping her for surgery.

(3) Jack follows the police car that has his only lead, the man who has killed the cop, and who knows something about the disappearance of Jack's daughter. (4:02:12a.m. shown on screen)

(4) Hospital admitting: Teri Bauer (mom) enters with Janet York's dad, asking if anyone by the name of their daughters has been brought in, a girl in a traffic accident. Nurse tells her there's a Jane Doe down the hall. The two parents take off down the hall.

(5) They rush through the doors and down the hall to find her in surgery. Look through the windows. Jack calls Teri, she updates him on what's happened, she needs him. Intercut scenes between Jack and Teri as they talk on the phone. Kim called a second time and sounded in trouble. She was in North Hollywood. Janet's in surgery. Jack says he's trying to find Kim, he'll explain later, just trust him. They will get through this. Jack continues driving after cop car. Teri watches the surgery, hoping Janet will survive, hoping Janet will know where Kim is.

(6) Back alleys of North Hollywood: (shown onscreen 04:06:45) two boys load Kim into the assassin's car, her hands bound and tape over her mouth. Assassin tells them to take her back to the compound, he'll meet them there, he'll give them the money then (20,000 grand). The two teens argue, one just wants to split, scared, the other one reminds him that he owes him. They get into the car.

(7) David Palmer, Campaign Headquarters: (shown onscreen time 04:06:58) Palmer looks over some data. Tells Patty, his assistant to go to bed. His daughter enters, she's made lattes. Polls open soon, daughter leaves room. His wife, Sherry, worries about their daughter, Nicole. Doesn't want him to talk to Nicole about the threat of a news story that is going to break on them: the fact that Nicole's brother, Keith, killed the boy who raped her.

(7A) Nicole and her dad drink latte, she's all excited about the poll, that he is going to win, her old school friends are flying in. He decides not to tell her about possible news story

(8) Counter Terrorist Unit: (onscreen time 04:09:32) Nina on cell phone to Jack, she warns him George coming after him. Jack at precinct, has to get to talk to this lead. Nina asks Tony for the contact number, they argue about whether or not they can trust Jack, she doesn't trust Tony. Nina defends Jack, Tony gives her the number grudgingly.

(9) Precinct: Jack talks with the sergeant in command, sergeant won't let Jack see the cop-killer. Jack talks the sergeant into letting him see the guy, just for a few minutes.

(10) GREEN LIGHT: Precinct: Sergeant leads Jack to the interrogation and holding room. Just as he is about to swipe the key card to allow entry, George Mason, Jack's superior, rushes into the corridor with other agents, and says hold it. Jack glares at Mason. (04:12:26a.m.)

(12 minutes into the episode) - Commercial break return to episode at 15:26

ACT TWO (return 16 minutes into episode)

(11) spit screen shows OR, assassin, Palmer and daughter, and van with Kim (shown onscreen time 04:16:28) The teens still arguing about Kim, Danny tells Rick that the guy is going to kill Kim, maybe already has, they'll just get paid and get out. Forget Kimberly. Rick upset.

(12) Mason and Jack enter a room at the precinct. He wants to know what he was doing at Dunlop Plaza, Richard Walsh is agent killed with Jack by sniper. They argue, Jack explains what happened: Walsh and Bailer were killed because they had info on the guy in the interrogation room, that this guy's somehow involved in the hit on Palmer. Mason says Jack sit down and wait, he'll talk to the suspect. Jack's impatient and angry, but he has no choice.

(13) Assassin's car stops at red light. Kim tries to get the attention of the trucker who pulls up beside them while the assassin is on the cell phone. The assassin holds a gun to her head and tells her to stop kicking the window. He peels off and into a parking lot. (18 minutes into episode)

(14) Assassin takes Kim out of the car and plops her into the trunk, he doesn't have time for this.

(15) Palmer's Headquarters: (hotel suite) (04:19:45) he paces, calls Maureen, waking her up, the audience just hears her voice; he wants to talk, meet him in the conference room on the third floor in ten minutes.

(16) Cop talks with Teri and Mr. York about Kim's disappearance and Janet's accident. Jack calls, intercut with Teri as she talks to him, he says he's at the Van Nuys police department and he thinks there's someone there who may have been with the girls, he'll explain later, he's waiting to talk to him, Jack tells her to talk with Janet as soon as she wakes up from surgery. He's got to go.

(17) Mason enters as Jack hangs up his cell phone. Mason informs Jack that the suspect only wants to talk to Jack. Jack asks if he can go in. Mason motions for him to do so.

(18) Jack in the interrogation room: makes sure the suspect knows the others are listening outside the glass window. Jack leans over and

whispers to the suspect. The suspect leaps up, attacking Jack. Cops rush in as the two wrestle. Cops get the suspect settled down as he screams that he wants his lawyer. Mason tells Jack to go cool off. Jack slips down the hall to an empty room for some privacy. He waits.

(19) Suspect taken into place his call. He calls Jack, Jack has slipped him a piece of paper with his cell phone number. Tells Jack that he must be at a pay phone on San Fernando Road in twenty minutes to answer it or the people who have Jack's daughter will know something's wrong. Jack must get him out of the police station now!

(20) U-TURN: Nina at Counter Terrorist Unit Office: on phone, Jack tells her that the suspect's name is Pentacoff, and she must run a trace on a pay phone near the San Fernando Road address that he was checking out earlier. She does so, without a warrant. Nina says that as soon as the assassin gang hears it's not Pentacoff, they'll hang up. Jack says they will hear Pentacoff's voice. Nina scoffs, asking if he's planning, a jailbreak? He doesn't reply, pausing, then just orders her to set up the trace. He hangs up, and slips back into the corridor. (Shown onscreen 04:25:32a.m.)

(25 minutes into episode) - Commercial Break.

ACT THREE (return 29 minutes into the hour)

(21) Split screen Palmer, Nina, Assassin car, police. (04:29:34a.m.) At precinct, Jack finds a cop, it's the partner of the dead cop, Jack says he needs to speak with the suspect again, cop says suspect been moved to a holding cell. He tells Jack that he wants Pentacost to go down for killing his partner, which means a clean interrogation. No more roughing up Pentacost. Jack agrees. The cop says he'll only let Jack speak to Pentacost with him present, he's got the access key. Jack agrees.

(22) They go into holding cell. Pentacost says no questions without his lawyer. Jack tries to strangle Pentacost, cop pulls him off, Jack then insults the cop, engaging the cop into a fight. As they struggle, Pentacost secretly lifts the access key off the cop. Jack leaves the room with the sergeant and other cop. They tell Jack to get under control. See Pentacost using access key to slip out of the police station.

(23) Hospital waiting room. Mr. York brings Teri some coffee. He says the doctors are removing fluid from Janet's spine, but she will be okay. They comfort each other.

(24) Palmer: outside conference room, security checks out Maureen.

(25) Inside the room, just Palmer and Maureen. They talk about the fact that they both have come a long way, why does she want to hurt his family with a rumor? The reporter, Maureen, because of their friendship, reveals her two sources. One, George Ferragamo, Palmer's son's therapist, and the second, an autopsy report that shows the boy his son murdered was in a violent struggle, and there's a hospital form that shows another boy entered a hospital that night with same type wounds. The handwriting was analyzed, and it belongs to his son, Keith. Palmer tells Maureen to do what she has to do, just know it is with consequences. (Shown onscreen 04:36:55a.m.)

Break for another commercial - (37 minutes into episode)

(26) Split screen: Rick and friend in van, Nina at computer, Palmer. (Shown onscreen 4:40:51a.m.) Senator goes to see his son who is asleep. Wakes him up and wants to know what happened the night Nicole was raped. Keith says his father has no right to ask that question because he was off politicking and someone had to take care of the situation. Keith refuses to tell his father anything. Palmer leaves upset.

(27) Mason apologizes to the cops about Jack, appreciate it if they handle things internally. Cop's partner enters, sergeant says the computer has him already checked out. Cop realizes his access card is gone. They rush to the holding cell.

(28) Hospital vending machine: Teri tells Mr. York about being upset with Kim who was failing algebra, they argued, she wished she hadn't said some things she had. Mr. York comforts Teri, and promises he will stay with her until they find Kim.

(29) Mason and cops uplink to GPS (global positioning satellite) to pinpoint Jack's location as he and the suspect they left the precinct at the same time. Go back ten minutes. Stills appear on computer

screen, they watch Jack get into a car, mark the car. Mason wonders where Jack is going.

(30) ROAD OF NO RETURN: Jack in Explorer. They hop out of car at the pay phone. He calls Nina, is she set to go with the trace? She answers yes - intercut. Phone rings, then they realize it isn't the pay phone, there's a cell phone underneath the pay phone. Now they can't trace the call. Pentacost answers the phone as Jack listens. The lead assassin tells him there are keys taped to the back of the pay phone; there is a car parked on a street around the block; there's a body in the trunk, get rid of it. The lead assassin hangs up. Jack looks at Pentacost in panic, Jack, wandering who is in the trunk, fearful it is his daughter. As they race around the corner to find the car, we cut to: (04:48:18a.m.)

Commercial Break - (48 minutes into the episode)

ACT FOUR (return 53 minutes into the episode)

(31) Split screen (shown onscreen 04:53:56a.m.) Teri and Mr. York, Nina. Jack and Pentacost running. They reach the car and Jack opens the trunk, blood everywhere, a body in a clear plastic. He opens the plastic, it's a body. Jack relieved. Mason arrives. Jack explains why he broke out Pentacost. Mason says tell him what is going on or he's throwing him back to the cops. Jack explains that there are people within the agency in on the Palmer hit, and that's why Walsh and Bailer were really killed. He thought Mason was in on it. Help him. Mason says they never had this conversation. He'll go question Pentacost while Jack handles the identification of the body.

(32) Jack in his Explorer, calls Nina, needs ID on body, get their best forensic guy on it. He's bringing in the body.

(33) Hospital: They're still doing surgery on Janet. Teri takes call from Jack (intercut) Jack be there in twenty minutes. Janet is their only link to Kimberly. She waits, exhausted.

(34) -writer didn't use-

(35) -writer didn't use-

(36) -writer didn't use-

(37) -writer didn't use-

(38) -writer didn't use-

(39) Assassin compound: Danny and Rick wait for the lead assassin to arrive so they can get their money. Assassin opens trunk, then goes over and asks about the other girl, says his people say she's at a hospital. Dan says, the other girl might not have been quite dead. Assassin says you're either dead or not, then shoots, executing Danny. Rick and Kim react horrified.

(40) CLIFFHANGER: Split screen, numerous ones. Hospital: Janet flatlines: (5:00:00a.m.) - Commercial break.

In the graphs above, you'll notice that the writers didn't necessarily use all the streets available for their episode's story. That's because their story didn't warrant them. As you can see, less scenes were used in *Gilmore Girls* and *West Wing* than in *24*. Why? Because in both of these drama tunnels, you have longer scenes within the episodes due to an abundance of dialogue per scene. In the action tunnel of *24*, you have less dialogue per scene because there is lot of action which means intercutting and more scenes to create the tension in the story.

Also note that in sequences where the action cuts back and forth quickly, I didn't list each scene separately, I just marked the *essence* of the scene and noted that the sequence was intercut. For example, in *24* on scene (5) I listed Jack's driving in his car and Teri at the hospital as the same scene even though the camera cut numerous times between Jack and Teri in their respective locations as they talked on the phone instead of writing each time they cut back and forth from Jack's car to the hospital as separate and new scenes. I could have listed it as two scenes, but since Teri answered at the hospital and most of the action remained with her, I just listed it as one scene. Simplify when you graph because an editor may have chopped one scene in the script into a dozen separate scenes. You'll find this especially true in action tunnels.

Okay, now it's time to apply what you've learned about graphing:

Exercise 16.A. From the two series you previously viewed and recorded, graph the six episodes thoroughly. This will really familiarize you with each of the two series. List the main plot (the story that dominates the most time within the hour) and the other plots within the episode. Re-examine the central questions you listed for these episodes in Chapter Five. This will help you with examining all the plots within each episode. Be sure you have a central question listed for each of the plotlines in each episode just as I have done in the previous graphs.

Exercise 16.B. For those writing an original pilot, graph the three episodes you viewed and recorded to familiarize yourself with the series for which you will write your second script. List the main plot (the story that dominates the most time within the hour) and the other plots woven in each episode. Re-examine the central questions you listed for these episodes in Chapter Five. This will help you with examining all the plots within each episode. Be sure you have a central question listed for each of the plotlines in an episode as I have done in the previous graphs.

Chapter Eight
Introduction to Plot

Yes, its finally time to delve into the fun and exciting world of plotting a story. So let's start with the basics:

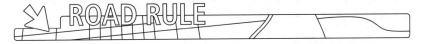

Road Rule #11: One and one fourth of a teleplay page equals one TV screen minute on average.

Thus, while you have 45-47 minutes to tell your one hour story (the other 13-15 minutes comprising the time for commerciasl) your teleplay will usually run somewhere between 56-64 pages.

There are exceptions, however, so if possible, you'll want to try and get your hands on several scripts of the series for which you are writing your sample teleplay to see what that particular show's page length averages per episode. For example, shows like *ER* average slightly longer in page length because the medical terminology consumes a lot of page space, but is often read rapidly when played out in the emergency room. Action shows might run longer as well because quick editing and camera movement used in such series plays out quickly on the TV screen, but might take longer to explain the action on page. For the most part, however, if you stay within the 56-64 page range, you'll be okay. Whatever you do, don't write under 56 pages because you'll have dead air time (nothing filling the TV screen).

So you have 56-64 pages to plot. How do you fill all those blank pages? Don't panic, all you need is your Writer's TV Road Map. It works for any and all TV genres whether you want to write a medical drama or a mystery. Every great TV episode follows such a map to tell its story.

The Writer's TV Road Map

Okay, now it's time to learn what those numbers represent on the graphs you made. Your plots are a series of streets which merge into their respective Central (?) Avenues. Each street on the Road Map equals one scene (or perhaps a sequence of *very* short scenes like in a MUSIC MONTAGE or when establishing shots of location or intercutting within action sequences). You create a new scene each time you switch time (for example: going from morning to late morning) or location (going from inside the courtroom to outside the courthouse) of your story.

Each set of ten streets or scenes forms one city block of the episode.

It will take four city blocks to construct your one hour script. Thus:

Act One = 1 city block (introduces the A-story, subplots, and any new characters; sets-up which character(s) the plot(s) is/are about)

Act Two = 1 city block (builds conflict & increases obstacles ending with the midpoint of the episode)

Act Three = 1 city block (continues to build conflict and obstacles, culminating in a crisis for at least one of the characters)

Act Four = 1 city block (wraps up all plots with the climax and/or resolution if contained series, or wraps up and sets up various plots if a continuing series, sometimes ending in a cliffhanger)

In your construction, integrate the plots and the characters so that each is dependent on the other. The plot is your system of roadways and the character is the driver zooming down your story's streets. Within the first few streets, compel the audience to care about your driver and his/her problem in the story (the protagonist of the episode); then tow him/her into opposition.

Falling Rocks

You must also include falling rocks (obstacles). Each falling rock along the journey must cause your driver to react, and it must keep him/her zooming forward in your story. To construct problems for your characters, you need to decide who or what is pushing those falling rocks off the cliff and in front of them.

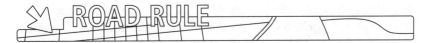

Road Rule #12: Villains come in all shapes and sizes, and they don't have to be human. Just look at the villains from Buffy the Vampire Slayer and Charmed? With Enterprise, the villains often are hostile alien life forms, and can come even in the toxic pollen. Nature can also be the villain in your story; blizzards, floods, earthquakes, and fires can be powerful villains, hurling numerous falling rocks at your characters.

Parallel Streets

These are your subplots which reflect and/or enhance the A-story plot. You have to weave these streets throughout your script, incorporating plot lines for the supporting cast and/or any new characters needed to execute your story. Depending on your TV tunnel, you will have about 2-6 subplots to juggle with your main or A-story plot. These subplots must merge with your main plot or with each other somewhere during the course of the story.

In *West Wing*, "The Fall's Gonna Kill You", the subplot of Donna worrying about the falling satellite from space symbolically reflects the central plot of the president's lie while also providing some much needed comic relief. This subplot merges into the main plot and premise in the final scene of the episode as Josh and C.J. discuss the fact that the President's lie could destroy them all.

All your subplots and your main plot in each city block must keep progressing the story as your characters drive towards the episode's climax. Your story's speed limit (tension) increases, compressing time shorter and shorter until real time for your characters often becomes reel time. This brings us to the need of the "ticking clock."

Ticking Clocks

A ticking clock is a story device which sets up tension and a need for immediate action by the character(s). It dictates that a character(s) perform a certain action by a specific time, or a grave consequence will occur. It is a major obstacle with a time limit attached. Often this device is set into motion by the story's villain or antagonist. A ticking clock(s) can help you plot your way through your story. Where you set it in motion depends on your story's individual needs.

The political action/thriller, *24*, created a whole series based on a ticking clock. Warned that an assassin is out to kill Senator Palmer on the day of the California presidential primary, Jack Bauer has just twenty-four hours to discover who is behind the hit and stop the assassin. In one of its individual episodes, it presented another ticking clock to help plot that episode:

In *24*, "4:00a.m.-5:00a.m.", Jack must break out a cop killer from a police precinct who is involved in the assassination plot in order to get him to a pay phone within twenty minutes so Jack can keep his daughter Kim alive.

Rest Areas

Although the risks rise as your incline (storyline) gets steeper, a city block may also need a rest area. This is a breathing space for your characters and for the viewer. These moments allow the characters to refuel before facing more falling rocks and dangerous curves, and also gives the viewer a chance to relate more strongly with the character. The rest area is often a reflective moment for a character or can also be a comic relief scene. It is a scene in which there is no (or very little) plot advancement. In these scenes, a character takes us into his/her thoughts and feelings, revealing more about that character and/or another character. In television, the rest area often plays out in a music montage, creating a mood in the audience through the music and images shown.

In *Enterprise*, rest areas occur when Captain Archer records his personal daily captain's log. These scenes often are about the captain's reflections and/or dilemmas of whatever is going on in each particular episode.

In *Once & Again*, rest areas occur during the black and white segments, when the character looks into the camera and reveals his thoughts and feelings.

It really isn't that hard to start plotting your story, once you begin to add all these elements. If you're still a little worried about your plot, then relax because there are a few tricks of the trade to help you with story ideas and to help you jazz up your plot(s).

Plot Gimmicks

You can use these within a series, within an episode, or within the rules of your TV world. If a series uses plot gimmicks weekly in their episodes, then you will have to incorporate such gimmicks into your own plots when writing for that a series. Below is a list of the most frequently used plot gimmicks in TV. They can be mixed and matched for added effect.

· Breaking the 4th Wall

· Character Daydreams, Dreams, or Fantasizes

· Documentary

· Flashbacks or Flashforwards

· Holiday Classics

· Homages

· Music Montage

· Out of Body Experience

· Parallel Plots

· Photographs

· Rashomon

· Reincarnation

· Runners

· Time Travel

Below are some examples of how other writers used these gimmicks to make their stories interesting.

1 Breaking the 4th Wall

This means the character(s) actually look into the camera and speak directly to the audience, and thus are breaking that fourth, unseen wall between the viewer and the character. This is a quick way to expose the true feelings of a character and reveal more about what is going on in his/her thoughts. It can also be used to add humor to a story.

Once & Again uses this plot gimmick as one of the rules within its TV world. These scenes are filmed in black and white (combining the documentary style) and are asides to the viewers. In these scenes, the character(s) talk to the audience about their feelings and thoughts. If you are writing a sample spec for this series, you would have to incorporate this plot gimmick in your own story so you don't break the rules of its TV world.

Likewise, *Moonlighting* often broke the 4th wall, but unlike the example above, they used this plot gimmick for humorous effects instead of dramatic ones.

2 Character Daydreams, Dreams, or Fantasizes

Here, the audience is taken into the daydream, sleeping dream, or fantasy of a character. This generally allows the writer a good way to escape the rules of the TV world for that episode because in a dream or fantasy, you can go as wild and crazy as you want. These gimmicks generally are used for humor or to show profound insight about a character or theme. They can also be used to add suspense to a story through premonition, or by playing the dream as if the scene is really happening, then revealing it's just a dream.

In *St. Elsewhere*, "Sweet Dreams", some of the resident doctors get involved in hospital dream research. The dreams of these doctors and how they are affected fuel the plots in this episode.

In *J.A.G.*, "Capital Crimes", this gimmick creates suspense as Lt. Col. Sarah "Mac" MacKenzie has a nightmare in which she is murdered in the park. This Teaser then reveals it is a dream, but when a colleague misses an appointment, Mac's nightmare becomes a psychic lead in which she follows clues in her dream to find the missing woman's body and her murderer.

In *Thirtysomething*, "Whose Forest Is This Anyway," as Nancy and her son Ethan develop a children's story, the scene cuts away to show Ethan as the character in the fantasy story they are creating.

3 Documentary

This is when the characters in the series are being filmed by a documentary crew in the course of the story. The camera shots then are focused just as if the episode was a documentary. The entire episode might appear this way, or just segments of it may appear in documentary style. This plot gimmick can provide character tension, reveal a character, and/or add lots of humor to an episode.

Third Watch's "Sex, Lies, and Video Tapes", a camera crew trails after Doc and Kim as they treat several gunshot victims.

St. Elsewhere's "Drama Center" shows a documentary film crew as they follow Dr. Craig around the hospital, providing a great amount of humor in the episode.

Homicide's "The Documentary" revolves its storyline around a documentary filmmaker, Brody, who follows the detectives around for twenty-four hours, revealing what a day in the life of a Baltimore detective is like.

4 Flashbacks or Flashforwards

This is when a character remembers something from his past, and "flashes" back. That is, the audience sees the character in the moment he is remembering. In this way, the audience gets to feel and experience the scene just as the character did. This can be more powerful, when used correctly, than just having a character tell about a past memory.

In *Any Day Now*, the series rules of its TV world require the writer to employ this gimmick and flashback to the childhood of the main characters. These flashbacks provide subplots which reflect the A and B-stories of the episode. It also provides great backstory to reveal why and how the characters turned out to be who they are today.

C.S.I. also uses this gimmick as a rule of its TV world. Here the detectives flashback to the crime as they piece together their interpretation of what happened by following the forensic clues.

You can also flashforward in storytelling. This is when we see a character projected into his future. Often, this gimmick combines with daydream or fantasy as a character thinks about what will happen if s/he makes a certain choice, then the story flashforwards to show what the character believes will happen. This is most often used for humor.

5 Holiday Classics

Every year around the holidays, you're sure to see a tribute to three of the most beloved Christmas stories of all time: Capra's "*It's A Wonderful Life*," Dicken's *A Christmas Carol*, and O'Henry's *Gift of the Magi*. These aren't homages, because the writer actually lifts the whole plot and inserts it into his/her own episode. These are popular because viewers find them familiar and nostalgic, and since these stories are in public domain (which means you can usu them and not be used) writers often take advantage of them.

In *Moonlighting*, "It's A Wonderful Job", a depressed Maddie has a chance to see what her life and the lives of those at Blue Moon Detective Agency would be like if she had sold the agency as she had originally intended.

Quantum Leap's "A Little Miracle - December 24, 1962" revisits the Dicken's classic as Sam leaps into the body of a wealthy and lonely contractor who is determined to demolish a local Salvation Army mission in order to build his high-rise. Sam and Al set out to "Scrooge" the contractor into changing his mind as they give him a visit by ghosts past, present, and future.

Little House on the Prairie retells the *Gift of the Magi*, with Pa making a saddle for Laura and Laura selling her horse for a stove for Ma in "Christmas At Plum Creek".

6 Homage

Homages are simply a tribute, and most homages are made to famous filmmakers, famous films, and/or film styles such as film noir and the musicals. This gimmick is almost always used for humor and generally written overly dramatically to provide such humor.

Thirtysomething's "South by Southeast," is a homage to Hitchcock's films as someone stalks Gary.

In *Moonlighting,* "The Dream Sequence Always Rings Twice" is an homage to the film, "The Postman Always Rings Twice" and to film noir in general.

In *Moonlighting,* "North By North Dispesto", A restless Ms. Dispesto gets to live on the edge, finding danger and excitement when she gets a piece of paper from a mysterious man as she attends a ball in Maddie and David's place. This is another tribute to Hitchcock, of course.

7 Music Montage

This is a series of shots and/or scenes shown as a song or music plays. Most often it is used to illustrate passage of time, but can also be used to help reveal a character. This gimmick evokes a mood and tone for the episode, and can really make a statement and hit an audience emotionally when used correctly.

The series *Homicide* often used this gimmick to create a mood of what the harsh life of the Baltimore detectives were like. *Moonlighting* also used music montages to create a sense of fun and humor in their stories.

8 Out of Body Experience

This occurs when a character is injured and becomes unconscious and/or dies briefly. The character's soul leaves his/her body, and either spends time with living people who can't see him/her, or visits those who have crossed over to the other side.

Providence's "Syd In Wonderland" and "Paradise Inn": while in a coma, Sydney visits her mother in heaven as the other characters worry whether she will survive.

St. Elsewhere's "After Life": Fiscus is shot in the emergency room. His out of body experiences let him visit Hell, Heaven, and Limbo as doctors try to save him.

9 Parallel Storylines

This is when a subplot not only reflects the main plot, but actually parallels it by telling a similar story through another character's POV.

In *Gilmore Girls*, "Double Date", the subplot of Lorelai agreeing to go on a double date with her best friend Sookie parallels the A-story plot of Rory double dating with her best friend, Lane. Both end up going on double dates they didn't want to be on, and both end up helping a friend at the expense of their own well-being.

10 Photographs

Here, the writer uses photographs to draw upon plot or to provide segues and commentary on scenes. This can be combined with Breaking the 4th Wall as the subject in the picture can look into the camera and speak, or with flashbacks.

Judging Amy uses family photographs as a segue between scenes and also to evoke a mood reflecting the characters.

In *Thirtysomething's*, "Date Night" use photographs in a flashback. The photographs come alive and the viewer sees how Hope and Michael first met.

11 Rashomon

This is an homage to the classic Japanese film Rashomon by director Akira Kurosawa. It is used so often that it demands its own separate category. The plot lifted from this film is that the *exact same* story is told or repeated several times, but from a *different* point of view. Thus, it is a retelling of the same event experienced by several characters, and the viewer gets to experience this event through each character's unique viewpoint.

Thirtysomething's, "Couples", Michael and Hope go to dinner with Elliot and Nancy. The dinner is then retold four times through each character's differing account of what actually happened. This reveals how each character's prejudice or feeling towards another character colors what really, and shows the deteriorating relationship of Elliot and Nancy in a very compelling way.

12 Reincarnation

This gimmick builds a story around the fact that certain characters have had a past life together. This can be a fun plot to use because you can explore why characters behave the way they do with each other by setting up a past history between the two characters that is from a whole other lifetime. This gimmick is most effective when it is combined with flashbacks to allow the audience to relive this past life with the character(s).

In *The X-Files*, "The Field Where I Died," reveals Mulder remembering a past life with Scully during the Civil War. His knowledge from that life time allows him to discover a hiding place in his current investigation.

In *Moonlighting's*, "A Womb With A View", the angel, Gerome, flicks on a television set in Maddie's office to reveal the numerous past life romances of Maddie and David, showing them to Baby Hayes who is waiting to be born.

13 Runners

These are stories which aren't tied up within the episode, but are carried throughout a story, just not always consecutively. Most romance plots are runners in a series.

In *Homicide*, the Adena Watson case, the brutal murder of a young girl, plagues Detective Bayliss throughout the series. It is not a storyline that continues every week, but pops up again in various episodes when new evidence or clues are uncovered in the case.

In *The X-Files*, the backstory of what happened to Mulder's sister serves as a runner in the series as occasionally a current case leads Mulder to follow up new clues in his sister's abduction.

In *Northern Exposure*, the storyline of Joel and Maggie getting together, serves as a runner for the series.

14 Time Travel

This is not a flashback to another time by a character thinking back on a memory, but rather a character *actually travels* to another place in time. *Quantum Leap*, of course, built each episode's plot around the time travel of Sam Beckett.

Elements Which Affect Plot

Basically, there are three factors within a series which will affect how you plot your story:

· Story Arcs

· Contained Series

· Continuing Series

1 Story Arcs

Every episode will have its own story arc, however, some series will also have story arcs which continue for several episodes, and/or for the length of the series. For example, the storyline of Nancy's cancer in *Thirtysomething* lasted through several consecutive and nonconsecutive episodes. *Wiseguy* uniquely implemented its series by carrying a story arc over the course of six or so episodes, and then moving its main character, Vinnie Taranova, into a whole new storyline and cast of supporting characters.

2 Contained Series

In a contained series, each individual episode wraps up all the plots (or almost all the plots) introduced in the first Act of the story. For this reason, they can be easier to write for because you don't have to worry about storylines that are continuing, or guess where the show's producers are going with such storylines. You might have an occasional plot, like a runner, that does run throughout the series, but the A-story is always wrapped up. If it isn't, then it becomes a two-part episode in which the main plot is concluded the following week.

Contained episodes are often found in the mystery tunnel, like *Law & Order* and *C.S.I.* Other tunnels which also plot their stories in contained episodes include *Touched By An Angel* and *Enterprise*.

3 Continuing Series

If a series is continuing, also known as episodic, it means it doesn't tie up most of the story lines, but carries several of them over into next week's episode. Some plots will be wrapped up within the hour, and some won't. This type of series often employs a cliffhanger at the end of the episode to keep the audience hanging on until the following week. Then, at the beginning of next week's episode, they generally run clips of what has happened previously on the show so viewers who missed an episode can keep up with that night's episode. Tunnels such as nighttime soaps like *Dallas* and *Knot's Landing* are always plotted in a continuing format. Other series which are episodic include *24* and *West Wing*.

Exercise 17. From the episodes you graphed in the previous chapter, go through each and list any plot gimmicks used. Are these gimmicks a rule of the series or just used within the a specific episode?

Exercise 18. Next, go through your graphs and highlight all the falling rocks in each story, then list any ticking clock(s) in each (if applicable). Be sure it is a true ticking clock (a major obstacle with a time limit) and not just a falling rock (obstacle).

Exercise 19. Now, think about your own story and plots. Do you need to use any of these plot gimmicks to make your story more effective? Remember, if the rules of the series for which you are writing or creating require you to use these plot gimmicks, you must do so.

Chapter Nine
TV Characters

The driver is the protagonist of the episode, and the one who will drive the A-story. In your sample spec and/or original pilot, the series's cast of characters will determine who you can choose to drive your story. There are three kinds of casts: solo, duo, and ensemble. Often the series' title will cue you as to what type of cast the series has.

1 Solo Cast

This is when a series chooses to tell it's A-story through basically the same solo character each week. This doesn't mean that there is only one character in the cast; it simply means there is only one character who is the focus or star of the series. There will be, of course, exceptions as occasionally a supporting player(s) will get the A-storyline, but this usually occurs later in a series, and is due either to the popularity of an actor playing the supporting character, and/or the fact that the star of the series is off filming a feature or on maternity leave.

A solo cast series is the easiest to plot because you have only one main character that will dominate most of your story's screen time. If you are a more linear thinker, you might want to consider this type of series for which to write.

Mystery and political thriller tunnels often employ this type of cast. Series such as *Magnum P.I., Alias,* and *The Education of Max Bickford* fit this type of cast. As you can see, the titles do give a big hint as to whether or not it is a solo show.

2 Duo Cast

This cast supports two main characters from which to spin the A-story. Obviously, this type will have the occasional exceptions for the same reasons as the solo cast, and a supporting character will sometimes carry an A-story instead of one of the subplots, but this is the exception not the rule. As a novice writer, always follow the rule.

In a duo cast, the relationship can be one of family, friends, romance, and/or colleagues. Cop and mystery tunnels often use this type of casting, pairing detectives or private eyes. Romance tunnels, likewise generally use this type of cast.

Series such as *Cagney & Lacey*, *Gilmore Girls*, and *Any Day Now* fall into this category.

3 Ensemble Cast

This type of cast of characters allows you more creative range, because there are many characters from which to derive the A-story. That is, the series is told every week from numerous viewpoints, or the viewpoint of a different character than the week before. This type generally has more subplots than the other cast of character types. Here, you will have an A-story, and maybe up to four to six subplots which means that even though the A-story will dominate, it won't take up most of the hour. All the plots in the episode will be more evenly divided. If you are good at juggling many things at once, then you might choose to write for this type of series.

Series in which the occupational arena (setting) prevails, and family drama tunnels most often use this type of cast for their series. *West Wing*, *ER*, and *Boston Public* comprise this category.

Types of Drivers

Every series will reflect basically four main types of characters. In television, however, your driver can change over the course of the series. S/he may start out as one type, but through the course of the series change character types as s/he grows and learns. This change of course, does not happen overnight, but over the course of many, many episodes.

If you are creating your own series:

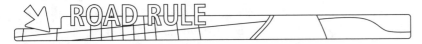

Road Rule #13: Give the audience a driver to care about, and one we can laugh and cry with along the ride.

All characters must be relatable to the audience. Your characters must have the same needs, desires, dreams, and problems that the viewer might have. This is what makes an audience identify with the driver of the episode and/or series. So how do you begin to make characters relatable? You or the creators of a series start by choosing one of these four character types:

· The Race Car Driver

· The Taxi Driver

· The Demolition Derby Driver

· The Anti-Car Driver

1 The Race Car Driver
This character excels in his/her environment, which is often highly specified, rarely, if ever, failing. For this reason, s/he often feels a sense of entitlement. S/he is packed full of confidence and self-esteem. This character is the prima donna, so to speak, of his/her arena. Things always seem to go his/her way. Other characters in the story admire and/envy this driver's special talent and intelligence, but they may or may not like the driver since sometimes this type of character can be arrogant and/or obnoxious. S/he pays attention to detail and is goal-oriented. This character is a leader and an overachiever. Examples of this type of driver include supersleuth of forensics, Grissom, in *C.S.I.*, Police Chief Jack Mannion in *The District*, and Dr. Mark Craig in *St. Elsewhere*. This character speeds along his/her own course, following his/her own map, with little or no need of approval from other characters because s/he is so certain of her/his actions. There will

most likely be only one race car driver per series because this driver should stand out from among the rest.

2 The Taxi Driver

The taxi driver is the regular guy/gal who's just like anyone who might get into his/her cab. As an audience, we can relate to this driver because S/he's one of us. S/he's the girl or boy next door with the usual everyday life problems, like Amy from *Judging Amy*, Dr. Greene from *ER*, and Donna Moss from *West Wing*. Most of the characters on television fall into this category.

3 The Demolition Derby Driver

This character has many breakdowns going into the story, and during the journey, s/he's getting slammed from all directions, always ending up on the bottom of the pile. With the demolition derby driver, fate appears to be against him/her. This driver has low self-esteem, especially when it comes to the opposite sex. Generally, they are self-deprecating and are acutely aware of their limitations, whether real or self-imposed. Sometimes, they are haunted by a tragic or flawed past. This character is the loner who finds it hard to trust others, and is the underdog who rarely triumphs in his/her attempts. S/he can be that lovable loser, or just a character who has one lousy break after another. This character sometimes has an addiction to overcome or one has been overcome. This character embodies the universal appeal of yearning for acceptance and/or justice in what appears to be an unfair world, and so immediately wins the viewer's sympathy because of his/her struggle throughout the episode or series. Characters like Jimmy in *The Practice,* Andy Sipowitz from *N.Y.P.D. Blue,* and Abby from *ER* are all characters of this type.

4 The Anti-Car Driver

Last, is the anti-car driver, the rebel. This driver doesn't always fit into society's norms because s/he just doesn't think like everyone else. This can be a good trait, or it can work against the character at times. S/he is the *oddball* of the cast and definitely marches to the sound of his/her own drummer. This character doesn't look for approval either, just acts on her/his own instincts which s/he believes are always right, just like the race car driver. They have a deep belief in themselves and how the world should be. Their beliefs sometimes cause this driver to be judgmental and/or self-righteous. Other anti-car drivers like to live in the moment which can bring judgement and/or teasing from the others. Whereas with the race car driver, the other characters in the cast envy and wish to be like the race car driver, with the anti-car driver, most of the other characters in the cast rarely understand him/her and certainly don't want to be "weird" like this character. This can prove frustrating for the anti-driver who just wants the rest of the characters to see the world as s/he does. They will, however, remain true to their convictions because these convictions define them. These characters will either be champions of a cause to which they commit their lives, or commit their lives to living only in the moment. They are not leaders or followers. They just drive along their own self-appointed road. Characters such as Maxine in *Judging Amy*, Fox Mulder in *The X-Files*, and Lorelai in *Gilmore Girls*.

As a character grows and changes, his/her character type can change as well. Having a demolition driver transform into a race car driver can reveal a strong character arc (which we'll discuss in the next chapter). Transforming characters into other types, of course, must be done over the course of many, many episodes so the growth and transformation is believable.

Pedestrians or Passengers

These are the characters who "support" the driver, as a series regular character (oppearing weekly or nearly weekly occasionally throughout the series) or a guest character (appearing only once) in the series. These characters illuminate the driver's personality and/or advance the plot. They also serve to bounce with dialogue off the main character, and/or are characters from which to derive humor, conflict, and information. Supporting characters can be fun to write because they can be less serious or driven than your hero, and can also be more quirky than your main driver.

In *Magnum P.I.*, Magnum is the driver of the series while Higgins, Rick, and T.C. form most of the supporting cast.

In *Gilmore Girls*, Lorelai and Rory are the drivers while the supporting cast includes Rory's grandparents, Luke, Lane, Sookie, Dean, Jackson, Paris, and a few other eccentric townsfolk and classmates.

In *West Wing,* the ensemble characters include President Bartlet, his wife, Abbey, Sam Seaborn, Leo McGarry, Josh Lyman, his assistant, Donna Moss, C.J. Cregg, Toby Ziegler, and Charlie Young, many of whom can be the driver one week and a supporting character the next. Additional supporting characters appear as well, but they are recurring characters since they aren't used weekly, such as Joey Lucas, Oliver Babbish, and the vice president.

Road Rage

Unlike feature film, in television, there isn't always a villain. That's not to say that the driver won't face obstacles; it just means that won't necessarily be hurled by a villain. You must still have dramatic conflict; it just won't be the result of a villain. Whether or not you need a villain will depend upon the TV tunnel, the rules of the series's TV world, and the particular story you are constructing. Villains are handy because they give the driver someone to race and/or crash with throughout the story, make your story easier to plot because as the villain or the driver sets out to achieve a goal, the other one attempts to foil that goal. Villains are often driven by their need to control the outcome of your plot. If you do have a villain, both your villain and your driver each need to have their own respective goal which must be in conflict.

When writing villains, remember that villains rarely see themselves as evil. They have reasons and justifications for the bad things they do. This is what makes them interesting and complex.

Types of Villains

There are basically four main types of villains:

· Road Rage Driver Villain

· Aggressive Driver Villain

· Sunday Driver Villain

· The Open Road villain

You can use any of these types to tell your story (if applicable) and you can have more than one villain in your story as long as it fits with the rules of the series' TV world for which you are writing and/or developing.

1 Road Rage Driver Villain

The road rage driver is a villain intent on destroying and literally killing your driver and/or other characters at any cost to achieve his/her goal. Anyone who gets in this villain's way is road kill. This type of villain rarely has a redeeming quality, but s/he can. Either way, s/he serves as an almost undefeatable foe for your driver. They are a villain to the end, 'til death do they part. Generally, his/her goal differs and/or is opposite of your driver's goal. Most of the creatures du jour on *Buffy the Vampire Slayer* would fall into this category.

Serial killer Jack - *The Profiler*
The terrorists - *24*

2 Aggressive Driver Villain

This villain is a competitor and arch rival of the driver, wanting to win whatever the driver is vying for: a job, an award, a love interest, property, …whatever the driver possesses or is attempting to possess. This villain should be as clever or more so than the driver then the competition is equally matched. Their goal must also be in direct conflict with your driver's. Because they are arch enemies, the villain and driver are determined to defeat each other. It's a fight to the end - just not a fight to the death, like our road rage villain.

J.R. Ewing - *Dallas*
Gregory Sumner - *Knot's Landing*
Angela Channing - *Falcon Crest*

3 Sunday Driver Villain

This villain is more of an aggravation to your driver. S/he causes irksome delays and situations for your characters. Sometimes, it's nothing personal and this villain type is unaware of his/her impact, and sometimes, this villain type enjoys making your driver's life miserable. This villain type isn't life-threatening, but at his/her best, can make your driver's life unbearable at times.

Miles Drentell - *Thirtysomething*
Frenchy - *The Ponderosa*
Paris - *Gilmore Girls*

4 The Open Road Villain

This simply means that the open road is the villain, that is, the villain is either a machine, an event, an unknown disease/illness, and/or nature which poses a threat to your characters in a particular episode. In *Baywatch*, the ocean serves as one of the villains that the lifeguards must battle weekly.

The wrecked train in *ER's,* "The Crossing"
The storm in *Dawson's Creek* 's, "Two Gentlemen of Capeside "
The tornado in *Any Day Now* 's, "One Hour of Drama"

Okay, so now let's put your newfound knowledge of characters to use.

Exercise 20. From the previous one or two series you recorded, list whether the series uses a solo, duo, or ensemble cast to drive its' plots. This is the cast you will use in your sample script. In addition, if creating your own series, list which cast type will you use.

Exercise 21.A. From the six episodes you recorded, list the type of driver used in each A-story. Next list the type of driver you'll be using in your sample script.

Exercise 21.B. From the three episodes you recorded, list the type of driver used in each A-story. Next, list the type of driver you'll be using to drive the A-story in your original pilot.

Exercise 22.A. List the supporting characters from the six episodes you watched. These are the characters you'll need to use in your sample script.

Exercise 22.B. List the supporting characters you'll need for your original pilot, the ones who will form your series' supporting cast.

Exercise 23. From the episodes you recorded, list any villain used (if applicable). Then list the type of villain your driver will fight against in your episode and/or series (if applicable.)

Chapter Ten
Character Development

Writing for characters on television is unique in this way: a writer has hours and hours of time to develop and layer a character, revealing bits of his/her personality over many episodes and if lucky, over many years. Thus, a viewer gets to really know the characters over the course of a series. Indeed, if the series runs for numerous years, the audience watches these characters grow up or grow old in front of their eyes. By tuning into a certain series, the viewer is in essence, inviting those characters into his/her home every week. Because of this, the audience begins to feel like they know these fictional people, and can come to really care about them.

Identification Please

Who is your driver? Never, ever get into the car with a stranger. You have to know the driver of your story or you won't be able to write him/her convincingly and consistently.

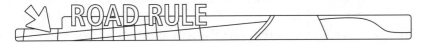

Road Rule #14: Know your characters and how they will react with one another! Stay consistent to the world and characters you create.

This is paramount to impressing producers. When writing for an existing show, you've got to know who the characters are so you can have them react consistently in the story you are creating. When creating your own show, you've got to know who your characters are so they will be consistent within your own pilot script. So how do you do this? By creating character dipsticks and a compass for the characters to follow.

1 **Character Dipsticks**
A dipstick consists of everything you know or have learned about the character for which you are writing. Dipsticks measure the

fundamental characteristics of each character whether he's the driver, the villain, or a supporting character.

A. His/Her approximate age

How old is the character? Pre-kindergarten (baby and toddlers) elementary school (Lauren in Judging Amy) high school (Rory in Gilmore Girls) young adult (Clark Kent in Smallville) or adult (Captain Archer in Enterprise) or senior (Grams in Dawson's Creek)?

B. Environment

Where do s/he live? Is it a futuristic world (*Dark Angel*) or historical (*The Ponderosa*) or contemporary (*West Wing)?*

C. Cultural background

Of what nationality or ethnic background do they come from? Example are: Irish (Danny McGregor from *The District*) African-American (Eugene Young from *The Practice*) and Korean (Lane Kim from *Gilmore Girls*)?

D. Relationships

What is the driver's relationship to the other characters in the story? Who are his/her friends? Who are his/her enemies? Who are his/her parents? Who are his/her classmates? You must know how characters relate to each other because their chemistry is very important. Learn and/or create their backstory (history with one another) to know how your characters will act and react with each other in a scene.

For example, are the characters childhood friends or sweethearts, or college roommates who haven't seen each other in twenty years? How does a character relate to his/her family? This will speak volumes about that character. Does one character have a kind of shorthand with his wife/husband or best friend? The audience learns about a character by how s/he relates to the other characters in her/his life.

E. Super or magical powers

Sometimes characters can have special powers, especially those in a fantasy or sci-fi series. It is important to list the powers that a certain character possesses so you will know how to use them in the story. (Prue, Phoebe, and Piper in *Charmed* or Clark Kent in *Smallville)*

2 Character Compass Traits

To know the characters you are writing, see their world through *their* eyes because each one will have his/her own limited POV (point of view). Examine a character's personality traits. These traits serve as compass points and direct a character's choices and reactions throughout the journey. Ask yourself, what are the character's strengths and weaknesses? What motivates the character? To create truly great characters, you must make them complex. You don't want your hero to be perfect anymore than you want your villain to be all evil (for the most part). Film director, Elia Kazan, said that when he looked at a hero, the first thing he asked was, "What's wrong with him?" Likewise, when he looked at a villain, he asked, "What is good about this character?" Asking these questions of your own characters will help to make them well-rounded and many layered.

To help with contrasting traits and to make sure the characters you create are different, you should read THE COLOR CODE by Dr. Taylor Hartman. In his book, he talks about four basic personality types (reds, blues, yellows, whites) and how they interact with one another. Most importantly, he theorizes that red personalities are motivated by power, blues by intimacy/passion, yellows by fun, and whites by peace. Knowing what motivates a character, gives you great guidance in the plotting of your story as well as in the development of your characters.

NOTE: THE COLOR CODE lists numerous character traits of each color personality. I highly recommend this book for your writer's reference library as it can be a great resource for creating characters.

Television series which garner critical acclaim and hold viewers interest over the years are ones which incorporate all four of these personalities in their main cast of characters. This is because when you put these four types together, you automatically create dramatic conflict.

Let's look at characters from the acclaimed medical drama, *St. Elsewhere.* This series won numerous awards because week after week, the writing, directing, and acting was brilliant, because the writers, Joshua Brand and John Falsey created marvelous, yet flawed characters, mixing its cast with the four personality types:

Dr. Mark Craig, one of the greatest of all television characters, is a red, and thus always motivated by power. He prides himself on being a brilliant surgeon (which he is), and demands excellence and perfection from those around him, especially his residents. The fact that he chooses to works at St. Eligius, an old county hospital that barely keeps open is interesting. He is organized, attending to every detail. A know-it-all, he runs his surgical department like Napoleon. To him, there is no excuse for ineptness, no room for mistakes. One must be perfect, or at least strive to be. He is usually insensitive because of his bluntness, sometimes even to his patients which often provides great humor in the series. (The race car driver)

Dr. Donald Westphall, is a blue, motivated by intimacy/passion. Blues are the people who change the world for the better. They fight for injustice whenever they come upon it, and Donald is no exception. Always taking up a cause, Donald can rub people the wrong way. He is judgmental and self-righteous, but a loyal and an honorable man. Compassionate, he takes care of the resident doctors as well as his patients, often neglecting his own needs. As an administrator, he works to implement programs within the hospital to help those less fortunate in the community. He is an idealist, and is always fighting the right battle. A lonely widower, he has dedicated his life to his job and his patients. (Demolition derby driver)

Dr. Daniel Auschlander, the chief administrator of the hospital, is motivated by peace, thus he's a white personality. He loves music and serenity, but rarely has time to enjoy either as he is always solving problems and running interference for Donald or Mark. The hospital peacemaker, Daniel is a quiet man who is kind, wholesome and dedicated. Throughout the series, he struggles to come to peace with the fact that he is dying of liver cancer. (Taxi cab driver)

Dr. Victor Ehrlich is a resident doctor who is motivated always by fun, which makes him a yellow personality. He's insensitive in a piggish, chauvinist way, always wise cracking and speaking before he thinks. He's always looking for the next big party. Kind of a klutz and perpetually late, especially for rounds, he serves as a persistent thorn in Dr. Craig's side. He's a oddball, a California surfer, who's hyperactivity constantly annoys those around him. He's always eager to please and get in Dr. Craig's good graces, and although he rarely succeeds, he is persistent. He's always looking to serve his own self-interests. (Anti-car driver)

In the examples above, I also include each driver type. This, however, doesn't mean, that all blues are demolition derby drivers or all yellows anti-car drivers. You have to examine what a character's true motivation in life is, to determine what his/her personality or color type is.

Another important question to ask of your characters, is how haveexperiences and relationships created his/her personality?

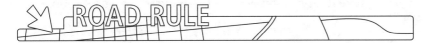

Road Rule #15: Know your characters most private moments.

Writer Graham Greene once wrote: "In every childhood, there is a moment when the door opens and lets the future in." Such a defining moment in a character's life is often a great start at developing why a character is the way s/he is. These moments can be tragic, inspiring, or one of revelation. For example:

In *The Practice*, Eugene Young's brother was wrongly imprisoned because a few policemen abused the justice system. From this trauma, Eugene felt impassioned to become a lawyer and fight for the guilty just as hard as for the innocent, because that's what guarantees that the justice system will work. That's what, in Eugene's mind, will ensure that no other innocent man suffers an injustice such as his brother did.

In *The X-Files*, Fox Mulder is haunted by the childhood memory of his sister's abduction from their home. Her disappearance sets him on a single-minded course as an adult to discover the truth of what happened to her.

In *Dawson's Creek*, a touching childhood memory of spending time with his father who loved films, created Dawson's dream of become a great filmmaker.

On the compass, a character's type (race car, taxi cab, demolition derby, or anti-car) is his/her "true north." That is, what category he/she falls in will determine how this character moves and reacts through the plot and series. For example:

In *ER*, poor Abby, a demolition driver, always gets slammed from one angle or another. First her ex-husband forgets to pay her medical school tuition so she's out of the program. Her mother's bi-polar illness often causes worry, mental anguish, and/or embarrassment for Abby. Having to be the adult in the mother-daughter relationship even as a child has led Abby to build an emotional wall to protect herself. As a result she is her own worst enemy, and thus when Luka falls in love with her, Abby eventually sabotages the relationship.

Let's examine the compass traits of the TV characters below:

Grissom in C.S.I. (Race Car)	Lily in Once & Again (Taxi Driver)	Jimmy in The Practice (Demolition)	Lorelai in Gilmore Girls (Anti-Car)
Intelligent	Sensitive	Gullible	Rebel
Show-off	Responsible	Loyal	Opinionated
Loner	Nurturing	Plain	Protective
Handsome	Sympathetic	Lonely	Smug
Dry Wit	Romantic	Low Self-Esteem	Sarcastic
Teacher	Good Listener	Not Book Smart	Smart
Tenacious	Protective	Compassionate	Independent

These are just some of the traits these characters reveal and exude in the course of their series. Next time you view a program, start really scrutinizing the characters. Get to know them as you would your own friends, only then you will be able to write them believably.

The Character Trinity

The most important factors to know about your character in regards to plot, whether it is your main plot or subplots, are:

1 His/Her Goal

2 His/Her Need

3 His/Her Fear

Think of these elements as the character trinity. You must create your driver with a very blatant goal and need, then put him/her on a one way street to achieve it. Your driver's goal fuels the A-story (action plot line) while your character's need can fuel an emotional subplot. The character's goal and need are two distinct elements. This goal and need most often conflicts with the character's fear and/or is motivated by it. In addition, the character trinity will be interlinked with the plot's premise.

Let's take a look at our examples:

In *West Wing*, "The Fall's Gonna Kill You" the A-story is about taking a poll to learn how the public will react to the president's not revealing during his campaign that he has MS. The goal is for the staff to find out this information while concealing why they need to know (thus not exposing the president's lie). The need of both the staff and president is to save themselves politically. The characters' fears are that the president may be impeached and they will be indicted. Notice how the character trinity interweaves with the premise of the story arc: "Lies destroy".

In *Gilmore Girls*, "Double Date", Rory's goal is help her best friend sneak out on a date with Todd while her need is for Lane to have a good time. Her fear is that Lane will be hurt if Todd doesn't like Lane. The character trinity is reflected in the episode's premise, "Lying can get you into trouble."

In *24*, "4:00a.m.-5:00a.m." Jack's goal is to get answers from Pentacost. His need is to find out what Pentacost knows about Kim's disappearance. His fear is that his daughter, Kim, has been kidnapped and may be harmed, by those plotting to assassinate the Senator. The premise, "Sometimes you must sacrifice personal happiness for the greater good," is interwoven in the character trinity.

In *Enterprise*, "Fight or Flight", Hoshi's goal is to adjust to her new surroundings. Her need is to be valuable to the crew. Her fear is that she will fail the Captain and crew, resulting in dire consequences for them all. The premise, "you must believe in yourself," is played out in the plot and reflected in the character trinity.

A character can also have a goal and need which drives the series, and not just the episode. For example:

In *The X-Files*, Fox Mulder's goal is to find out about the government conspiracy involving alien abductions so he can learn the truth about his sister's disappearance. His need is to be absolved from his sister's abduction. His fear is that he will never find his sister.

In *The Fugitive*, Richard Kimble's goal is to find the one-armed man, but his need is to prove his innocence. This is what drives the plot and emotion of each and every episode. His fear, of course, that the FBI will catch him before he can prove his innocence.

In *Law & Order*, the goal of the detectives and lawyers is to find and put the criminal in jail, while the need is to see that justice is served. The fear is usually determined by the whatever issue is being examined in the episode. For example, in "Ritual" McCoy fears by being lenient with the defendant, he might encourage vigilantism.

The Character Arc

What a character learns in the course of the episode, story arc, and/or the series is called the character's arc. This is what is executed through the premise of your story. It can be any character, not just the driver of the story, although it most often is the driver.

In *West Wing*, "The Fall's Gonna Kill You", the characters are beginning to realize, "Lies destroy."

In *Gilmore Girls*, "Double Date" Lane and Rory learn, "Lying will get you into trouble."

In *Enterprise*, "Fight or Flight", Hoshi learns to believe in herself, and that to survive new surroundings, one must adapt.

In *Law & Order*, the criminals learn that crime doesn't pay (at least most of the time).

For those of you creating your own series, keep in mind what your character will learn in the course of the series. This isn't something you'll use in your pilot, of course, but a direction to think about when developing your sample episodes. For example, in *Buffy the Vampire Slayer*, Spike, started out as a true villain for Buffy, but through the course of the series, falls in love with her because she could not be corrupted by the evil she fights. His love for her transformed him to "the good side" so to speak, and illustrated his character arc for the series.

Character Tics

It's always fun to create a character tic for one on your characters. A character tic is a trait or quirk unique to that particular character, like Sherlock Holmes's famous hat and pipe. A character tic readily identifies a character to the audience. Always let a character's tic play into the plot whenever possible. Often tics are exhibited in voice distinctions. For example:

In *Moonlighting*, Ms. Dipesto would often answer the phone at Blue Moon Detective Agency, talking in riddles.

In *St. Elsewhere*, the janitor calls himself, Mr. Entertainment, and converses by singing or speaking song lyrics.

One popular character tic is to create a character that the audience *never* sees, but that the other characters know and talk about, like Dr. Oliver London in *St. Elsewhere* or Robin Masters in *Magnum, P.I.* Be imaginative, and have fun with this device when developing one of your characters. Just remember, if you give them a tic, it's with them for the course of the series.

Character Tags

Once you begin writing the actual script, there is a technical format to follow in regard to characters. When a new character steps onto the page for the *first* time, introduce his/her name in CAPS and sum him/her up in a one or two sentence character tag (description) which sticks in the reader's mind. You want a reader to immediately grasp who this character is. When you write for an existing series, you only write a character tag if you introduce a new character not already on the series. If you are creating your own characters for an original series, you will have to provide a character tag for every character you introduce in your pilot script.

Remember those brief descriptions of the *Enterprise* crew listed for the television bible in Chapter Six? That's basically what a character tag is. For example, a possible character tag for these characters could be:

CLARK KENT: 16, yes, he's Superboy, just without the cape, suit, and the flying bit. At least for now, because he's just a typical teen, well sort of. With super powers that he has to hide from his peers, Clark doesn't exactly fit in. He isn't sure why he is the way he is, which makes him even more insecure during these awkward teenage years. Yearning to be like everyone else, Clark's got some growing up to do before he's ready for his date with destiny. *(Smallville)*

JORDAN CAVANAUGH: 30-ish, think "Erin Brockovich in Quincy's lab coat,"* only feistier, and definitely more sexy. She's a medical examiner who's too impatient to wait for the detectives to solve the crime. Stubborn, sardonic, and smart, she's a frustrating combination of traits which suits her combative personality well. *(Crossing Jordan)*

*(quote taken from TV Guide - Fall preview 2001)

GRISSOM: remember those geeks in your high school science lab? Well, now one of them has grown up into a handsome forensic detective. This forty-ish scientific Sherlock is more stubborn than a pit bull when it comes to outsmarting the criminal. His dry wit and cocky attitude doesn't always fly well with the higher-ups, but his clever mind plus his desire to mentor make him a hit with his crime team of constantly learning scientific sleuths. *(C.S.I.)*

Make each character sound original and distinctive. You'll use these tags later in the actual script, so do the work here. That way, you won't have to slow your momentum during your first draft when you're focusing on plot.

Recap

1 Know the characters' true north, color type, dipstick, and major compass traits. This will keep you writing the character consistently. It will also assist you in knowing how the driver will react in each scene and/or situation. You must insure the characters are driving their own vehicles rather than being bused by you, the writer. Characters must follow their own needs in the plot, not the writer's needs.

2 Make sure each character you create is unique and fun. Have him/her complement and contrast other characters in the script.

3 Characters must be believable and consistent to keep viewer's interest. This doesn't mean a character can't grow and change, but s/he must do so in a way which is believable.

4 Make your characters relatable. Be sure to include universal appeal when creating your characters and your story. Don't make them perfect. They must have flawed as well as enviable traits.

5 Create a moment from the character's past which truly defines who s/he is.

6 Make your character tics unique and fun.

7 Make your character tags memorable. Really sum up the essence of your character in the most exciting way possible.

For ideas on developing intriguing characters, examine those characters from the classics of literature, television, and feature films. These characters have endured the test of time and have been successful for a reason. They can give you a great sense of how to create lasting stories and unforgettable characters.

NOTE: In the exercises below, for those writing for an existing series, you will answer the character questions based on your observation of the series' characters for which you are writing. These exercises will help you learn more about the characters and help you get to know them better so that you can write them consistently and convincingly. For those writing an original pilot, you will do these exercises to create the characters for your own series. These exercises require a great amount of time and thought: *do not do them all in one session!* Work at your own pace, but whenever you feel tempted to hurry along, that's the time to stop and return to the exercise another day.

Exercise 24. Create a character dipstick for the driver of each plot line in your episode, regardless of whether it is a sample spec or original pilot. Include the measuring marks A-E, especially noting the relationships and backstory between the main characters in your story.

Exercise 25. Now make a character compass for these each of these drivers. Remember, don't make a character perfect; s/he must have some traits which are flawed. What is the true north (character type) of your character? Is s/he motivated by intimacy (blue) power (red) fun (yellow) or peace (white)?

Exercise 26. Look for traits in the supporting cast which clash with the driver's traits to help develop humor and/or conflict in your story. In addition, for those of you creating your own series, make sure you create the character's major life-changing or life-directing moment.

Exercise 27. If applicable, create a character dipstick and character compass traits for your villain. What is your villain's true north (road rage, aggressive driver, Sunday driver, or open road)? What is his/her color type, if applicable? Make sure it clashes with your driver's color type.

Exercise 28. From three or six episodes you graphed, write what the A-story driver's goal, need, and fear is in each episode. Is there a character trinity that runs through the series?

Exercise 29. For the episode you are writing, list your own driver's goal, need, and fear. Next, write what the your driver's character arc (or what another character is going to learn) during the course of the episode (if applicable). Review your premise to see what idea or moral needs to be embodied in the character. Include any other goals by characters in the subplots.

Exercise 30. If applicable, write down your villain's goal and/or need in your story and/or series (unless it is an open road villain) and make sure it conflicts with your driver's goal and/or need.

Exercise 31.A. For those writing for existing series, create a character tag for any new supporting characters you are introducing in your episode.

Exercise 31.B. For those creating an original series, sum up your driver, villain, and any other supporting characters that you will use in your pilot script in a one to three sentence tag.

NOTE: Don't write a character tag for a character who appears briefly in your script. For example, if you have a waiter whose only function is to take a dinner order from your main characters, and then is never seen again in the episode, you obviously wouldn't need to describe such a character. You only need to write character tags for main and supporting characters, characters integral to your plot.

Chapter Eleven
Act One

So now that you know the characters, it's time to have them enter the plot. The first city block on your TV Road Map forms Act One and comprises the first 13-22 pages of your teleplay, streets1-10. This is where you introduce any new characters and set-up which character(s) this particular episode will focus on. If you're writing for a solo or duo cast series, it will always be about the star character(s). If you are writing for an ensemble cast series, you'll have a choice of which character will dominate your particular A-story.

Act One is also where you will introduce or continue character relationships and establish the episode's plots in the most fascinating way possible without giving away all of your story. Here, you set-up most of the subplots as well as hurl a few falling rocks (obstacles) your character's way. There probably will be no time for rest areas in Act One unless in the Teaser(see below) to reflect the tone of the series and/or to reveal something more about a character. Act One can also be a great place to set up a ticking clock to drive the tension and/or suspense throughout the whole episode.

NOTE: For those creating an original pilot, this is where you establish the series' arena (setting) and its genre.

Road Rule #16: Your first scene sequence is crucial so think visually! Hook the viewer from the beginning frame!

The Teaser

This is the opening scene or scene sequence of Act One which "teases" the audience into staying tuned and not switching the channel. It sets up what the episode is about, establishes the theme and tone of the episode, and/or reveals something more about a character.

In your script, the Teaser will be your first 1-4 pages of Act One. Most often, the Teaser is followed by the series' main credits and title, then the show breaks to commercial. The Teaser exists to grab and hold the audience's attention through the commercial break (and the reader's attention so that he'll keep turning those pages). Your TV tunnel will greatly affect what the Teaser will be. For example, if you are writing an episode for *Law & Order*, your Teaser will always include: a crime in progress being interrupted or a crime being discovered. In the next scene, the detectives arrive at the crime scene, find a lead, and end the scene with a snappy dialogue line from one of the detectives. Most cop and mystery genres open with the crime in the Teaser. *Six Feet Under* is a family drama-comedy with dark humor depicting the lives of a family who own and operate a funeral home. It uniquely uses its Teaser to show a character who is about to die. This character will be the body that the series cast will prepare for burial in the course of the episode, and a subplot that will intertwine with their own storylines.

Let's take a look at the Teasers from the graphed examples in this book:

In "The Fall's Gonna Kill You", the story sets-up White House Counsel, Babbish, who "interrogates" C.J. Kregg: has she ever *knowingly* lied about the president's health? At the end of the two scenes, C.J. admits she has *unknowingly* lied to the public about the president's health on numerous occasions. *(West Wing)*

This Teaser cues the viewer that the episode is going to be about the serious ramifications of the president's lie, and that the rippling effect of this omission has begun. It lets us know that we are going to experience one of the rippling effects through C.J.'s point of view. Main credits roll, then the story resumes after a commercial break.

In "Double Date", the Teaser is simply Rory and Lorelai in the kitchen, performing their morning routine sans (without) dialogue. *(Gilmore Girls)*

This Teaser reveals more about the characters, and while it doesn't set-up the story, it does depict the harmony between the characters, subtly hinting that this oneness will be tested during this episode. The main credits roll, followed by a commercial break. Then, Act One continues.

In "4:00a.m.-5:00a.m.", the Teaser comprises action and story that picks up where last week's episode left off: doctor's look at the spine X-rays of Janet York, then they rush her into surgery as Jack follows the police car that has his only lead; a suspect in, the assassination plot on Senator Palmer; a suspect who knows, something about the disappearance of Jack's daughter. *(24)*

The Teaser raises the questions: Will Janet survive? Will Jack be able to interrogate the suspect? Will the suspect lead Jack to the assassin? To his daughter? All these questions invoke the viewer's attention, and keep the audience watching to see what will happen next. This Teaser is not followed by a commercial break as the series format is not set-up this way. Instead, the Teaser leads into the rest of Act One.

In Act One, there are two important plot points or On-Ramps you must construct: the Tow-Away Zone and the Green Light.

Tow-away Zone - The Catalyst

The first important plot point in Act One is the catalyst which should come somewhere between page one and five of your TV script. On your TV Road Map, it falls within the first few streets (1st- 4th Street). This street is where your driver is towed or pulled into the story. It's what spins each plot line and sets up each story's central question, the

A-story, the B-story, the C-story, etc…For the A-story in a contained episode, this scene is almost always found in the Teaser. When you have only one hour to tell a story, you don't want to waste time getting to your main story. Again, in a mystery or cop tunnel, the crime is going to be the catalyst or Tow-Away Zone of the story.

Let's review our examples:

In *West Wing*, "The Fall's Gonna Kill You", the Tow-Away Zone for the A-story is when Toby tells Josh to request a secret poll (4th Street). The Tow-Away Zone for the B-story is when Babbish questions C.J. about what she knew and when she knew it. The scene ends with C.J. admitting that on many times she has lied to the American public about the president's health. (2nd Street)

Both these scenes encompass the continuing story arc's central question: "Will this lie destroy them all?" while each Tow-Away Zone spins its respective question: "How will the American public react to the lie?" (A-story) and "How much trouble is C.J. in; will this lie ruin her career?" (B-story). Each Tow-Away scene above runs about 3 minutes.

In *Gilmore Girls*, "Double Date", it is the scene in which Lane asks Rory to get Dean to set her up on a date with his friend Todd. (2nd Street)

This scene follows the Teaser, and sets up the A-story central question, "Will Lane and Todd hit it off?" It comes after the commercial break. This scene also establishes a small subplot: that Lorelai has a business exam coming up and is having difficulty concentrating (setting up the D-story central question, "Will Lorelai ace her exam?", while the exam is the catalyst). This subplot provides some comic-relief for the awkward tension between Lane and Rory when Lane asks such a favor.

In "4:00a.m.-5:00a.m.", *24*, it's the scene in which Jack follows the police car which transports his suspect. This man is his only lead in finding the assassin, and maybe locating his daughter. (3rd Street)

This main Tow-Away Zone spins the series central question, "Will Jack stop the assassin from killing Senator Palmer?" as well as spins the A-story central question: "Will the suspect lead Jack to the assassin? To Kim?" It falls at the end of the Teaser.

Green Light - The First Turning Point

The Green Light generally falls somewhere within the first eleven to fourteen minutes of the episode, and will fall approximately between pages 12 - 20 of your teleplay. It is the first turning point of your script, and occurs on the 10th Street On-Ramp. This is where your driver (hero) or another character hits the gas and zooms into the action. Maybe s/he doesn't want to drive into the action, but s/he commits to the conflict nevertheless. On this On-Ramp, one of your drivers is hurled a crisis and/or dilemma, and often must make a choice in regards to the plot. Here, there must be more at stake and more emotional impact than before for your driver. 10th Street marks the end of Act One and precedes the commercial break, thus it must be compelling enough to keep the viewer from changing channels during the commercials.

While the examples below depict different genres, the basic plotting for their respective 10th Street On-Ramps is the same:

In *West Wing*, "The Fall's Gonna Kill You", the Green Light scene is when C.J. and Babbish review her press release about the president's health. The two are interrupted by his secretary who hands C.J. a note. Babbish asks what's in the note, and C.J. stares at him, replying, that the sky is falling (12 minutes into the episode).

This scene interweaves the comic-relief subplot of the satellite with the threat of destruction to the White House staff's careers. Here, C.J. is presented with the crisis that she has publically lied about the president's health and that she may be indicted (B-story) while the symbolic storyline of the satellite (D-story) serves as a great act out line to the commercial break.

In *Gilmore Girls*, "Double Date", the Green Light is when Rory asks Dean to ask Todd to go out on a date with Lane. The four can double date, Rory suggests. Dean is hesitant, but reluctantly agrees (13 minutes into the episode).

This scene commits Rory to the action of the A-story plot; she "hits the gas" and encourages Dean to get Todd to go out with Lane.

In *24*, "4:00a.m.-5:00a.m.", the Green Light occurs when the sergeant is about to let Jack into the holding cell to interrogate the suspect when Jack's superior, George Mason, arrives to stop Jack (12 minutes into the episode).

In this scene, Jack has definitely committed to the action of the plot when he is suddenly hurled a crisis: the arrival of Mason who isn't likely to let Jack see the suspect. In fact, Mason is more likely to arrest or fire Jack at this point in the story.

On-ramp Signposts

To ensure that your 10th Street On-Ramp is strong enough to keep the viewer from switching channels during the commercials, follow the signposts below. Incorporate all five in your Green Light scene:

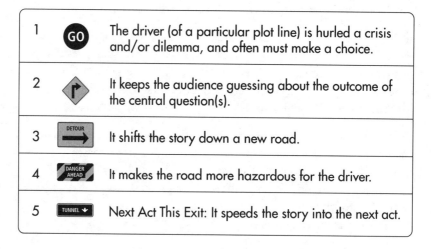

1	GO	The driver (of a particular plot line) is hurled a crisis and/or dilemma, and often must make a choice.
2		It keeps the audience guessing about the outcome of the central question(s).
3	DETOUR	It shifts the story down a new road.
4	DANGER AHEAD	It makes the road more hazardous for the driver.
5	TUNNEL	Next Act This Exit: It speeds the story into the next act.

NOTE: These signposts are derived and/or adapted from the turning point's functions Linda Seger lists in her book *Making A Good Script Great*, a marvelous book on screenwriting.

Let's review our sample episodes to see how the writers developed these signposts to create their respective 10th Street On-Ramps:

In *West Wing*, "The Fall's Gonna Kill You", it used all the signposts to make an effective act break:

(1) C.J. is hurled a crisis: she's realizing how much trouble she could be facing, and she is given the note that the sky is falling.

(2) It does keep the audience guessing about what is going to happen next to C.J. and everyone else.

(3) It shifts the story down a new road as these two plot lines merge.

(4) It makes the road more hazardous as the ramifications of the lie hit home for C.J.

(5) It definitely speeds us into the next act as the audience eagerly waits to see what will happen to C.J. and the staff.

In *Gilmore Girls*, "Double Date", the signposts are met in this manner:

(1) Rory makes the choice to ask Dean about getting Todd and Lane together.

(2) The audience now wonders what will happen on the date, so it does keep the viewer guessing.

(3) It shifts the story onto a new road, because now it looks like the four teens will double date.

(4) It makes the road more hazardous because Dean worries about Todd not having a good time, and Rory worries whether Lane will get her feelings hurt if the date is awful.

(5) It speeds the audience into the next act as the viewer waits to see if Lane and Todd will hit it off.

In *24*, "4:00a.m.-5:00a.m.", the writer uses the signposts to make a very strong act-out:

(1) Jack is hurled a crisis when Mason stops him from interrogating the suspect.

(2) It definitely keeps us guessing because now it looks like Jack won't even get to question the only lead he has to the assassin and to his daughter's whereabouts.

(3) It shifts us down a new road as the viewer wonders how Jack will get the information he needs when he can't even talk to the suspect.

(4) It makes the road very hazardous, because if Jack can't talk to his only lead, how is he going to find the assassin, stop the hit on Senator Palmer, and find his daughter who may have been kidnapped?

(5) It certainly zooms us into the next act as the audience waits anxiously to see how Jack will get to the suspect.

The City Block of Act One

Look again at the graphs in this book, and let's examine their first city blocks to see which plot lines were established, and how much story time each one dominates. In:

West Wing's, "The Fall's Gonna Kill You", sets up five plot lines:

C.J. and Babbish plot (1st, 2nd, 10th Streets)

Satellite plot (3rd, 5th, 10th Streets)

Poll plot (4th, 5th Streets)

Tobacco plot (3rd, 6th Streets)

Sam speech plot (4th Street)

This city block establishes who the episode is going to focus on since it is an ensemble cast, weaves in the themes of the episode (which we'll discuss in a later chapter) introduces several subplots, all which reflect, parallel and/or enhance the story arc's central question: "Will this lie destroy them all?" This whole city block runs approximately 13.5 minutes. I listed the plots in descending order, depending on how many streets they used. The C.J. plot and the satellite plot take up most of the *scenes* in Act One, but this doesn't necessarily mean they take up most of the TV *screen* time. It's just an indicate of which plots might be dominating this act.

Gilmore Girls, "Double Date", also sets up four plot lines:

Lane date plot (2nd, 10th Streets)

Lorelai business exam plot (2nd, 3rd, 4th Streets)

Sookie date plot (5th Street)

Lane & Rory lie plot (1st Street)

The first city block establishes the A-story plot of Lane and Todd, and the B-story plot which parallels it; the subplot of Sookie and Jackson. It also establishes the subplot of Lorelai's upcoming business exam. This city block runs approximately 16 minutes. If we look at our graph, we can see that while the business plot line is also two scenes, they appear to be short scenes by our notes. Thus, the Lane date plot dominates, and is an indicator that this is the A-story plot. The Teaser, while not directly spinning the Lane & Rory lie plot, thematically falls to that plot line since the harmony between Rory and Lorelai will be broken with the deception.

In *24*, "4:00a.m.-5:00a.m.", four plot lines are established:

Jack and suspect plot (3rd, 5th, 8th, 9th, 10th Streets)

Hospital plot: Janet surgery; Teri waits (1st, 2nd, 4th, 5th Streets)

Kim kidnap plot (5th, 6th Streets)

Palmer's son plot (7thStreet)

Act One establishes that Jack has to get to the suspect and find out what he knows; that Janet is still fighting for her life in surgery; that Kim is now in the hands of the assassin; that Palmer must find out if the rumor about his son is true, and how to stop this story from making it into the news. Act One runs 13 minutes. The dominate plot is the Jack and suspect plot, which is indeed the A-story plot of the episode.

As I mentioned at the beginning of this chapter, Act One will also include several falling rocks for your character(s) to help set-up and build the plots. These obstacles may be set into motion by the villain, another character, and/or by the driver.

Let's look at the falling rocks used in the Act Ones of our graphed examples:

In *West Wing*, "The Fall's Gonna Kill You":

(1) C.J. has lied on many occasions to the public about the president's health.

(2) A satellite is hurling to earth, and Donna fears it will crash in a populated area.

(3) Josh suddenly realizes covering up the president's illness may be seen as a fraud perpetrated upon the American public just as the tobacco company perpetrated a fraud that nicotine is not addictive.

Here, two of the obstacles are created by the president who withheld the fact that he has multiple sclerosis during his campaign. The other obstacle symbolically reflects the story arc's central question: "Will this lie destroy them all?"

In *Gilmore Girls*, "Double Date":

(1) Lorelai serves as an obstacle to Lane by repeatedly interrupting Lane and Rory as Lane tries to talk Rory into helping her get a date with Dean's friend, Todd.

(2) Lorelai must solve a problem at work before she can return to her studying.

(3) Also, Sookie nervously faces the obstacle of setting up a date with Jackson. (Sookie is her own obstacle here)

(4) Dean serves as an obstacle for Rory as she must convince him to get Todd to go out with Lane even though Dean thinks the two are not well-suited.

In *24*, "4:00a.m.-5:00a.m." obstacles abound:

(1) Janet is wheeled into surgery, and so will not be of use in finding out where Kim is.

(2) Jack's only lead is a suspect who has just killed a cop; and the cops aren't too eager to share the suspect.

(3) Kim, who is bound and gagged, is placed into the assassin's car.

(4) The rumor that his son may have committed murder is about to hit the press, presenting a several obstacles for Senator Palmer.

(5) Jack's superior, George Mason, is hunting Jack and suspects Jack might have something to do with the deaths of two agents.

(6) The police sergeant refuses to let Jack talk to the suspect.

(7) Mason finds Jack and stops him from interviewing the suspect, Pentacost.

Here, almost all the obstacles are created either directly or indirectly by the assassin. Palmer's obstacle spins from the reporter who has discovered that Palmer's son may have murdered someone.

As you can see from the examples above, the action/thriller tunnel has more obstacles than the drama tunnels, that's typical. The genre you've selected will directly affect how many obstacles you'll need in your plots.

In addition, Act One can be a good place to set up a ticking clock to help establish tension and suspense in the episode. From our three examples, none choose to use this device in their respective Act Ones.

The Recap

Act One contains the Teaser, the Tow-Away Zone, and the Green Light scene. The main Tow-Away Zone is the catalyst which spins the A-story of the episode and its central question, occurring somewhere in the first few streets of Act One. Each of your subplots, however, will also have their own Tow Away Zone. The Green Light scene falls on the 10th Street On-Ramp, and is the scene in which your driver must face a choice, crisis, and/or dilemma. It must incorporate all five story signposts in order to be effective enough to hold the viewer's attention through the commercial break. While Act One is mostly about the set-up of the episode's story, it also will have a few falling rocks (more if it's an action/thriller, or action/adventure tunnel) and possibly a ticking clock. Altogether, Act One will run approximately 12 - 17 minutes, and usually comprises the first 13-22 pages of your teleplay.

Exercise 32. Examine the three or six episodes you graphed earlier. List the Teaser, and the A-Story's Tow-Away Zone. Did the Tow-Away Zone fall within the Teaser? If not, on what street did it occur?

NOTE: Think about the A-story's central question. What is being answered in the climax of the episode? Only the scene which truly zooms your driver in that direction can qualify as the catalyst of the A-story.

Exercise 33. Next, list the 10th Street On-Ramp (Green Light) of each episode. What time in the hour did they occur? Note how they incorporated the signposts used on 10th Street. A strong act out will encompass all five. How long was each episode's Act One?

NOTE: 10th Street will be the scene which precedes the first commercial break after the opening credits have been seen (those listing the guest stars, writer, director, etc...).

Exercise 34. From the three or six episodes you graphed, now list each of their plot lines in their respective Act Ones. How many plot lines did each episode set up? Which plot in each dominates to become the A-story? Are any of the plot lines continuing from existing episodes, or were they created and contained within the episode you graphed?

TV Road Map (page 222)

Remember, each street represents one scene or a series of *very short* scenes. You'll only need to write one or two sentences per street to break down the heart or point of each scene. As you construct your plot, keep in mind:

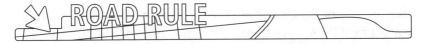

Road Rule #17: Your character must leave each scene needing more than when s/he entered it!

This is what assists you in building tension within your plots. Make sure to follow this Road Rule as you begin constructing your story.

NOTE: As you block out your Act One, you might not need to fill in every street on your TV Road Map. That's okay. Series heavy on dialogue will use less streets on your TV Road Map than those series heavy on action as we've already noted in the graphed examples in this book. Only use the streets (scenes) your story requires, no more, no less.

Exercise 35. Fill in your premise, central idea, and main central question on the TV Road Map Form. Also copy the goal and need for the driver and the villain (if applicable) of your story onto the form. Next, list the Teaser and the A-Story Tow-Away Zone. Then, fill in your 10th Street. Make sure your driver's goal is serviced by the two major plot points of Act One. Make sure your 10th Street answers all five story signpost questions for a strong act break.

As you juggle the main plot and its subplots, make sure each has enough falling rocks and/or ticking clocks to heighten the tension. You must keep raising the incline that your characters have to drive on.

Exercise 36. List any other plot(s) you want to construct to mirror and complement the A-story. Introduce all or most in your Act One. Remember, they will each have their own Tow-Away scene. With this in mind, it should be easy for you to fill in the rest of the streets for Act One on your TV Road Map. Use the A-story central question to keep you on track for your main plot.

Now, it's time to scrutinize Act Two.

Chapter Twelve
Act Two

In the city block of this act, you must build upon the plotlines that you set up in Act One, increasing your story's tension. In addition, if your story requires another subplot that you didn't have time to introduce in Act One, then introduce it here early in the act. Make sure your subplots balance and enhance your A-story plot. Remember, you'll probably be juggling more subplots if you are writing for an ensemble cast series than if you are writing for a duo or solo cast series.

The Act Two city block comprises 11th - 20th Streets on your TV Road Map. Each street in this block, just as in Act One, must lead into its respective Central (?) Avenue. As your character travels along these roads, s/he must have enough "falling rocks" or obstacles to complicate Act Two. While Act One is about establishing your plots, Act Two is about building them so you probably won't have time for a rest area. Again, your TV tunnel will help determine how many obstacles you'll need for your story. In an action tunnel, you must make sure the villain is hurling enough obstacles in the driver's path. In the drama tunnels, you'll use less obstacles to build your story, as these tunnels contain more dialogue and character moments than action.

Each city block in Act Two will comprised anywhere from 10 to 16 pages, averaging somewhere between 8 to 12 minutes of TV screen time. In each of the four city blocks of the teleplay, as the speed limit increases or suspense increases, the story constantly rises up a steep incline by heightening the jeopardy, making the driver's road more difficult to navigate. This is how you keep these 10-16 pages building. In addition, each city block must also set up the next city block (remember story signpost 5: Next Act This Exit) which brings us to the major plot point of Act Two:

The U-turn: Midpoint

The last scene of Act Two is the 20th Street On-Ramp which shoots onto one of your plots Central (?) Avenues. In a solo cast series, it shoots onto the A-story central question. In a duo or ensemble series, it can shoot onto any of your plots. 20th Street forms the midpoint of the one hour episode, and turns the story into an *unexpected* or *opposite* direction. In other words, it's your U-Turn. This midpoint scene immediately precedes the mid-hour commercial break, and generally falls between 22 to 24 minutes into the episode or somewhere between pages 26-30. It must set up Act Three and be strong enough to fuel the second half of the episode (Streets 21st - 40th).

Like 10th Street, 20th Street must also encompass the story signposts listed in Act One to ensure its act out is strong enough to hold the viewer's attention through the longest commercial break in the hour.

Let's take a look at the 20th Street On-Ramp in each of our examples, and see how each encompasses the five story signposts:

In "The Fall's Gonna Kill You": 20th Street occurs when the First Lady and President argue; why didn't he tell her he was going public about his illness? He gently informs her he had to because she had filled out a form for their daughter's college, a form on which she didn't mark that he had MS. (*West Wing*)

(1) Abbey, the First Lady, is hurled a crisis; her husband's whole political career could be ruined when he admits he has multiple sclerosis and didn't reveal his illness about it during his campaign - and it's her fault that he must come forward now.

(2) It keeps the audience guessing because not only is the president in for a tumultuous ride, but now so is she.

(3) It shifts the story down a new and unexpected road because now she is implicated in the omission.

(4) The road is more hazardous to them both now as the president has no choice but to go public before word leaks out about his illness.

(5) This scene zooms us into the next act as we wait to see what happens when Abbey speaks with the White House Counsel and how this will affect their careers and their marriage.

In "Double Date": the U-Turn scene occurs: when Jackson forces Rune to go on the double date. (*Gilmore Girls*)

(1) Lorelai and Rune are hurled a crisis and a choice as they get stuck on this date together, both choosing, for their own reasons, to go.

(2) It keeps the audience guessing because now it doesn't look like Jackson and Sookie will have a good time since Rune is being such a jerk.

(3) It shifts the story down a new and unexpected direction because the viewer wasn't expecting anyone to object to going out with Lorelai, an attractive and personable woman.

(4) The road is more hazardous because Lorelai is stuck on a date with someone who doesn't want to be with her, and Sookie's attempt to win Jackson's affections are threatened by his cousin's foul mood.

(5) This scene zooms us into the next act as we wait to see what will happen on this horrible date.

In "4:00a.m.-5:00a.m.": 20th Street occurs when Jack gets Tina to put a trace on the pay phone, and she realizes Jack is planning to break Pentacost out of jail. (*24*)

(1) Jack is faced with a crisis: he must get Pentacost out of jail and to the pay phone or the assassin will know something's wrong; he chooses a jailbreak.

(2) It keeps the audience guessing: how is Jack going to free Pentacost and sneak him out of a precinct of cops who are keeping an eye on the suspect who murdered one of their own?

(3) It shifts the story down a new and unexpected road because who would expect that Jack would break Pentacost out of jail?

(4) The road is more hazardous to Jack who is risking his career and his life to free the cop murderer in hopes Pentacost will lead him to the assassin and to whoever has kidnapped his daughter.

(5) This scene really zooms us into the next act as we wait to see how Jack is going to get Pentacost out and if they can make it to the pay phone in time.

The story incline or jeopardy becomes steeper on these 20th Street On-Ramps because of these strong act outs. Here, the characters have committed more deeply to the plot, and they will each have to face the consequences of their actions in the next act, Act Three.

The City Block of Act Two

Let's study the city block (story sequence) of Act Two from our graphed examples. These are the plot lines each episode serviced in their Act Twos:

West Wing's "The Fall's Gonna Kill You" continues with five plot lines for the episode, substituting the tobacco and First Lady plot:

Sam speech plot (11th, 12th, 13th, 15th Streets)

First Lady, Abbey, plot (18th, 19th, 20th Streets)

Poll plot (20th Street)

C.J. and Babbish plot (14th Street)

Satellite plot (16th Street)

The Sam speech plot dominates the top of Act Two while the Abbey plot dominates the end of Act Two. Both plots were a mere mention in Act One, but now construct most of Act Two. This helps build their plot line since neither were constructed in Act One, while holding the audience's suspense on the other three plots which were the focus of Act One. Notice the tobacco plot line from Act One is dropped for this act, which makes room for the Abbey plot line. All, except the Sam speech plot, continue to build or reflect the central question: "Will this lie destroy them all?" This city block runs 9 minutes in length.

Gilmore Girls, "Double Date", also builds its four plot lines:

Sookie date plot (11th, 0i^{Uh}, 17th, 18th, 19th, 20th Streets)

Lane date plot (15th, 17th Streets)

Lane & Rory lie plot (15th, 17th Streets)

Lorelai business exam plot (11th Street)

While Act One sets-up the desire for the dates, Act Two builds the excitement of the double dates with the B-story now dominating. The middle of the act establishes the Rory and Lane fib. This city block also runs 9 minutes in length.

In *24*, "4:00a.m.-5:00a.m.", the following plot lines are continued:

Jack and suspect plot (12th, 16th, 17th, 18th, 19th, 20th Streets)

Kim kidnap plot (11th, 13th, 14th, 16th, 19th Streets)

Hospital plot: Janet surgery; Teri waits (16th Street)

Palmer's son plot (15th Street)

The beginning of the city block re-establishes Kim's kidnapping and constructs this plot more, then picks up the A-story where Act One left off with Jack at the precinct. The A-story dominates Act Two, but keeps constructing all the plots that it set-up in Act One. This city block runs about 9.5 minutes in length.

Now, let's look at the obstacles presented in each of our examples:

West Wing's, "The Fall's Gonna Kill You" presents four obstacles:

(1) C.J. is the obstacle as Babbish attempts to help her with her statements. (14th Street)

(2) Chicago people want Sam to make a specific quote in the speech he is writing, but he refuses. (15th Street)

(3) No one, including Charlie, seems concerned that a satellite is crashing to earth, further frustrating Donna. (16th Street)

(4) Abbey learns it was her fault the president must go public. She must now speak with the White House Counsel. (20th Street)

So basically each of the four plots are given an obstacle to move each of the subplots and the A-story plot forward.

Gilmore Girls', "Double Date" also adds four obstacles:

(1) Michel is an obstacle as Lorelai attempts to study. (11th Street)

(2) Lorelai is an obstacle for Sookie who must convince Lorelai to go on a double date with her and Jackson and his cousin, Rune. (11th Street)

(3) Lane doesn't have permission to go on the date with Todd so they must lie to Lorelai about their plans for the evening. (15th Street)

(4) Rune doesn't want to go out with Lorelai because she is too tall. (17th & 18th Street)

Notice how these obstacles fuel their respective plot lines, by adding more conflict to each story. There's also a rest area on 14th Street as Sookie reveals her feelings for Jackson and that she is so nervous he won't like her.

In *24*, "4:00a.m.-5:00a.m." creates six more obstacles for its characters, and sets up a ticking clock:

(1) Rick wants to forget the money and leave, while Danny insists they get the money. (11th Street)

(2) Mason refuses to let Jack talk to the suspect, and insists on questioning Pentacost himself. (12th Street)

(3) Kim is the assassin's obstacle as she tries to get help. (13th Street)

(4) The assassin threatens to shoot Kim, then locks her in the trunk of his car. (13th and 14th Street)

(5) Janet's still in surgery so Teri can't talk with her until she's out and awake. (16th Street)

(6) Jack has twenty minutes to get Pentacost out of jail and to a pay phone...tick, tick, tick. (19th Street)

This last obstacle sets up a new ticking clock (an obstacle with a set time limit that demands a character perform a certain action by a specific time, or a grave consequence will occur) for our hero. Notice how this ticking clock adds tension and pushes the story forward with momentum.

Exercise 37. List the 20th Street, U-Turn, for each of the three or six episodes you graphed. How did this scene turn the story in an unexpected direction? How long did the Act Two city block run in each?

Exercise 38. Next, list all the subplots and on which street they occurred for each of these three or six episodes. Notice how each subplot increased its tension or jeopardy, a æz¬…—zøᵃΩ¬{3ubplot reflected or enhanced the A-story plot.

NOTE: Do not skip the above exercise. I know you are excited to structure your own Act Two, but it is important to see how each episode builds its own jeopardy and suspense to keep an audience's attention before you map out your own story.

Exercise 39. On the TV Road Map, list what will be your 20th Street (midpoint). Be sure it is a strong act out, and sends your character and story skidding into a new and/or unexpected direction. Use all the story signposts, and be sure your U-Turn sets up the next city block, Act Four.

Exercise 40. Now go through the TV Road Map, and fill in the scenes for your Act Two's city block. Include your subplot(s) which will be

more evenly distributed if you are writing for an ensemble cast series. Make sure your incline rises (jeopardy) by adding the needed obstacles. Use a ticking clock if your story warrants one.

Congrats! You've structured your Act Two! You're halfway to the finish line!

Chapter Thirteen
Act Three

Act Three consists of Streets 21-30. Each city block in Act Three will be comprised of 9 to 15 pages (averaging 11-18 minutes). Act Three will also increase the story's speed limit (tension/suspense) by adding more obstacles. Like Acts One and Two, this city block must also set up the next (and last) city block of your story, Act Four. In Act Three, you'll continue to weave the A-story plot with the other plots, merging several or all plot lines on the 30th Street On-Ramp. 30th Street should encompass all of the story signposts just like 10th and 20th Streets do. It is the major plot point of Act Three.

Road of No Return
The Obligatory Scene

30th Street is the *Road of No Return* in which Act Three peaks. It's a One Way Street; at which there is no going back once your hero drives onto it, and nothing can ever be the same again. Your driver must drive onto this street with some threat to him/herself or to someone s/he cares about, or with some consequence to achieving his/her goal. S/he either makes a conscious choice to enter the action "full speed ahead!" or is forced into the action by an event or other characters. The 30th Street On-Ramp occurs anywhere from page 40-48 in your teleplay. 30th Street zooms the character into the motion of the episode and/or continuing story's climax. The final crash (confrontation) in Act Four is now inevitable. The question set up on the A-story Central (?) Avenue will be answered soon in Act Four if it is a self-contained series, and reverberated if it is a continuing or episodic series.

NOTE: Often, a secret or discovery is revealed on 30th Street because obviously there is no going back: one can't un-reveal a secret and/or unlearn a discovery once it is known.

This 30th Street On-Ramp generally falls around 36-38 minutes into the episode, and includes all five story signposts as well:

In *West Wing*, "The Fall's Gonna Kill You": Abbey meets with Babbish, accusing him of trying to further his career. He quickly reminds her that he isn't the one who lied. In one week, they will be going public, and she better be ready to answer some tough questions because what's about to happen is going to be huge. (Notice the ticking clock: one week and a major crisis is upon the all - tick, tick, tick).

This 30th Street On-Ramp follows these signposts:

1   Abbey faces a choice; she can work with Babbish and help herself, or continue being hostile which won't help her or her husband.

2   Keeps the audience guessing: what will happen in a week when the president goes public?

3   It shifts the story down a new road as the First Lady now legally enters this messy cover-up.

4   It makes the road more hazardous for Abbey because she is the one who lied on Zoey's college form, a form which can now be used as legal evidence against her and possibly her husband.

5   It most certainly speeds the story into the next act as the audience waits to see how this lie will affect the First Lady.

In *Gilmore Girls*, "Double Date": the 30th Street is set in Luke's diner as Lorelai escapes her date to hang out with Luke; Rune wants to go bowling and tries to convince Jackson to bag the date; Sookie asks Jackson to stay; Lane's mom passes by the window to see Lorelai in the diner *without* the girls. Mrs. Kim confronts Lorelai about the girls' whereabouts, then storms off to find her daughter.

1   Sookie faces the crisis of Jackson leaving with Rune, but Jackson chooses to stay and start their date over; Lorelai faces a crisis as she realizes her daughter and Lane lied to her and Mrs. Kim (discovery revealed to both moms).

2   It keeps us guessing; now it looks like Sookie and Jackson may hit it off, and continues to keep us guessing if Luke's going to finally ask Lorelai out on a date.

3   It shifts the story into a new direction as the lie is revealed; Jackson and Sookie are finally having a good time on their date.

4   It makes the road more dangerous for Lane and for Rory who are about to be confronted by their mothers.

5   It definitely shifts us into the next act as the audience waits to see if Luke will ask out Lorelai, if Jackson and Sookie will get together, and how much trouble are Lane and Rory in?

Here, Mrs. Kim and Lorelai make a discovery: the girls have lied to them, thus the girls' secret is revealed which speeds us towards the climax in Act Four.

In *24*, "4:00a.m.-5:00a.m.", the 30th Street is the scene in which Jack and Pentacost race to the pay phone. Jack is on his cell to Nina to set up the trace, only the phone rings and it isn't the pay phone. There's a cell phone under the pay phone. Now they can't trace the call. The assassin tells Pentacost to take the keys taped to the back of the pay phone and find the car around the corner, then get rid of the body in the trunk of the car. Jack looks at him in panic, what body? Who's in the car? Pentacost doesn't know. As the two race to find the car, Jack fears he will find his daughter, dead.

1   Jack's hurled two crises: one he can't trace the call, and two, there is a body in the trunk. Is it his daughter?

2   It really keeps the viewer guessing about the story: now the viewer wants to know, who's in the trunk?

3   It shifts us down a new road as Jack races to find out who's in the trunk and how does this body fit into the assassin's plot?

4   It is definitely more dangerous for Jack because he isn't able to trace the call and outwit the assassin, and now there's a body in a trunk and it might be his missing daughter.

5   It zooms us into the next act as the audience definitely doesn't want to channel surf. They want to know who is in the car trunk.

Notice the discovery revealed on the 30th Street in *24*: There's a body in the trunk. They've set it up nicely because we've seen that Kim was put into the trunk of the assassin's car earlier in Act Two. It makes for a very exciting act out, and pushes the story into the climax in Act Four.

The City Block of Act Three

Let's study the city block (story sequence) of Act Three from our graphs:

In *West Wing's* "The Fall's Gonna Kill You" continues with only four plot lines, dropping the C.J. - Babbish plot and the satellite plot, and returning to the tobacco plot:

First Lady, Abbey, plot (21st, 30th Streets)

Poll plot (22nd, 25th Streets)

Sam speech plot (24th Street)

Tobacco plot (22nd Street)

At the beginning of this sequence, the numerous storylines are revisited and the tobacco subplot is sidelined for now. In the middle of the sequence, Sam stands his ground about the speech, and Josh furthers the rippling effect by bringing Joey into the circle of secrets. The end of Act Three is punctuated by Abbey who is forced to admit her lie to the White House Counsel. This city block runs 11 minutes.

Gilmore Girls, "Double Date", builds and merges these plot lines:

Sookie date plot (21st, 23rd, 24th, 30th Streets)

Lane date plot (22nd, 25th, 30th Streets)

Lane & Rory lie plot (30th Street)

Lorelai and Luke plot (30th Street)

In this episode, Act One was about the set-up of the date, Act Two about the preparation of the date, and Act Three depicted the actual dates in progress. Notice how these four plots merge together on 30th Street. This will often happen when writing for solo or duo cast series. This act also drops Lorelai's exam subplot to bring in the runner plot and its central question: "Will Lorelai and Luke *ever* get together?" This city block runs 12 minutes.

In *24,* "4:00a.m.-5:00a.m.", the following plot lines are continued:

Jack and suspect plot (21ᵗʰ, 22ⁿᵈ, 27ᵗʰ, 29ᵗʰ, 30ᵗʰ Streets)

Palmer's son plot (24ᵗʰ, 25ᵗʰ, 26ᵗʰ Streets)

Hospital plot: Janet surgery; Teri waits (23ʳᵈ, 28ᵗʰ Streets)

Kim kidnap plot (30ᵗʰ Street)

This city block sequence mostly focuses on the jailbreak, playing out the twenty minute ticking clock. The Palmer's son plot continues to build as well. Notice how two of the four plots merge on 30ᵗʰ Street. This city block runs 18 minutes, and is longer than usual because it takes another commercial break within this block midway into the Act. (This is most likely because it requires more advertisers as it tries to make its place in the ratings.)

Okay, so what obstacles are hurled at the characters in their respective Act Threes?

In *West Wing*, "The Fall's Gonna Kill You", the writer hurls three obstacles at the characters:

1   Sam still refuses to add the line to his speech even though some powerful people argue for him to do so. (24ᵗʰ Street)

2   Joey has a new interpreter, and so Josh asks the interpreter to excuse them, not knowing if he can trust the guy. Joey, who is deaf, must now only read Josh lips. (25ᵗʰ Street)

3   Abbey is elusive and hostile towards Babbish who must get to the truth. (30ᵗʰ Street)

This scene sets up the ticking clock that they have one week to get prepared to go public about the president's MS, and if the First Lady (and the others) aren't prepared, disastrous ramifications can occur to her career (and to the others' careers). There is one rest area, shots of D.C. which create a mood of power, and reflects what is at stake for these characters.

In *Gilmore Girls*, "Double Date" hurls four falling rocks:

1   Sookie is her own obstacle as she can't stop chattering to Lorelai, nervously ignoring her date. Rune is the obstacle for Lorelai having a good time. (21st Street)

2   Todd's personality is the obstacle as Lane wonders what she ever saw in this guy. (22nd Street)

3   Rune presents another obstacle, he's leaving to go bowling, and demands Jackson come with him. (30th Street)

4   Lorelai is presented with the obstacle that the girls have lied to her and Mrs. Kim. (30th Street)

There are no ticking clocks presented here, but there is a short rest area as Luke and Lorelai hang out on 30th Street, observing Sookie and Jackson and wishing they could have that feeling again of courting someone new.

In *24*, "4:00a.m.-5:00a.m.", six obstacles are presented:

1   The obstacle is that Jack must get Pentacost out of the cell so Jack picks a fight with Pentacost and then the cop so Pentacost can pickpocket the cop's access card and escape. (22nd Street)

2   Maureen Kingsley, a reporter, has evidence that Palmer's son committed murder, and she's intent on breaking the story. (25th Street)

3   Palmer's son is an obstacle as he refuses to discuss with his father whether or not he did kill his sister's rapist. (26th Street)

4   Cops realize Pentacost has escaped with Jack's help and now are after Jack and the suspect. (27th Street)

5   Jack's superior pinpoints Jack using GPS and chases after him. (29th Street)

6   The assassin has placed a cell phone under the pay phone, and uses that to make the call so Jack can't trace it. (30th Street)

There are two ticking clocks working here, one for the episode and one for the series: one is the twenty minutes that Jack has to get

Pentacost to the pay phone; and one is the ticking clock that Jack has twenty-four hours to stop a hit on Senator Palmer.

There is a rest area here on 28th Street when Jack's wife, Teri, guiltily confides to Mr. York some of the last things she said to her daughter. It's a character moment, and it gives the audience a chance to breath before the story confronts the viewers with more obstacles and action.

Exercise 41. List the 30th Street from the three or six graphs you made. Did these Roads of No Return incorporate all five signposts? How long did the city block run in each of these episodes? What subplots were juggled with the A-story plot? Which plots merged on 30th Street?

Exercise 42. Now list your story's 30th Street on the TV Road Map. Use all five signposts so that this Road of No Return will speed the viewer into the last city block, merging several or all of the plot lines and setting up the climax of the episode in Act Four.

Exercise 43. Now fill in the scenes for the rest of your Act Three. Remember, Make sure your incline rises (jeopardy) and your story's speed limit (tension or suspense) increases. Use a ticking clock if your story demands it. Include a rest area if needed.

Hooray! You've just structured your Act Three! One more act to go!

Chapter Fourteen
Act Four

Streets 31-40 form Act Four and will range from 11-14 pages. The last city block consists of three construction areas: the climax, the resolution, and the cliffhanger of the episode. This should be your easiest act to construct because you already know your ending. If you are writing for a continuing series, you will still be building plot as well as possibly setting-up some storylines for the next week. You may have a rest area and some more obstacles, but mainly this act is about merging plots together in the climax and/or resolution of the episode. In other words, your story, or literary highway, is about to end.

The Climax

In Act Four, most of the streets will merge into the episode's climax. The climax is the scene the audience anticipates throughout the episode, story arc (which may occur over many episodes) and/or the series itself. Most often the climax will occur at the top of Act Four, in the scene just following the commercial break, 31st Street, but it doesn't have to. Let your story and the graphs of the series you are writing for guide you.

Let's look at the final crash or clash in these episodes:

In *West Wing*, "The Fall's Gonna Kill You": the president explodes at Leo, needing to vent. Leo calms his friend, then fills him in about the poll. The president sends Leo to get Sam who is about to be let into the secret circle of the lie. This climax resounds the Central (?) Avenue: "Will this lie destroy them all?" and forms the A-story climax. (35th Street) The B-story climax falls on 33rd Street, merging with the C-story.

Notice above that some of the central questions are not answered, but instead are left unanswered to fuel next week's plots.

In *Gilmore Girls*, "Double Date", the climax occurs as Lane's mom finds and confronts Lane. (31st Street)

In *24*, "4:00a.m.-5:00a.m.", the climax is Jack opening the trunk to find lots of blood and a body wrapped in a plastic sheet. (31st Street)

The Resolution

The resolution simply sums up and completes the story. This is where you close any plots you didn't have time for in the climax, and that need to be concluded in this episode. In this scene(s) you allow the driver and other characters to absorb all that has happened to them, and/or what is going to happen to them. It is also a place to spin a new plot or a cliffhanger.

In *West Wing*, "The Fall's Gonna Kill You" : the resolution of Sam's speech is wrapped up on 36th Street; the resolution of the Donna/ satellite subplot is wrapped up on 40th street.

In *Gilmore Girls*, "Double Date", the resolution of Jackson and Sookie, they've now had their third date and are totally in love occurs on 35th Street, and the resolution of Lane's subplot is wrapped up on 33rd Street and 36th Street.

In *24*, "4:00a.m.-5:00a.m.", the Pentacost plot is wrapped up for the episode on 31st Street as a new subplot is spun: trying to I.D. the body.

The City Block of Act Four

Okay, let's review our graphs and see how the plots were concluded and/or continued:

In *West Wing*'s "The Fall's Gonna Kill You" returns to six plot lines:

Poll plot (31st, 34th, 35th, 40th Streets)

First Lady, Abbey, plot (32nd, 33rd, 35th Streets)

Satellite plot (32nd, 40th Streets)

C.J. - Babbish plot (33rd, 40th Streets)

Sam speech plot (35th, 36th Streets)

Tobacco plot (34th Street)

This act runs 14 minutes. In the beginning of the act, the A-story or poll plot commands most of the act. Notice how the Donna/satellite subplot merges with Abby's subplot; and then later with the C.J. subplot. C.J.'s plot line also merges with the Abby subplot. The act ends with the satellite subplot, the C.J. subplot, and the Josh/poll subplot crashing into each other. In addition, the rippling effect grows as now Sam will be told the secret. There's also rest area on 34th Street as Josh confides his concerns to Leo who attempts to remain more optimistic. The act adds only three new obstacles:

1   Donna's told the crashing satellite may even contain plutonium, so now she's more fearful. (32nd Street)

2   C.J. admits to seeing Abbey give an injection to the president during the campaign. (33rd Street)

3   President is angry with Leo for telling the First Lady they were going public before he could.

A new ticking clock is created on 31st Street as Joey has ninety-six hours to create, activate, and analyze a poll while the story arc's ticking clock continues: one week until the President tells the public.

In *Gilmore Girls*, "Double Date", services all five plot lines:

Lane & Rory lie plot (31st, 32nd, 35th, 38th, 39th, 40th Streets)

Lane date plot (31st, 32nd Streets)

Sookie date plot (37th Street)

Lorelai business exam plot (37th Street)

Lorelai and Luke plot (40th Street)

This act runs 9.5 minutes, and returns to all its plot lines, with the Rory and Lane plot line the main focus. Notice how several of the plot lines merge together on 32nd, 35th, 40th Streets. The end of the act continues to tease viewers with the runner plot as to whether or not Luke and Lorelei will get together. It also presented several more obstacles:

1   Lane and Rory are confronted about lying and the date is abruptly ended. (31st Street)

2   Lane is grounded, so she and Rory can't hang out. (34th Street)

3   Mrs. Kim is an obstacle to Lorelai who tries to get Lane's mom to not be so strict.

On 33rd Street, there is a rest area with Rory and Lane as they sneak a brief visit since Lane is grounded.

In *24*, "4:00a.m.-5:00a.m.", drops the Palmer plot, and focuses entirely on the other three plots:

Jack and suspect plot (31th, 32nd Streets)

Hospital plot: Janet surgery; Teri waits (33rd , 40th Streets)

Kim kidnap plot (39th Street)

This act runs 8 minutes. The beginning action opens with the episode's climax, and a new lead - the dead body. The end of the act heightens the suspense that Kim has been kidnapped by some very serious and cold-blooded people as another murder is committed, and sets-up the next week's episode with:

The Cliffhanger

Here, the character drives off the cliff and is left suspended in mid-air, so to speak until the following week's episode. In other words, you hurl the driver into a mess of impending doom that won't be resolved until the opening of the next week's episode. The cliffhanger teases an audience into remembering to watch and tune into the series the following week to see how the driver escapes the peril. It almost always appears within the resolution of one of the plots, and falls on the last or second-to-last scene of the episode, on 39th or 40th Street.

The cliffhanger is an optional plot point, dependent on the genre and format of the television series. Contained series rarely use this plot device (except to further fuel a romantic runner plot) but continuing series must employ it. The only exception to this rule is when a contained series is written in as a two-part episode (an episode which is told in two hours, telling the second hour of the story the following week). Then you would need a cliffhanger at the end of part one.

Series such as *Law & Order* or *Enterprise* don't need cliffhangers because they wrap up their main plots within the hour. Series which are episodic in nature, will use this device, nighttime soaps and action-thrillers most especially. TV series such as *Dallas* and *24* all use cliffhangers. Perhaps the best use of cliffhangers in a series is found in *Quantum Leap*. Each episode ends with a cliffhanger of where and who Sam Beckett has leapt into, teasing the audience to tune in next week to see how Sam gets out of his immediate predicament. In addition, the series uses the last week's cliffhanger as the opening teaser in the next week's episode.

Here's the cliffhangers from our graphed episodes:

In *West Wing*, "The Fall's Gonna Kill You", it comes on 40th street as Josh uses the analogy of the satellite, that satellites fall from space weekly and have never landed in a populated area or done any real damage; he guesses they are due for a hit.

This cliffhanger is found within the episode's resolution of the poll plot and the C.J. plot.

In *Gilmore Girls,* "Double Date", the cliffhanger is when Luke hints that he and Lorelei should hang out again sometime.

This cliffhanger falls in the resolution of the A-story and C-story plots.

In *24,* "4:00a.m.-5:00a.m.", the cliffhanger is when the assassin kills Danny as Rick and Kim watch horrified - is this what will happen to them? (39th Street) and Janet as she flatlines. (40th Street)

By using these three major plot points of Act Four, you will effectively merge your plots for a powerful episode.

Exercise 44. From the three or six episodes you graphed, pick out the climaxes and resolutions of the various plots. How long did the third acts run in each? Do these episodes use cliffhangers? If yes, what are their cliffhanger?

Exercise 45. Fill out Act Four on your TV Road Map, include the climax, resolution, and/or cliffhangers of each of your plots, merging the necessary plots. What plots, if any, are you continuing or setting-up for the following week's episode? Look at all the plots you established in the course of your episode, and be sure to dead end those you need to.

Chapter Fifteen
Themes

A theme is a dominate idea which pervades throughout an episode, continuing story arc, and/or a series. Like winding roads, they intersect your plot, weaving in and out of your story to enrich your premise and reflect your character's emotions. Themes usually spin from a character's need.

In *West Wing,* "The Fall's Gonna Kill You", the theme of impending doom and destruction is symbolized in the Donna satellite subplot that the sky is falling. This theme resounds in the title and in the cliffhanger of the episode, enhancing the premise, "Lies destroy." (The president's need to be the leader of the country spins this theme)

Gilmore Girls' "Double Date" explores themes of romance, love, friendship, trust, and honesty which are all woven into the plot lines of the episode. (Lane and Sookie's need to be romanced spins these themes.)

24's "4:00a.m.-5:00a.m." weaves themes of family, isolation, betrayal, and good vs evil. Jack's need to save Palmer and his daughter spins these themes.

Enterprise's "Fight or Flight" winds the theme of adaptability as the subplot of the alien worm Hoshi transplanted from a planet to the ship merges with Hoshi's own need to adapt and find her place among the crew of the Enterprise.

In addition, themes can also wind throughout a series:

In TV's *The Fugitive*, the themes of justice and redemption wind throughout the series as Richard Kimble searches for the one-armed man (his goal). His need to prove his innocence helps spin the theme of justice.

In *The X-Files,* themes of conspiracy, betrayal, justice, truth weave through most of the series's plots.

Buffy the Vampire Slayer uses themes of good vs. evil enriching the premise, "sometimes you have to sacrifice personal happiness for the greater good."

Smallville weaves themes of family, isolation, suffering, loneliness, and friendship as Clark Kent tries to come to terms with who he is and what his destiny will be. This enhances one of the series premise, "sometimes you have to sacrifice personal happiness for the greater good." This premise, as you see, is a popular one with our do-good heroes (heroes who serve mankind).

Once & Again depicts themes of friendship, romance, love, and family, all which reflect the series premise: "love conquers all."

All these themes touch the audience because the viewer can relate to them to varying degrees. Develop your themes through the desires of your characters and wind them through your plots to compel the viewers to root for your characters.

Exercise 46. Review your notes from the three or six episodes you graphed. What themes wind through each episode and series? How do these themes illuminate the plot(s) and the premise? Through which character's need are they depicted?

Now think about your own teleplay. What themes will enrich your story and plots? Look at your driver's need, goal, and/or premise as these will define the themes useful for your story.

Exercise 47. Now make a list of one to three themes for your story (and/or series if applicable) that will enhance your plots and your premise. Write these themes on a note card, highlighting your main theme. Keep them in sight as you write your episode to keep you focusing on these winding roads. Which character(s) will carry the theme(s)?

Exercise 48. Now that you know your themes, go through your TV Road Map and wind these themes throughout your scenes.

The Pit Stop Principle

Give yourself a round of applause! You just outlined an entire one hour episode for TV! Now it's time for a Pit Stop.

Exercise 49. Don't touch your TV Road Map - don't even think about your story for at least 1 week!

I know, I know, you are anxious to start writing your episode and continue to the next chapter, but trust me, these days off from your story will save you lots of rewriting. You've done an enormous amount of preparatory work, so take a bow. You've earned this writer's break.

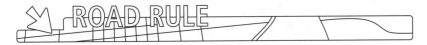

Road Rule #18: Never zoom past a Pit Stop. Pull over and rest to refuel your creativity!

A Pit Stop will allow everything you've read, written, and created in these past fifteen chapters to absorb into your thought processes. When you go through your first checklist in the next chapter, you want to do it with a fresh outlook and renewed energy. Not rushing at this point will save you a great amount of tuning-up or restructuring later. So close the book now, go have some fun, and I'll see you in a week.

Chapter Sixteen
Checkpoint Charlie

Okay, you've taken a Pit Stop (no cheating, only proceed if you have set your TV Road Map aside for at least a week) and you're ready to proceed with a clear, refreshed, and objective mind. The outline is where you want to catch your structure mistakes, not in your one hour teleplay where you'll have 56 - 64 pages to wade through. Therefore, take this chapter seriously and really examine your TV Road Map for any flaws.

Exercise 50. Using the criteria below, scrutinize your outline. Does your TV Road Map pass every checkpoint listed below? If you answer no to any question, then you've wandered off plot. Rework any outline scenes necessary.

1   Is your Teaser (opening sequence) a "grabber", hooking the audience from the first scene(s)?

2   Does your main Tow-Away (1st, 2nd, or 3rd Street) set up the A-story Central Question Avenue? Have you created Tow-Away Zones for each of your subplots?

3   Have you given your driver(s) a blatant goal and need in the episode?

4   Is your driver(s) actively driving along his/her plotted streets. S/he can't be a passenger in the story!

5   Does your driver "hit the gas" and zoom into the plot at the Green Light (10th Street)? Is your driver hurled a crisis and/or dilemma? Must s/he make a choice here?

6   On 10th Street, is there more at stake, more emotional impact for your driver than before?

7 Does your 10th Street On-Ramp incorporate all five story signposts? Is it compelling enough to hold the viewers' attention throughout the commercial break?

8 If applicable, is your villain in opposition with your driver's goal and need?

9 Highlight the falling rocks you have created on your TV Road Map. Do you have sufficient obstacles to sustain your Act One plots?

10 Have you created enough subplots for your main plot, and do these subplots reflect, parallel, and/or enhance the A-story? Do all these plots in Act One reveal the scope of the whole episode? Do they effectively set-up your Act Two?

11 Does your 20th Street U-Turn (midpoint) in Act Two speed the driver/story in an unexpected or opposite direction? Is it strong enough to fuel the second half of the episode?

12 Does your 20th Street incorporate all five story signposts to create an act out strong enough to hold the viewers' attention throughout the longest commercial break?

13 Do you have sufficient obstacles to sustain your Act Two plots? Is your story's incline (jeopardy) rising? Are each of your plots building to effectively set-up your Act Three?

14 Is your 30th Street On-Ramp the strongest? Does it leave your driver in the most jeopardy? Does your driver move onto this street with a threat to her/himself, someone s/he cares about, or to achieving her/his goal? Is your driver forced into the action and/or commits to the action on this street?

15 On your 30th Street, is there no going back once the character commits to the plot here? Are there fewer choices for your driver as s/he enters this road? Does it set into motion the episode's climax in Act Four?

16 Does your 30th Street incorporate all five story signposts to create an act out strong enough to hold the viewers' attention throughout the commercial break?

17 Do you have sufficient obstacles to sustain your Act Three plots? Is your story's incline (jeopardy) rising? Are each of your plots building to effectively set-up your Act Four?

18 Are your character'(s) commitments rising as well ?

19 In your Act Four, is the episode's climax full of action that is bigger and better than the rest of the action in your story? Do you have enough obstacles here to conclude and/or set-up the next week's episode?

20 In your Act Four, have most or all of the plots merged together in the climaxes and resolutions of your episode?

21 If it is a contained series, have you wrapped up all your plot lines here in Act Four?

22 If it is a continuing series, have you wrapped up the necessary plots, and set-up the continuing plots (runners) for future episodes?

23 If applicable, is your cliffhanger strong enough to pull in the audience for the following week? Make sure it does.

24 If you have a ticking clock, is it ticking?! Did you truly set it into motion?

25 Do your rest areas reveal something more about the character(s) or create a mood which reflects your theme(s) and/or story?

26 Does your plot prove your premise, and is it embodied in a character who will fulfill that premise in your story's climax?

27 Do your parallel roads (subplots) and winding roads (themes) reflect and/or enrich the main plot? Do these plots and themes compel the audience to care about your characters? Does your theme(s) spin from the character'(s)s need(s)? If there are certain

themes in the series for which you are writing, have you incorporated these themes into your story as well?

28　Is any scene on your outline just duplicating another scene? If so, cut one of them. It's littering your literary highway.

Now that you're confident each city block is building and leading into the next city block, that your 10th, 20th, and 30th Streets each accomplish all five story signposts, and speed towards the answer to your Central (?) Avenue, then zoom to the exercise below. It's time for all your hard work to turn into some creative fun. When!

Exercise 51. Write your Act One (1st - 10th Streets). Really work on creating drivers and plots the viewer (and reader) will care about and want to watch. Once you've finished this exercise, you should have your first 13 to 22 pages, depending upon your story.

Chapter Seventeen
Dialogue

Dialogue is a precious tool for the writer. It can pull in the viewer, making him or her laugh and/or cry. As a writer, it can also be the most challenging and the most fun part of the script to write, especially in television where you have years to develop and perfect a character's speech rhythm and vocabulary peculiarities. The tone, characters, and tunnel of the series will cue you as to how to write dialogue for that particular series. For the most part, however, follow:

Road Rule #19: Arrive late and leave early in your dialogue.

Zoom into the dialogue as fast as you can, and keep the story moving along your story's streets. Don't waste time having characters chat about nothing unless that is a rule of its TV world. If creating your own series, concoct a rhythm in the dialogue that complements the genre.

Dialogue Style

The type and style of dialogue you use in your episode will mainly depend on these five factors:

- The Character's Compass Traits and Dipsticks
- The Characters' Relationships
- The Specific Rhythm/Tone of A Series
- The TV Tunnel
- The Network or Cable Station It Airs On

Let's look at how these factors affect the style of a series' dialogue.

1 The Character's Compass Traits and Dipsticks

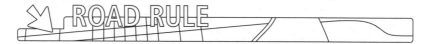

Road Rule #20: Don't take your audience out of the script by using dialogue uncharacteristic to the character!

A character's traits and dipstick data will most definitely affect their dialogue. Obviously, if a character is an adult, s/he will speak differently than a child of three. An Australian, British, or Russian character, for example, will have vocabulary unique to each one's own country. A character from the Bronx will speak differently than one from Texas. A character's race, culture, social status, and occupation will also influence her/his dialogue. These factors give diversity to the characters' vocabulary, and flavors the dialogue. A British person will refer to her/his apartment as a flat, to cigarettes as "ciggies" or "fags". They go "on holidays" or "to hospital" (dropping the article in each) instead of saying they are going "on a holiday" or "to the hospital." A doctor will speak differently from a waitress, cop, or a lawyer, as each will have their respective occupational jargon and education to factor into the dialogue equation. These differences may sound subtle, and they are, but they are what will make your characters sound real and believable to viewers. We live in a global world where anyone can be just a keyboard away from any culture and/or race. We have a plethora of information sent to us each day on the airways. Your audience is more educated than ever, so you better know your stuff in order to keep up.

2 The Character's Relationships

The relationship between characters will always dictate dialogue style as it is a two-way street regardless of whether they are siblings, spouses, friends, enemies, competitors and/or colleagues. Many characters will have a certain shorthand or dialogue rhythm with each other.

For example, in *Gilmore Girls,* the style of Lorelai and Rory is to often go off on tangents, creating a lot of dialogue diatribe. They chatter in a shorthand, which is often sarcastic or ironic. It's a shorthand of humor that only they usually understand and appreciate.

Thus, as you start writing your characters, remember their backstory and the relationships they have with the characters around them so you can enrich their dialogue.

3 The Specific Rhythm/Tone of A Series

Each series will have a certain rhythm and/or style to its dialogue. The best way to learn what that is to really study the series's dialogue.

West Wing has the unique rhythm of using repetitious dialogue. One character often passes on the same dialogue to another character as the characters move through the White House, even repeating the dialogue word for word. This gives the show a very unique dialogue print.

In the eighties, *Moonlighting* marked its dialogue with rapid-fire dialogue that overlapped. Thus, two characters often talked at the same time. They also used many of the dialogue devices we'll be examining, such as puns, parodies, and breaking the fourth wall. This all made the show especially unique and clever. (As you can imagine, however, one hour scripts for this show required a writer to write many more pages than normal because of the overlapping dialogue.)

4 The TV Tunnel

Genre also plays an important role in the rhythm and pacing of your dialogue. An action tunnel requires less dialogue than a family drama simply because it is an action series. It wouldn't make sense to slow or stop the action just so characters could converse about their daily problems whereas in a family drama, a scene might strictly consist of two characters talking about their problems written with no or little action in the scene.

The vocabulary used in a particular series's dialogue is also directly related to its TV tunnel. A series set in a specialized arena will incorporate vocabulary unique to that setting. For example, in *The Practice*, legal terms will speckle the dialogue, while in *ER*, medical vocabulary will abound:

```
          OLIGARIO
Her blood gas is back up. PH
is 7.1.


          GREENE
She's acidotic.
```

("Last Call" - *ER*)

NYPD Blue introduced audiences to a whole new police vernacular. Words and terms such as "skel" and "short eyes" flavored the dialogue and brought the audience into a more realistic world of the detective while *C.S.I.* introduces the viewer to a whole new vocabulary, that of the forensic scientist.

If you are writing an historical piece, then time and place will affect your dialogue. The characters in *Ponderosa* can't be talking about walkmans and DVD players. Use common sense when writing dialogue. If you're writing an historical piece or a character whose regional dialect is different from your own, then do some research. Historical diaries are great for learning the vocabulary and rhythm of the language of a certain time.

5 The Network or Cable Station It Airs On

Each network or cable station has its own set of rules and standards that it goes by. These standards will also affect your dialogue. The major networks such as ABC, NBC, CBS, and FOX (although FOX is a little edgier) are more conservative in the language and subject matter that they allow to be aired whereas cable channels such as HBO and Showtime can air more adult language and content. Warner Bros. strives for the teen and family audience, so their series reflect fairly clean (no obscenities) dialogue. The audience a particular network or cable channel is aiming for, will influence its series' dialogue.

For example, Pax markets to the family audience, so you won't hear certain dialogue that you would hear on HBO because there is no obscenities allowed. Thus, your characters better not sound like Tony Soprano if you're writing for *Doc*.

Watch and really listen to the series you want to write for. See what is acceptable and consistent to that series. If you're writing an original pilot, then study the various series produced by a specific network and/or studio so you can get a really good idea of what's acceptable and preferable to them. This will give you a guideline of what to do in your own dialogue and where to try to sell your script.

As you take in these five factors when writing, what's next? How do you write great dialogue? The answer is through practice and through the use of dialogue devices.

Dialogue Devices

These devices can make your script dialogue more fascinating, more dramatic, and/or more funny. You can let them stand alone or mix and match them however you choose.

· Act Out Lines

· Alliterations

· Breaking The 4th Wall

· Character Asks A Question

· Character Answers With A Question

· Character Defends Him/Herself

· Character Gives Advice

· Character Gives Order

· Character Makes An Exclamation

· Characters Makes An Observation

· Character Misinterprets Conversation

· Character Misinterprets Scene

· Character Talks To Her/Himself

- Clichés
- Comebacks
- Complaints
- Compliments
- Interrupt Character
- Interrupt Scene
- Monologues
- Narrators
- Puns
- Put-Downs
- Quotes
- Repeating Dialogue
- Segues
- Signature Lines
- Ultimatums
- Verbal Parody
- Verbal Toppers
- Words Which Sound Funny

1 Act Out Lines

This is the last line of dialogue in an act, or the last line of the Teaser. It usually gives a punch to the dialogue, acts as a cliffhanger, and/or creates suspense:

At the end of this episode, the last line in Act Four creates a suspense:

```
                MULDER
You know they say three
species disappear from the
planet each day. It makes you
wonder what ones are being
created.
```

```
                                    SMASH CUT TO:
The sewer tunnels, the water glistens like a primordial
soup. Flukeman's eyes pop open and stares hideously into
the camera.
```
("The Host" - The X-Files)

As the detectives study the crime scene of a priest who has been shot in the confessional -

```
                BRISCOE
        I wonder how many Hail Mary's
        that rates.
```
("The Collar" - Law & Order)

This last line of the Teaser, as always with *Law & Order*, provides a punchline of dark cop humor.

2 Alliterations

An alliteration is a repetition of initial sounds in adjacent words or syllables.

After Holling stands up to the boys at the bar and admits he hates sports, and that he would rather watch cooking shows, his wife, Shelley admits she's proud of him -

```
                SHELLEY
        Oh, yeah, it took a humongus
        set of peach pits to do what
        you did tonight.
```
("Birds of a Feather" – Northern Exposure)

3 Breaking The Fourth Wall

When a character turns and speaks directly into the camera, that is known as breaking the fourth wall.

In *Once & Again*, it is in the format of the series that throughout the episode there will be short black and white segments in which the characters speak directly into the camera, and reveal what s/he is really thinking or feeling. This is often juxtaposed against visuals of whatever the character is doing in the story.

In this episode, Karen battles with depression. Walking in the snow, she is hit by a car. As she lays crumpled in the snow, bleeding, we cut to see her laying naked and curled up, like a baby in the womb. She looks into the camera, and we hear her thoughts -

```
              KAREN
    It's been so long since I sat
    and felt the sun on my
    face…If I rest now, will that
    be okay?
```

("Gardenia" - *Once & Again*)

4 Character Asks A Question

Here, you build the lines off a question:

While on stakeout, the new detective, Kellerman, and the seasoned veteran homicide cop, Munch are stuck together watching and waiting for the suspect:

```
              KELLERMAN
    You don't think much of me,
    do you Munch?

              MUNCH
    Actually, I have no opinion
    of you, one way or the other.
    You have yet to appear on my
    radar screen.
```

("Stakeout" - *Homicide*)

5 Characters Answers With A Question

Here, you build your conflict and/or humor from the character's response, using a question.

As Max starts down the corridor of the college, his secretary calls after him:

```
              LORRAINE
    Can I have a word with you?

              MAX
    Which one?
```

("Save The Country" - *The Education of Max Bickford*)

6 Character Defends Her/Himself

Here, a character defend her/his ideas, beliefs, and/or actions.

Sam and Josh part ways on the street, but then stop as they each try to justify their ideals to their jobs -

>   SAM
>   Josh, what are you doin'?
>
>   JOSH
>   (beat)
>   I don't know.
>   (beat)
>   What're <u>you</u> doing?
>
>   SAM
>   Protecting oil companies from
>   litigation. They're our
>   client. They don't lose legal
>   protection 'cause they make a
>   lot of money.
>
>   JOSH
>   I can't believe no one ever
>   wrote a folk song about that.
>   (Verbal Topper)
>   ("In the Shadow of Two Gunmen", Pt.1- *West Wing*)

Here, both the characters defend their current jobs while both really know that each one needs to believe in something more than just making great money for what they do.

7 Character Gives Advice

With this device, one character counsels another. Notice the subtle way in which Weaver advises Greene.

After Doug brings in a woman he spent the night with who has died of a drug overdose, Carrie Weaver worries that maybe Doug is in no condition to be treating patients:

>   WEAVER
>   I know Doug is your friend…
>
>   GREENE
>   He got a tox screen, it came
>   back negative.
>
>   WEAVER
>   How about his blood alcohol?

A beat. Greene didn't think about that -

```
                    GREENE
          He's fine.


                    WEAVER
          Good. Because he's putting a
          chest tube in a fifteen-year-
          old right now.


                    GREENE
          He may need some help.


                    WEAVER
          Good idea.
```
("Last Call" - *ER*)

8 Character Gives Order

When Lt. Reed argues that he needs a real trial run to test the weapons, not just a computer simulation, Captain Archer orders:

```
                    ARCHER
          …Find Mr. Reed something to
          blow up.
```
("Fight or Flight" – *Enterprise*)

9 Character Makes Exclamation

When Nina confronts Jack about the key card, her persistence leaves him no choice but to take her hostage -

```
                    NINA
          What are you doing?!


                    JACK
          I'm sorry, Nina, I'm sorry.
     (Repeating dialogue)
```
("6:00a.m.-7:00a.m." - *24*)

10 Character Makes Observation

As Mulder and Scully scope out a case -

```
                    MULDER
         Maybe these people aren't
         disappearing. Maybe they're
         being hunted and the hunter's
         working the train station.

                    SCULLY
         And what happened to your
         theory of spontaneous
         combustion?

                    MULDER
         Maybe it's not so
         spontaneous.
```

("Soft Light" - *The X-Files*)

11 Character Misinterprets Conversation

In this situation, two characters have a conversation in which one character is speaking on one topic and the other character is speaking on a completely different topic, yet neither realize it.

Abbey, having just returned from a trip, walks towards C.J.'s office as she comes across Donna. The two walk together for a moment as they each walk toward different offices. Donna worries about the satellite that is crashing towards earth while Abbey has just been to see the White House Counsel who has presented to her how much trouble she and the president are in for concealing his multiple sclerosis.

```
                    DONNA
         How was the trip?

                    ABBEY
         Well, I got a medivac
         helicopter named after me…How
         are you?

                    DONNA
         I'm fine, but there's a giant
         object hurling its way toward
         us at a devastating velocity.

                    ABBEY
         Tell me about it.
```
("The Fall's Gonna Kill You" - *West Wing*)

The two then part and continue on their way, neither ever realizing what the other one is talking about.

You can also use this device not only to add humor, but to further your plot and build tension as the audience awaits the misinterpretation to be realized.

12 Character Misinterprets Scene

In *St. Elsewhere's*, "Attack", Roberta thinks she's having a confidential conversation about her new marriage with her friend who is the hospital operator, when in fact, she has accidentally hit the intercom. As Roberta speaks about her and Ehrlich's love life, the whole hospital hears. This provides much comic relief at Ehrlich's expense in the episode.

13 Character Talks To Himself

This can be used to provide another bit of exposition or for humor.

After Ehrlich spends the day trying to propose to Roberta, he botches it in the end, and upsets her. She apologizes for ruining his life and runs into the bedroom, locking the door. As she cries, Ehrlich tries to apologize, but there's no consoling Roberta. As Ehrlich leaves, he mutters to himself -

```
                    EHRLICH
          Ehrlich, you're a pig.
```
("A Pig Too Far" - *St. Elsewhere*)

This serves as a running gag throughout the episode, and throughout the series as well as Ehrlich is always being called "a pig" by his peers due to his insensitivity to women.

14 Clichés

Cliches are phrases which we have heard so much they have become trite. Whereas in screenplays, we moan if we hear a cliche, in television, you can spin them for funny or interesting dialogue.

While on stakeout, Giardello attempts to find out what is bothering Pembleton:

```
                    GIARDELLO
        You're yelling a lot lately.
        At the drop of a hat, you
        yell.

                    PEMBLETON
        Why would I yell if someone
        dropped his hat?
```

("Stakeout" - Homicide)

Kellerman arrives to take the next shift, and Munch opens the door -

```
                    KELLERMAN
        Here we are, home sweet
        homicide.
```

("Stakeout" - Homicide)

15 Comebacks

A comeback is a sarcastic or humorous response by one character to another.

As the detectives check in with Lt. Fancy about a case:

```
                    FANCY
        …You'll have assistance from
        the highway patrol cops, and
        you can use Martinez.

                    SIPOWITZ
        That kid's making into an
        okay cop.

                    FANCY
        Yeah, don't give him any bad
        habits.
```

("Personal Foul" - NYPD Blue)

16 Complaints

Here, a character makes a criticism or objection to someone.

The Craig's babysit for Jack. To soothe the baby's cries, Dr. Craig reluctantly and wearily reads young Petey a bedtime story.

```
          DR. CRAIG
...and Goldilocks said, please
don't cry anymore Baby Bear
because I have to perform
bypass surgery in the
morning.
```
("The Women" - *St. Elsewhere*)

Often, complaints are used as disparagements, humor, or to make the character more relatable.

17 Compliments

On television, characters often compliment each other. This can be a true compliment, or an offhand compliment.

```
        ONE OF THE
        LONE GUNMEN
That's why we like you
Mulder. Your ideas are
weirder than ours.
```
("E.B.E." - *The X-Files*)

18 Interrupt the character

Here something or someone interrupts the character.

As Jack puts a gun to Nina's back and orders her to follow him out of the building -

```
         NINA
Jack, I don't understand -

         JACK
- Stop talking, I'll explain
everything once we get out of
here.
```
("6:00a.m.-7:00a.m." - *24*)

19 Interrupt the scene

Here, something or someone interrupts the scene. In the episode below, David, Maddie, and Camille, in a madcap chase, try to escape the crooked detective. They lock themselves in the detective agency with Agnes, only to turn around and find the crooked cop holding a gun on them.

```
                    CROOKED COP
          How about this scenario: I
          shoot the four of you…I wipe
          my prints off the gun…I put
          the gun in Camille's dead
          hand.


                    DAVID/MADDIE/
                    CAMILLE/AGNES
                  (ad lib protests)

The group braces for impact as the crooked cop starts to
shoot when suddenly a PROP MAN grabs the gun from him -


                    CROOKED COP
          Hey, what are you doing?!


                    PROP MAN
          Sorry, babe, we're on a very
          tight schedule here. Props
          gotta go back in the prop
          room.
```
("Camille" - Moonlighting)

Suddenly, the room is swarmed by set builders who start dismantling the Blue Moon Detective Agency set, **breaking the fourth wall** as well, as the crooked cop **complains** that they haven't even finished the story yet.

20 Monologues

This is when a character gives a long speech, or monopolizes the dialogue. Most often, it's in the form of a toast, a eulogy, or some other ceremonial speech, but it can be a character who goes off on a tangent, ranting as s/he espouses her/his beliefs, thoughts, and/or feelings. In the famous turkey episode, the medical residents sit down with their mentors to eat Thanksgiving dinner in the hospital cafeteria. The camera pans the doctors, ending on young Pete, an infant who has recently lost his mother:

```
                WESTPHALL
        ...Thanksgiving is a day when
        each...of us should thank the
        powers-that-be for allowing
        us to be here. Existence is
        something we too easily take
        for granted, and whatever
        else we have or don't have,
        we are the living, and the
        rest of it's gravy.
                (a beat)
        And pass the potatoes,
        please.
```

("A Wing and A Prayer" - *St. Elsewhere*)

21 Narrator

Onscreen narration is when a character talks to the audience in this manner: the character's voice over (VO) is heard over various visuals. The character may or may not be in the scene as s/he talks, but if s/he is in the scene, s/he isn't speaking the words we are hearing. This dialogue device can set a tone, give us insight into the character, and also reveal exposition. Narration can play throughout the episode, or serve as book ends (used only at the beginning and the end of the episode). You will need to type "VO" which stands for "voice over" after the character's name in the dialogue like this:

```
            NARRATOR (VO)
```

In *Moolighting*, the show used title cards to add humor and supply segues to the next scene. In the episode below, as the titles appeared on the TV screen, voice over narration, **parodying** "*The Adventures of Rocky and Bullwinkle*" narrator, is heard:

```
            NARRATOR (VO)
        And suddenly...Maddie and David
        find themselves embroiled in
        one of those silly chases
        they like to do on
        Moonlighting...
```

(It's Maddie's Turn To Cry- *Moonlighting*)

Narration combined with flashbacks is a great way to reveal exposition. By flashing back, the audience gets to experience the *emotion and/or humor* of the scene, rather than just the *telling* of it.

Parodying also combines well with this device. In addition, juxtaposing the narrator's dialogue with the visuals can add humor, especially when you write the opposite of what an audience expects.

22 Puns

Some series' dialogue thrives on puns, *Gilmore Girls* for example loves playing with words as did *Moonlighting*. A pun is simply the humorous use of a word in a way that suggests two or more interpretations.

In the dialogue below, Maddie calls David into her office and demands to know what's with all the buxom blonds in the reception area? David asks to whom she is referring, teasing her more:

```
                MADDIE
     That flock of floosies, that
     bevy of bimbos that -

                DAVID
     - That mass of maracas? You
     wouldn't perhaps be referring
     to the candidates that I'll
     be interviewing later this
     afternoon for the job of au
     pair?

                MADDIE
     Au pair? What au pair?

                DAVID
     What au pair! Or two pair, or
     three pair -
     (pun)

                MADDIE
     - Enough!
```
               ("A Womb With A View" - Moonlighting)

Notice the use of **alliteration** at the top of the dialogue as well as having **one character interrupt another character.**

23 Put-Downs

A put-down is a bit like name calling, or a type of insult.

While performing surgery, Ehrlich seeks advice about being newly married to Roberta, a hospital candy-stripper. Already, he is attracted to another women. His mentor starts to reprimand -

```
            CRAIG
    Ehrlich, you've been married
    two weeks. You've made a very
    serious commitment to a
    lovely, young girl.

            EHRLICH
    But she wants to be a doctor
    -

            CRAIG
    That looney tunes!
```

("After Dark" - *St. Elsewhere*)

24 Quotes

On television, characters often quote from well known works of literature.

After Westphall finally faces that he will have to eventually place his ten year-old autistic son into a group home, he rocks Tommy as he reads from *The Runaway Bunny* in *St. Elsewhere's*, "Drama Center"-

```
            WESTPHALL
    "..If you run after me, I
    will become a bird and fly
    away from you, said the
    little bunny. If you become a
    bird and fly away from me,
    said his mother, I will be a
    tree that you come home to…"
```

Westphall hugs his son, emotional over what is the inevitable: that as a doctor, hospital administrator, and a widower whose daughter is going off to college, he will no longer be able to care for Tommy at home.

25 Repeating Dialogue

You can repeat a line of dialogue, either in the same scene or throughout the story, using it to payoff somewhere in the script. Often, if it is repeated, it's repeated three times because in comedy, three is the magic number.

In *Gilmore Girls*, "Double Date", Sookie begs Lorelai to go on a double date with her, Jackson, and Jackson's cousin. Reluctantly, Lorelai finally agrees:

                    SOOKIE
          Thank you! Thank you! Thank
          you! You will not regret
          this.

                    LORELAI
          Pick another phrase.

                    SOOKIE
          You will not have to pay.

                    LORELAI
          Much better.

Notice the magic number of three. Also, the order by Lorelai.

26 Segues

A segue is a shift directly into the next scene or next act. You can have many different kinds of segues, though quite often they will be in the form of a declaration, an order, a question or a threat:

As Mason stares at the satellite feed of Jack escaping with Pentacost:

                    MASON
          Where are you headed, Jack?
                              ("4:00a.m.-5:00a.m." - *24*)

27 Signature Lines

Sometimes, a character will use a certain catch phrase which, when used repeatedly by only that character, comes to be known as a "signature" line. When an audience hears this line, they immediately think of that particular character. If it's successful, it becomes part of our language.

                    BARACUS
          I pity the fool!

                              (*The A-Team*)

Quantum Leap uses this signature line every time Sam leaps into a new body and a new dicey predicament:

```
                    SAM BECKETT
          Oh, Boy!
```

Dragnet brought us:

```
                    SERGEANT FRIDAY
          Just the facts, Ma'am.
```

28 Ultimatums

While ultimatums can also come from any character, often the villain issues them to dictate a character's doom.

As Jack and Nina arrive at an isolated oil field, Jack waits for the terrorist's next instruction:

```
                    TERRORIST
          Take her out and shoot her.
                              (Order)
                    JACK
          No!             (Exclamation)

                    TERRORIST
          It's your choice, Jack. Nina
          or your daughter.
```

As Nina pleads with Jack who hesitates, the terrorist reaffirms his ultimatum:

```
                    TERRORIST
          - Just do it! Kimberly's dead
          if you don't - Just shoot
          her!
```
("6:00a.m.-7:00a.m." - *24*)

29 Verbal Parody

A verbal parody is a comical or satirical *verbal* imitation of someone or something.

Lorelai **complains** about Sookie only discussing her love life:

```
                    LORELAI
          - Of course, if she tells me
          the story of how Jackson
          cultivates his own meal worms
          to help fertilize his plants
          one more time, I'm going to
          Romeo and Juliette them both.
                      (Parody)
                ("Double Date" - Gilmore Girls)
```

30 Verbal Toppers

This is a line of dialogue that caps off a section of dialogue. Think of it as the punctuation mark to the conversation.

In this episode, Fiscus stops Ehrlich, laughing -

```
                    FISCUS
          Ehrlich, who's your designer
          here, Calvin Swine?   (parody)
```

Fiscus points out that someone has drawn a pig on the back of Ehrlich's lab coat with the words: "Ehrlich, you're a pig."

```
                    EHRLICH
          This is not funny, whoever is
          doing this, it's not funny,
          enough's enough. I'm not an
          animal, I'm a man!    (parody)


                    FISCUS
          And if anybody here agrees
          with that, please oink.
                    (Verbal Topper)
                ("A Pig Too Far" - St. Elsewhere)
```

31 Words Which Sound Funny

You can also get humor from using words which sound funny together:

When one of the recurring and most cantankerous characters, Mrs. Huffnagle dies, seemingly killed by her hospital bed which sandwiches her, Ehrlich replies:

```
                          EHRLICH
            ...Huffnagle on the half-shell.
                          ("Murder, She Rote" - St. Elsewhere)
```

As David enters the office, he sees all the activity and asks Agnes -

```
                          DAVID
            Is the blond dervish still
            whirling?
                          ("Between A Yuk And A Hard Place" - Moonlighting)
```

Conclusion

As illustrated from all these examples, you can combine dialogue devices with each other to strengthen the dramatic conflict, suspense, and/or humor in your dialogue. Get familiar with spotting these devices as you study dialogue. It takes time and experience to learn to write dialogue well. By applying these devices, you can make your dialogue an enjoyable read.

Dialogue Signposts

To test your dialogue as you write, check it against these signposts:

1 Is it revealing backstory, information on, or the personality of a character?

2 Is it giving the viewer more information in your plot or subplots?

3 Does it have to be said in dialogue, or would it play better to show rather than tell?

4 Is the line of dialogue really necessary, or can it be eliminated altogether?

5 If it's a joke, *is it funny?*

Examine each line, especially the first and last lines of dialogue in a scene. Can you cut them and zoom right into the scene? Most likely, the answer is yes. Remember, just because television allows you more time with dialogue, doesn't mean that you want to waste a line of dialogue with inconsequential chatter, unless of course, that is the style of a particular character or series.

Exercise 52. Pick a scene that you've already written for your script with the longest amount of dialogue. Go through this scene, reviewing ONLY the dialogue. Rewrite it using any of the dialogue devices that make your dialogue stronger.

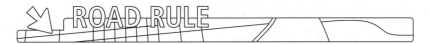

Exercise 53. Next, go back through the same scene, and rewrite the dialogue again. This time apply

Road Rule #19: arrive late and leave early in your dialogue. Use the dialogue signposts: if any piece of dialogue does not correctly follow them, dump it! It's littering your page. Once you've rewritten the dialogue, reread your scene. Listen to how much tighter it sounds and how your pacing has improved.

NOTE: *Don't* start rewriting the whole script yet, just this one scene. The rewrite comes in a later chapter.

Now, with your new knowledge of dialogue, it's time to:

Exercise 54. Write your Act Two (11th - 20th Streets). This Act should consist of about 10 to 16 pages. Include the dialogue devices discussed in this chapter. Keep your driver on course and zoom the story into the next city block, Act Three. Keep building the necessary subplots as

well. By the time you finish, you should have somewhere between 23 to 38 pages of your one hour teleplay written.

NOTE: Don't worry about making your dialogue perfect. This is just to help familiarize you with dialogue devices. Keep focusing on getting the plot and characters onto the page.

Chapter Eighteen
Prose: Your Information Highway

All the words on your page that aren't dialogue, sluglines or character names, make up your prose. In other words, it's the words you use in describing your scene or the action of your scene, the information you give to the reader. In the excerpt below:

```
EXT. CARPORT - NIGHT
```
(This is your slugline.)

```
- as a blue sedan screeches to a halt and the
passenger door flies open.
```
(This is your prose.)

See how economical? Notice how the word choice builds tension, giving a sense of urgency to the action described by using strong verb choices.

Often, the prose is neglected in scriptwriting, but it shouldn't be. Every word counts in your final draft. You want your whole script to be a terrific read for executives, producers, and agents.

Prose Signposts

To ensure your prose is on the right track:

1 Capture the tone and genre for which you are writing. If it's an action tunnel, make sure your action reads in an exciting way. If it's a family comedy, make sure your prose reflects humor when applicable.

2 Keep your page balanced: don't flood your pages with ink (blocks of lengthy paragraphs). Break up the action with dialogue or with line spacing.

This makes your script a more appealing read as well giving it a professional appearance. In those series that fall in the action/adventure or action/thriller tunnel, you might be tempted to fill the page with overly detailed descriptions. Keep it simple and clear and succinct.

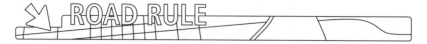

Road Rule #21: Less is more! Especially in your prose.

3   Keep your prose between 2 to 4 lines *per paragraph*, and try not to exceed 6 to 8 lines *per scene* unless you have a long action sequence. Remember, you can break up prose blocks with dialogue or line spacing. Make sure what you write is clear and understandable to the reader; just do it succinctly.

4   Choose *action* verbs over *linking* verbs. Load your script with strong and interesting word choices.

Don't write: Jack *is searching* for an escape route from the sniper's fire.

Write: Jack struggles to escape the whizzing bullets of the sniper.

5   Eliminate excess words. Don't describe every bit of action, only what is necessary. For example:

```
INT. WAREHOUSE - NIGHT

Jack sneaks along the dark building, making
sure it is all clear to enter the next room.
Moonlight steams through various windows as
Jack follows after the suspect, peering in
various rooms. Suddenly, he sees the suspect.
The suspect fires at Jack who dodges behind a
beam, narrowly missing him. Jack fires a few
shots back, then rushes towards the door that
Pentacost has just fled as the hunt
intensifies.                        (70 words)
```

You can describe the same action just as efficiently by rewriting it this way:

```
INT. WAREHOUSE - NIGHT

Moonlight streaks into the darkness as Jack
cautiously stalks the suspect. A flash of
light, their eyes lock. Pentacost shoots and
```

```
Jack dodges behind a beam, returning fire,
then races after Pentacost.          (32 words)
```

By eliminating unnecessary words which drowned the reader, we described the same action using half the words. You could also take the prose block above and split it up with dialogue.

Screen Directions

Screen directions are just that - they tell the reader how the action is directed, and they are always capitalized. In your teleplays, you will rarely use them at all unless applied with a specific plot gimmick. Otherwise, it's the television director's job to decide how to frame the scene.

CLOSE ON: Close-Up of the character or object named.

INSERT: used for extreme close ups to show a note or a clue.

FLASHBACK: lets reader know the story is moving back in time.

FLASHFORWARD: lets reader know the story is moving ahead into the future.

BACK TO PRESENT: lets reader know the story is moving to the present again. Always follows a flashback or flashforward scene.

LONG SHOT: camera shoots to show the distance of the scene.

PAN DOWN: Camera moves down the scene.

PAN TO: Camera pans or moves to another part of the scene.

PAN UP: Camera moves up the scene.

Sometimes, you will also have certain directions at the end of your scene just preceeding the next slugline:

DISSOLVE TO: this dissolves us into the next scene and is used most often to indicate a passage of time, for example, moving from day into night. It can also by used to span longer amounts of time, maybe cutting to a scene twenty years later.

SMASH CUT TO: this "smashes" or *cuts very quickly* into the next scene, and is generally used for humor or suspense. It just indicates you want to cut more quickly into the next scene than normally.

CUT TO: cutting to another part of the action or another character *within* the same scene.

In addition, you must always capitalize your SFX (sound effects) as well. This helps the sound editor out when he's looking for the sound effects in a script. For example:

...a JACKHAMMER POUNDS

...a phone RINGS

...MUSIC MONTAGE

Also in your prose, you can direct the rhythm of the scene to indicate a pause before a character responds or the action resumes. For example:

The patient absorbs the doctor's diagnosis. A beat. She looks up tearfully.

"A beat" is a common term to cue the actor and/or director that a dramatic pause is needed. It's a punctuation mark to the scene. You don't want to overuse this, or every moment will appear dramatic and soon you'll be writing melodrama. It's a bit like using an exclamation mark in your writing. You want to do so sparingly so that when you do use it, it stands out for the effect that you want.

Exercise 55. Pick a scene that you've written that is heavy on descriptive blocks. Go through the scene using the prose signposts to make your prose stronger and leaner. Be sure to capitalize all sound effects. If using screen directions, do so sparingly. Rewrite only this scene, then reread your new scene. Notice how much more powerful it is.

Exercise 56. Now write your Act Three (21st- 30th Streets). This Act should consist of about 9 to 15 pages. Again, keep your driver(s) on course and zoom the plots into the last city block of Act Four. Make sure your 30th Street uses all five On Ramp Signposts. Once this act is finished, you should have about 45 to 48 pages of your one hour teleplay written.

Remember, just focus on structure and character. If you attempt to focus on being perfect with structure, character, dialogue, prose, and format all at once, you're going to get lost. Just keep putting words on the page, and don't worry whether or not each word is brilliant. You'll have plenty of chances in your many, many rewrites to sweat about the finer details.

Chapter Nineteen
The Scene

A scene is one of the story elements used to write a script. You create a new scene each time you switch location (even if the next scene is just in the next room) or time of day (even if the next scene is just a few minutes later). The length of a scene in television may vary from 1/8 of a page to 6 pages, that is, from a few short seconds to several minutes. Most of your scenes, however, will probably range from _ of a page to 4 pages. Too long a scene could create a fidgety viewer who might decide to channel surf. You have to keep your scenes and story moving forward.

Just as in the overall plot, each scene has a beginning, middle, and end. Likewise, each scene also needs a rising incline (jeopardy) which grows steeper in each individual street (scene).

Let's examine some scenes from our graphs:

West Wing, "The Fall's Gonna Kill You": on 25th Street, Josh meets with Joey Lucas. She has a new deaf interpreter. Josh asks him to leave (beginning of scene).

At a table, Joey reads Josh's lips as he informs her of the president's MS. They need a secret poll to know how to go public with the illness (middle of scene: incline rising).

Joey grasps the enormity of the situation, then agrees to do a poll (end of scene: incline peaked).

Gilmore Girls, "Double Date": on 4th Street, at the Inn, Lorelai attempts to study for her business exam (beginning of scene).

Michel interrupts her; there's a problem, they are overbooked. He keeps badgering her about this problem, preventing her from studying (middle of scene: incline rising).

Lorelai solves the problem so Michel will stop complaining (end of scene: incline peaked).

24, "4:00a.m.-5:00a.m.": on 12th Street, Mason and Jack enter a private room at the precinct and argue (beginning of scene).

Jack relents, and tells Mason that the two agents were killed because they discovered the suspect is somehow connected to the Palmer assassination plot (middle of scene: incline rising).

Mason refuses to let Jack see the suspect, and announces he will interrogate Pentacost. Jack's upset, but is forced to sit and wait (end of scene: incline peaked).

Although each of the above examples are from different genres and formats, each scene is constructed the same way: with a beginning, a middle and an end.

As you construct your plot, keep in mind:

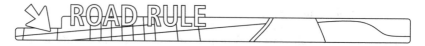

Road Rule #22: Arrive late and leave early in your scenes.

Just as in your dialogue, you want to enter a scene at the last possible second and leave it as soon as you possibly can. In addition, it's important to remember:

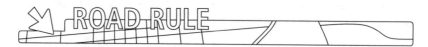

Road Rule #23: Your character must leave each scene needing more and/or knowing more than when s/he entered it!

In our examples above, this road rule plays out like this:

Now Joey knows the president's secret, and tells Josh how she will construct the poll questions to give them the numbers they need. Josh and the president need her to be discrete. (*West Wing*)

Now Lorelai knows about the problem and has solved it. She needs a quiet place in order to study. (*Gilmore Girls*)

Now Mason knows part of why Jack has been breaking protocol. Now Jack must wait, unable to speak to Pentacost and find out what the suspect knows. *(24)*

As you construct your scenes, think about them in terms of telling their own mini-story. When your character enters the scene you are writing, that's the most important scene to him/her. Your characters don't know what is coming next, so don't write them as if they do.

Slippery When Wet – The Oblique Scene

So what makes a scene unique? Chances are whatever you think of first, that's what every other writer's going to think of too. Really dig deep for ideas. Think of at least three or four ways to approach the same scene, then discard the first three because by your fourth attempt, you've probably come up with something fresh.

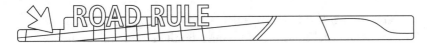

Road Rule #24: Write the unexpected scene. Keep surprising the audience (and your driver) in a believable manner.

Forget the *obvious* and write the *oblique* scene by sliding your driver in an unexpected direction, especially when writing a comic scene because it is the unexpected that tickles our funny bone and makes us laugh, or when writing a suspenseful scene because it is the unexpected that jumps out to scare us.

The best way to achieve writing a unique scene is to take a scene familiar to an audience and put a spin on it, slide it in a direction they aren't expecting. When you watch TV, pay attention to what scenes catch you unexpectedly, and what scenes bring a surprise laugh or sudden chill. Take note, because this is what you want to do in your own scripts to create comedy, suspense, and drama.

In *Gilmore Girls,* "Double Date,": Jackson and Rune arrive to take Lorelai and Sookie on a date, but Rune freaks out when he sees Lorelai, calling her an Amazon woman.

Here, the writer spins the scene in the surprised direction because Lorelai is an attractive and sexy woman pursued by many of the men in the series, so it's unexpected that her date would find fault in her appearance, and thus provides the viewer with some laughs.

24, "6:00a.m.-7:00a.m.": Janet's father, Alan York, goes into the hospital room to be with his daughter after her grueling surgery. Janet opens her eyes and asks for her mother. As Mr. York approaches, she then asks where is her father? Wham! Suddenly, viewers realize the man we've known as Janet's father really isn't Alan York. This imposter suffocates Janet. Now viewers know something our hero's wife doesn't: this imposter is really one of the terrorists. Now Teri Bauer is in danger too.

Here, the writer took a cliched hospital scene and really led the audience down the path, then crashed the viewer into another direction with a totally unexpected event, heightened the suspense, and increased the jeopardy.

Forgive me while I depart to a live-action film example because it is the quintessential example of taking a familiar scene the audiences has viewed dozens of time and sliding it into a surprise direction for a huge laugh:

Indiana Jones tries to escape the market place, but a man looms ahead slicing the air impressively with his swords. The audience is pumped for (and expects) a martial arts battle - How is Indiana going to get out of this one? Indiana frowns; it's been a tough day. He takes out his pistol and shoots the guy. It's a brilliant and unexpected spin, and the audience roars with laughter. (*Raiders of the Lost Ark*)

NOTE: This is how a writer should write the oblique scene. Unfortunately, this wasn't a scene written in the script. It came about when Harrison Ford showed up for an eight hour day of stunt work.

Ford, however, had the flu, and only had one hour of work in him. Thus, the scene was improvised so Ford could go to his hotel and recuperate.

Don't count on serendipity to make your scenes memorable ones. Come at the scene from an unlikely direction - it's your job to envision scenes like these. This is how you create comedy, suspense, and drama. Push yourself to write original and memorable scenes. Each and every street must keep the viewer riding along with your driver.

What scenes in television have made an impression on you? What made them memorable? In television, you get to create powerful scenes every week for characters that audiences know and love. Take advantage of that fact, and keep your scenes original and interesting.

In *St. Elsewhere,* "The Last One", the writers ended the series with a beautifully poignant scene. Dr. Westphall comes home from work, only he isn't a doctor, he's a construction worker. Dr. Auschlander turns out to be his father who sits with Tommy. Westphall says hello to his autistic son, musing, "I wonder what he thinks of all day." As Westphall goes into the kitchen, Tommy holds a snow globe. Inside, we see the building of the hospital, St. Eligius. The whole series has been the imagining of a young boy with autism.

Certainly, one of the most talked about scenes of the eighties was Bobby Ewing's return to *Dallas.* When actor Patrick Duffy wanted off the series, the writers decided to kill off the character. After a season of poor ratings, the writers convinced Duffy to return to the show. Only there was one little problem, Bobby Ewing was dead. So the writers opened the season with this original scene:

Pam, Bobby's wife, awakes to hear the shower running. She goes into the bathroom and hesitantly opens the door. Bobby turns and smiles. The whole last season is presented as a nightmare that Pam had.

While the example above might be a bit extreme, it certainly wasn't typical. Be creative as you write, and keep the viewers guessing, not only as to where the story is going, but also as to where the scene is going.

During the outline process, your focus is first on plot, but when writing a scene, focus on the characters and dialogue. Make your driver smash into a scene head-on by hurling something emotional at him, or something unexpected. Your job as the writer is to make your driver's life difficult for those 56-64 pages. Take that job seriously.

Exercise 57. Choose the longest scene you have written so far and rewrite it from three different approaches using the three Road Rules in this chapter. Number each attempt. Don't edit any of your ideas as you write, just write whatever comes to mind.

Once you've written these three different versions (plus your original draft) *take a two day Pit Stop*. **Do not** proceed to the exercise below until you have "tuned-up" your imagination. You must approach your work with fresh eyes.

Exercise 58. Now that you've had several days to clear your mind, read your four scene attempts. Which one reads the best? Which version sounds the most fresh and interesting? Most likely, the draft you choose won't be your first attempt. Insert the scene you like best into your teleplay before moving to the next exercise.

Exercise 59. Knowing each scene has its own beginning, middle, and end, attempt to write the oblique scene as you write the last block: Act Four (31st - 40th Streets). Make sure you follow the plot points of Act Four for each of your plots. Be sure your main climax proves your premise. Use a cliffhanger at the end if the series format requires it. Your completed script should range between 56-64 pages.

Chapter Twenty
The Rewrite

Congratulations! You've finished your first television script. It's time to clean up your streets. Now, the real work begins. As you go through the exercises in this chapter, keep in mind: there are plenty of writers who will make sure their script has flawless plots, fully layered characters, unique scenes, great dialogue, and strong prose. They put in the extra hours, rewriting and polishing their teleplays. These writers are your competition so:

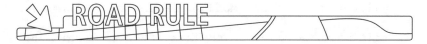

Road Rule #25: Rewrite! Rewrite! Rewrite!

You want to drive through your script using the checklists below. Drive through only one checklist at a time. **DO NOT** attempt to check your scripts scene by scene using all the checklists at once. You need to approach it from an overall view, and then move inward. Take appropriate Pit Stops between each "drive" through your script. Don't start a new pass when you're tired of your script (and you will get tired of it - that's when you know it's time to take a Pit Stop).

Structure Checklist

If you diligently structured your Road Map, your plot should be on track, but it's smart to make sure your characters didn't drive off the road as you were writing. Fix any crumbling streets in this first rewrite.

Exercise 60. Go through your script using the checklist below, and scrutinize your structure. Examine only your plots.

1   If any two scenes accomplish exactly the same thing, cut one, no matter how brilliant it may be - lose it!

2   Does your Teaser truly hook the viewer (or reader) in the first few pages?

3   Have you written your scenes so each city block has its own incline (jeopardy or what's at stake) which is rising? Does your city block also increase each plot's speed (tension)?

4   Have you created enough falling rocks for your characters within each city block?

5   Are your Green Light, U-Turn, & Road of No Return On-Ramps strong enough to speed your story into their respective city blocks and hold the viewer's attention through the commercial breaks?

6   Have you embodied your premise in a character which proves the premise in one of your climaxes?

Character Checklist

Now that you have passed through your teleplay and inspected it for structure, do the same with your characters.

Exercise 61. Using the checklist below, examine your characters and ONLY your characters.

1   Have you set-up from whose POV the story will be about for the episode?

2   Is your driver(s) consistent to his/her world, dipstick, true north and character compass?

3   Are your supporting characters and villains consistent, if applicable?

4   Are your characters unique and interesting? Are they relatable to your audience?

5   When you first introduced your characters, did you make their character tags memorable?

6   Have you created a worthy adversary for your driver, if applicable? Does your antagonist have a forceful goal and/or emotional need which is in direct conflict of your driver's goal and/or need?

Scene Checklist

Do not proceed unless you've taken a few days off.

Exercise 62. With the checklist below, evaluate your script scene by scene.

1   Does each scene have its own beginning, middle, and end? Is it building as well?

2   Have you written the oblique/unexpected scene, or a scene the audience has experienced many times?

3   Is your character leaving each scene, knowing and/or needing more than when entered it?

4   Do you arrive late and leave early in each of your scenes, or can you jump in faster and/or exit more quickly?

5   Have you hooked your viewer for the next week's episode with your cliffhanger (if applicable)?

Dialogue Checklist

Have you taken an appropriate Pit Stop? You want to have refueled your creativity before taking on the dialogue.

Exercise 63. With the checklist below, rewrite your dialogue.

1   Does the dialogue vary or sound like the same character?

Go through your teleplay reading *only* one character's dialogue at a time. Highlight the main characters and their dialogue using different colors. This helps illuminate inconsistencies in the character's dialogue and speech patterns. Repeat this process with each character in your script, checking each line:

    a   Is it consistent for your character compass traits and dipstick?

    b   Is it consistent with the character's relationship to whomever is speaking?

    c   Is it appropriate for the series and/or network?

Now, continue to examine the dialogue as a whole:

2   Do you need to jazz up your dialogue in the scene by using more of the dialogue devices discussed in Chapter Seventeen?

3   Does each line of dialogue fulfill at least one of the dialogue signposts listed in Chapter Seventeen?

4   If it is a comedic line, is it FUNNY?!

5   Are you arriving late and leaving early in your dialogue within each scene?

Go through the dialogue within each scene and find the one line which is the fuel (essence) of that scene. Circle it. Then go back through the scene and toss as many unneeded lines before and after that line as you can. This is the time to look for repeating lines which don't need to be repeated. For example: "I can't believe you did that. What were you thinking?"

You don't need both of these lines; one does the job. Remember, if it is the style of the serie's dialogue to often repeat lines, that's the only time it's okay. Follow the rules of the series.

Are we there yet? Are we there yet? Are we there yet? Almost.

Prose Checklist

Hooray! It's time for that last polish.

Exercise 64. Follow the checklist for your prose.

1   Are you choosing action verbs and other strong word choices?

2   Have you eliminated all excess words?

3   Are you describing action that isn't necessary to describe? If the answer is yes, eliminate it.

4   Is the action you are describing clear to the reader?

5   If you included screen directions, did you do so sparingly? Be sure to capitalize them.

6   Is your action broken up so that it doesn't look as if you've flooded your page with ink?

7   Have you captured the genre's tone in your prose?

8   Have you capitalized any SFX (sound effects) in your script?

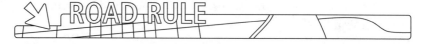

Road Rule #26: Your first five pages must read brilliantly!

Exercise 65. Polish your first five pages again to ensure they are an exceptional read!

You did it! You survived the rewrite process. Be proud of your hard work, your script reflects all your efforts. Hopefully, it will pay off - literally.

Everybody's A Critic

This is fortunate for you because it's time to hand your scripts out to trusted friends to read. Choose friends who are brave enough to tell you what works and what doesn't in your teleplay. After you get their notes, take another Pit Stop to absorb the notes before polishing your script for the final time. The more time away from your script, the more objectively you can approach your polish. You might not use all the notes you get, but if you consistently get the same note on a certain area of your script, odds are, your friends are right.

Exercise 66. Polish your script regarding the comments you received, then set your first teleplay aside and take another Pit Stop.

Exercise 67. Once you've refueled your creativity, then begin the process again. Go back through this book and complete the necessary writing exercises for your second script. Once you have completed your second one hour teleplay and its rewrite, then proceed to the last chapter.

Give yourself a round of applause. You've put in some very hard work. The time has come to send your scripts out into the world.

Chapter Twenty-One
TV or Bust!

Now that you've written, rewritten, and polished your scripts repeatedly until both read brilliantly, it's time to send them out. First, you'll have to send a query letter or make a cold call to get permission to submit your script to a series producer, and/or agent.

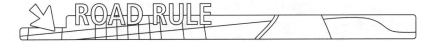

Road Rule #27: Never send your script to a producer or an agent without first getting permission!

How do you get permission? By contacting agents and producers. You can get names of producers and studio executives from *The Hollywood Creative Directory of Producers* and *The Hollywood Creative Directory of Agents.* The directories list who works where and what their title is, the studio/producer's (or agents) office address, phone number, and what films and/or television series they have produced. They are handy books to have for a writer without an agent, but each costs about eighty dollars. You can purchase both books from Samuel French bookstore in Hollywood. You can also get a list of agencies and their addresses/phone numbers (*without* specific names of agents) from the Writer's Guild of America for only a couple of dollars. In addition, the *WGA Journal* also will periodically run listings of each television series currently on air and contact information so it might be a good idea to check for the periodical at your local library.

The Query Letter

This is a letter in which you make your request for submission. If you have written an original pilot script, you most definitely want to get an agent before you pitch your series anywhere. You need an agent to protect your interests. For those who have written two sample scripts of existing shows, I would also recommend finding an agent first and let them send your scripts out, but you're welcome to try to pitch to series's producers if you like. In your query letter, include as succinctly as possible:

1 That you have two one hour scripts you would like the agent or producer to read. If speaking/writing to a series producer, let them know you are a devoted fan of the show and would like to pitch to them, after of course, they review your sample scripts. If you are speaking/writing to an agent, let them know that you are a writer seeking representation.

2 List any previous writing positions, credits, awards, and/or nominations you have acquired (even if it's not in the TV medium). You want to prove you are marketable as a writer.

3 Thank the person for his/her time for considering to read your script.

4 Just send the query letter, *do not* send your script until invited to do so by the producer or agent you queried.

It's okay to send out multiple query letters. Hopefully, you'll receive positive responses, although it might be several weeks or even a month before you receive a reply. If you live in the Los Angeles area, make some cold calls. Introduce yourself to the assistant and briefly list any credits you have as a writer. Tell them you have a script you'd like to send. Be especially nice to these assistants as these are the people who will read your scripts first, and help you get your foot into the door. Be respectful of their time.

Exercise 68. Send out query letters and/or make cold calls to get your scripts read. Repeat this exercise until you have someone reading your script.

Keep a list of who and when you sent letters or made calls.

The Script Submission

You've finally received permission to submit your script, sent it off, and now it's being read by an assistant. These assistants are trusted by the agent or producer to find the next "hot" writer. They are your next speed bump in the road. If they like your scripts, then they will pass it on to the agent or producer for whom they work.

As s/he reads your teleplay, you will be judged on story structure, characters, dialogue, style, and humor (if applicable). If you haven't received a response three weeks after sending your scripts, then call. Don't pester, but be persistent. These people are extremely busy, and might have forgotten your script.

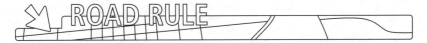

Road Rule #28: Don't take rejection personally!

There are too many factors determining why someone passes on your scripts other than your talent or the quality of your scripts. Don't be shy (but don't be defensive) when rejected. Ask for an honest critique of the script. Thank the reader for his/her time. If your script is rejected, send it to the next agent on the list, and keep sending until you find an agent who says yes. If a producer doesn't like your scripts, then s/he won't call you in to pitch for the series.

NOTE: If you receive enough feedback listing the same problems, then rewrite and polish that script before sending it out again. Wait until you have several of the same negative comments, however, because you don't want to tailor your script to someone who's already rejected it.

Let's say your scripts are received enthusiastically because you've followed the *Writer's Road Map #4: Writing The One Hour Teleplay* in a creative and successful way, proving your talents as a writer. Then zoom onto the express lane. You're on your way!

The Pitch

If a producer likes your scripts, then you will get a meeting to pitch your story ideas in hopes of landing a freelance assignment (and eventually a staff job). If an agent likes your original pilot, then you will pitch your series around town. For your story pitch, follow the story signposts in Chapter Four, giving the beginning, middle and end of your story. If it is an ensemble cast, create story ideas for several different characters. That way, if they have several Josh Lyman stories, for example, then you could quickly start pitching a story for Leo McGarry or Donna Moss. When pitching your series idea, follow the series signposts from Chapter Four. Capture the flair of the studio's style to which you are pitching.

Exercise 69. Using all five road flags, write your pitch for your each story idea or your series idea. Give the pitch flair. Then practice speaking it aloud just as you would present it in the meeting to producers. You can leave the written pitch behind with producers when you leave the meeting.

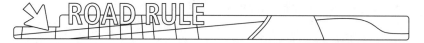

Road Rule #29: When you pitch, whether verbally or written, do so with enthusiasm! You are the one selling your screenplay. Don't be a doormat. Wow them!

In Conclusion

Get your scripts out there; get them read. Establish a network of contacts, because even more than talent and, can be it's *who you know!* Build and keep relationships with Hollywood producers and agents. Your career depends upon it.

Each studio has its own signature style. Find the one that matches your own talents as a writer. Your career is what *you* make it. There'll be bumps along the way, but if you have the endurance to stick with it, and follow the *Writer's Road Map #4: Writing The One Hour Teleplay*, this area of writing can be a very rewarding and fun career. Good luck!

Glossary

antagonist: the character who opposes the driver (hero).

backstory: any information or events that have happened to a character before the scene opens.

character arc: the learning curve (arc) of a character, i.e., what a character learns in the course of the story.

city block: a story sequence composed of ten streets (scenes). It has its own beginning, middle, and end with obstacles.

cliffhanger: optional plot point in tv series to keep audiences guessing, used to tease an audience into remembering to watch the next episode, the last or second to last scene in an episode.

colloquialism: an expression relating to a certain time or region.

compass points: the major and minor character traits which establish a character's personality.

denouement: the conclusion of story plot lines.

dialogue devices: writer's tools to jazz up the dialogue, making it more interesting.

exposition: information needed by the audience to understand the story or a character's motivations.

Est. shot: establishing shot; this is sometimes used to set up a location.

EXT.: exterior; describes the location in the slugline and is always abbreviated in capital letters.

flashback: a scene which flashes back in time; a technique used to give exposition.

genre: the category of the story being told, i.e., a comedy, a western, a mystery…

graphing: to outline scene by scene a film or script, listing the essence of each scene, who is in the scene, where and when the scene takes place, and what time the scene falls in the film (by minutes) or script (by page).

greenlight: 10th Street, the last scene of Act One; the scene where the driver (hero) must commit to the story. He speeds into the action full speed ahead.

high-concept: a story idea which can be conveyed in one or two sentences with a hook that makes the story easily recognized as becoming a blockbuster movie. For example, *Ghostbusters* and *E.T.*

hook: a twist that makes the story idea fresh and original.

INT.: interior; describes the location in the slugline; always abbreviated in capital letters.

juxtapose: to place side by side for comparison.

music montage: a series of scenes without dialogue where music plays over the images. Often used to illustrate time passing, characters falling in love, etc.

oblique scene: to write a scene that is unexpected, surprising the audience and/or a character.

payoff: an outcome which has been set up by the previous scene

pitch: to tell a story idea to executives/producers/agents as succinctly and enthusiastically as possible, including the hook and the universal appeal of the story.

point-of-view: (POV) through whose perspective the story is told; generally through the hero's perspective.

premise: what the writer communicates to the audience, i.e. what the writer wants to convey by telling the story. The premise is always embodied in a character who fulfills it at the end of the script.

prose: the description or action in the scene, i.e. everything on the script page that isn't a slugline or dialogue or a character name.

protagonist: the main character of the story, the driver.

query letter: a letter sent to acquire permission to submit a screenplay. Include the point of the letter, information about the writer, a brief synopsis of the script, and any acclaim the script has garnered.

resolution: a conclusion or result of the storyline.

road map: the writer's outline.

road of no return: 30th Street, the last scene of Act Three; the scene (street) in which the driver must make a choice which implies severe consequences. It is a street that once he/she drives onto, there is no going back.

running gags/devices: a tool to setup and payoff certain story elements. Often they are used as comic relief, or foreshadowing.

scene: (street) a story unit generally lasting between two to four pages. A scene changes any time the story moves to a new location or a new time.

screen directions: written in capital letters; these are shots listed in the script. For example, CU (a close up) or LS (a long shot). Use sparingly, if at all!

screen narration: information given to the audience via a character speaking directly to the audience, or written visually on the screen.

slugline: the line which introduces each scene. It is always written in capital letters and includes whether the scene is exterior or interior, its location, and the time of day. For example: INT. SEWER PIPES - MIDNIGHT or EXT. CENTRAL PARK - LATE AFTERNOON.

street: in this book, a street equals one scene or a series of very short scenes.

synopsis: a brief summary of a story, introducing the hero and major plot points. It should be told in the most exciting way. It's a script's calling card.

tag: the description given to a character when he/she is first introduced in the script. The tag itself is not capitalized, but the character's name is (but only the *first* time he/she appears on the page. Always include the character's specific age in the tag.

teaser: a scene or series of short scenes which introduce the movie in an exciting way to grab the audience's attention before settling into the story.

theme: a dominant idea which resonates throughout the script, intersecting the plot, and enhancing the characters and the premise.

tic: a bizarre or eccentric trait given to a character.

ticking clock: a story device which sets up tension and a need for immediate action by the character. It dictates that a character perform a certain action by a specific time, or a grave consequence will occur. Often this device is set into motion by the story's villain or antagonist. For example, VILLAIN: "Deliver three million dollars in one hour or I'll blow up the bus."

timeline: a list of important moments in a character's life, and how they shaped his/her personality. It also includes any important relationship which shapes/has shaped the character. It's a character's backstory.

tow-away zone: 1st to 4th Street, Act One; it is the story's catalyst; the scene in which the driver is towed or pulled into the story.

u-turn: 20th Street, last scene of Act Two; it is the scene which turns the story in a totally new or unexpected direction.

voice over: (VO) is used when a character's voice is heard, but the character is not seen. For example, if character A talks on the phone to character B who is not seen, the writer would type: CHARACTER B (VO), then follow with the character's indented dialogue. (OS) is also used in this way = Off Screen.

TV-ography

In television, the producers are the writers, so below is a list of producing/writing credits. Executive producers are the head writers of a series. Sometimes there's an "&" listed and other times the word "and" listed. The "&" means a partnership whereas the word "and" infers that additional writers or producers worked on the series, but not as an exclusive partnership.

7th Heaven: created by Brenda Hampton; executive producers Aaron Spelling, Brenda Hampton, E. Duke Vincent; co-executive producers Catherine Le Pard, Joel J. Feigenbaum; producers Burt Brinckerhoff, Chris Olsen, Jeff Olsen, Joel Wallenstein, Ron Darian; co-producers Naomi Janzen, Sue Tenney; associate producer Shelley Hull. Spelling TV. Warner Bros.

24: created by Joel Surnow & Robert Cochran; executive producers Brian Grazer, Joel Surnow, Robert Cochran, Tony Krantz; co-executive producers Stephen Hopkins, Howard Gordon; producers Andrea Newman, Cyrus Yavneh; co-producers Michael Loceff, Robin Chamberlin; associate producers Bob Johnston, Paul Gadd. Imagine Entertainment. FOX.
"4:00a.m.-5:00a.m." written by Chip Johannessen; directed by Winrich Kolbe. "6:00a.m.-7:00a.m." written by Andrea Newman; directed by Bryan Spicer.

The Adventures of Rocky & Bullwinkle: producers Ponsonby Britt, Jay Ward; writers Chris Jenkyns, Ted Key. Jay Ward Prods.

The Agency: created by Michael Frost Beckner; executive producers Gail Katz, Wolfgang Peterson, Shaun Cassidy, Michael Beckner; supervising producer Doug Palav; producers Ed Zuckerman, Mason Alley, Melissa Rosenberg, Vivienne Radkoff, Robert D. Simon; co-producers Joe Lazarov. Studios USA. CBS.

A.K.A.: created by Marilyn Webber & Michael Gleason, producers Michael Grais & Mark Victor, Michael Gleason, Marilyn Webber, Kurt Fehtke, Eric Larson. PAX.

Alias: created by J.J. Abrams; executive producers Alex Kurtzman, J.J. Abrams, John Eisendrath, Ken Olin, Roberto Orci; supervising producers Jeff Pinkner, Jesse Alexander; executive consultant Chad Savage; producer Sarah Caplan; co-producers Vanessa Taylor, Daniel Arkin, Tiffany Rocquemore-Delorme; associate producer Nicole Carrasco. Touchstone Television. Fox.

Ally McBeal: created by David E. Kelley; executive producers Bill D'Elia, David E. Kelley; co-executive producers Alice West, Pamela Wisne; producers Jack Philbrick, Roberto Benabib, Constance M. Burge, Jeffrey Kramer, Jonathan Pontell, Ellie Herman, Pam Jackson, Kayla Alpert, Kim Hamberg, Mike Listo,

Steve Robin; associate producers Roseann Keris, Pam Jackson. Twentieth Century Fox TV. Fox.

Angel: created by David Greenwalt; executive producers David Greenwalt, Joss Whedon, Gail Berman, Sandy Gallin, Fran Rubel Kuzui, Kaz Kuzui; producer Kelly Manners; co-producer Tim Minear. Mutant Enemy, Greenwolf Corp., Kuzui Enterprises, Sandollar Television. Warner Bros.

Any Day Now: created by Deborah Joy Levine & Nancy Miller; executive producers Bill Finnegan, Deborah Joy Levine, Gary A. Randall, Nancy Miller, Sheldon Pinchuk, David Calloway; supervising producer Bob Lowry, Valerie Woods. Paid Our Dues Prods. Lifetime.

The A-Team: created by Frank Lupo & Stephen Cannell; executive producers Stephen Cannell, Frank Lupo; supervising producer Jo Swerling, Jr.; producers John Ashley, Patrick Hasburgh; associate producers Steve Beers, Rob Bowman, Alan Cassidy, Gary Winter. Stephen J. Cannell Prods. NBC.

Baywatch: created by Michael Berk & Douglas Schwartz and Gregory J. Bonann; executive producers Michael Berk, Douglas Schwartz, Gregory J. Bonann; co-executive producer David Braff; supervising producer Paul Cajero, David W. Hagar; producers Deborah Schwartz, James Pergola; co-producers Craig Thomas Kwasizur, Kevin Beggs. The Baywatch Company, Tower 12 Prods. NBC.

Beverly Hills 90210: created by Darren Star; executive producers Darren Star, Aaron Spelling, Michael Braverman; co-executive producers John Eisendrath, Jessica Klein, Laurie McCarthy, Doug steinberg, David Stenn, E. Duke Vincent, Paul Waigner, Steve Wasserman; producers Michael Cassutt, Ann Donahue, Richard Gollance, Chip Johannessen, Dinah Kirgo, Larry Mollin, Jon Pare. Spelling TV, Torand Prods. Fox.

Black Sheep Squadron: created by Stephen J. Cannell; executive producer Stephen J. Cannell, producers Philip DeGuere, Donald P. Bellisario, Chuck Bowman, Alex Beaton, Ken Pettus, Milt Rosen. Stephen Cannell Prods. NBC.

Boston Public: created by David E. Kelley; executive producers David E. Kelley, Jonathan Pontell; co-executive producers Mike Listo, Kerry Lenhart, John J. Sakmar; producers Alicia Martin, Daniel Cohn, Jeremy Miller, Adam Armus, Douglas Steinberg, Phillip Neal, Peter Burrell; co-producers Sean Whitesell, Chuck Conway. Twentieth Century Fox TV. Fox.

Buffy the Vampire Slayer: created by Joss Whedon; executive producers Joss Whedon, Fran Rubel Kuzui, Gail Berman, Kaz Kuzui, Marti Noxon, Sandy Gallin; supervising producer Jane Espenson; producers Gareth Davies, David Soloman, Douglas Petrie; co-producer David Fury. Mutant Enemy, Sandollar Television, Kuzui Enterprises. Warner Bros, then UPN.

Cagney & Lacey: created by Barbara Corday & Barbara Avedon and Barney Rosenzweig; executive producers Barney Rozenzweig, Terry Louise Fisher,

Georgia Jeffries; producers Richard M. Rosenbloom, Barbara Corday, Jonathan Estrin, Peter Lefcourt, Shelly List, Barbara Avedon; writers Del Reisman, Aubrey Solomon. Orion TV. CBS.

Charmed: created by Constance M. Burge; executive producers Aaron Spelling, Brad Kern, Constance M. Burge, E. Duke Vincent; co-executive producer Nell Scovell; supervising producers Peter Hume, Sheryl J. Anderson; producer Jon Pare, co-producers Peter Chomsky, Daniel Cerone. Spelling TV. Warner Bros.

China Beach: created by William Broyles, Jr. & John Sacret Young; executive producers William Broyles, John Sacret Young, John Wells; producers Lydia Woodard, Terry McDonnell, Susan Rhinehart, Carol Flint, Rod Holcomb, Ann Donahue. Wells Prods. ABC.

Combat!: series developed by Robert Pirosh; executive producer Selig J. Seligman, producers Robert Altman, Robert Blees, Richard Caffey, Burt Kennedy, Gene Levitt, Richard Maibaum, Robert Pirosh; associate producers Lou Morheim, Georg Fenady. Selmur Prods. ABC.

Crossing Jordan: created by Tim Kring; executive producer Tim Kring, co-executive producers Samantha Howard Corbin, Ian Bledorrnan; supervising producer Todd E. Kessler, producer Dennis Hammer, co-producer Gary Glasberg, writers Diane Ademu-John, Damon Lindelof, Jill Blotevogel. NBC Studios. NBC.

C.S.I.: created by Anthony Zuiker; executive producers Ann Donahue, James C. Hart, Jerry Bruckheimer, Carol Mendelsohn, Anthony Zuiker; co-executive producers Sam Strangis; producers William Petersen, Cindy Chvatal, Danny Cannon; co-producers Andrew Lipsitz, Elisabeth Devine, Josh Berman, Tish McCarthy. Alliance Atlantis. CBS.

Dallas: created by David Jacobs; executive producers Philip Capice, Larry Hagman, Leonard Katzman, Lee Rich, David Jacobs; co-executive producers Joel J.Feigenbaum, supervising producers Peter Dunne, Arthur Bernard Lewis, James Brown, David Paulsen. Lorimar. CBS.

Dark Angel: created by James Cameron & Charles H. Eglee; executive producers James Cameron, Charles H. Eglee, Rene Echevarria; co-executive producers Rae Sanchini, Majorie David, Ken Biller; supervising producer Patrick Harbinson; producers Stephen Sassen, Janace Tashijan, Michael Angeli. Cameron/ James Eglee Prods. Fox.

Dawson's Creek: created by Kevin Williamson; executive producers Kevin Williamson, Greg Berlanti, Greg Prange, Paul Stupin, Tom Kapinos; co-executive producers Jeffrey Stepakoff, Gina Fattore; producers David Blake Hartley. Granville Prods. Warner Bros. "Two Gentlemen of Capeside" written by Jeffrey Stepakoff; directed by Sandy Smolan.

Diagnosis Murder: created by Joyce Burditt; executive producers Fred Silverman, Dick Van Dyke, Dean Hargrove, Chris Abbott; producer Don Gold; creative consultants Joel Steiger, Steve Brown, Teri Curtis Fox. Fred Silverman Co. CBS.

The District: created by Jack Maple & Terry George; executive producers Denise Di Novi, John Worth, Terry George; supervising producers Jack Maple, Pam Veasey, consulting producer Craig T. Nelson. Studios USA TV. CBS.

The Division: created by Deborah Joy Levine; executive producer Deborah Joy Levine, co-executive producer Aaron Lipstadt; supervising producer Barry Schkolnick; co-producers Judy Feldman, Sarah Gallagher; consulting producer Kimberly Costello. Viacom Prods. Lifetime.

Doc: producer Michael Prupas; executive story editor Joan Considine Johnson; produced by George Bloomfield, Marilyn Stonehouse; writer Ken Hanes, David A. Johnson, Gary R. Johnson, Joan Considine Johnson, John Posey, Edward Tivnan. Pax TV, USA. Pax.

Dragnet: created by Jack Webb; executive producer Jack Webb; producers Robert A. Cinader, William Stack, Jack Webb, Robert C. Dennis. Mark VII Ltd., Dragnet Prods. NBC.

Dr. Quinn, Medicine Woman: created by Beth Sullivan; executive producers Beth Sullivan, Carl Binder; co-executive producers Chris Abbott, Sara Davidson, Philip Gerson, Tim Johnson; producers Benjamin Benedetti, John Liberti, Eric Tuchman. Sullivan Co. CBS.

Ed: created by Jon Beckerman & Rob Burnett; executive producers David Letterman, Rob Burnett, Jon

Beckerman; co-executive producers Tom Spezialy; producers Bob Brush, Kathleen McGill, Merrill Karpf. Worldwide Pants Inc. NBC.

Education of Max Bickford: created by Dawn Prestwich & Nicole Yorkin; executive producers Joe Cacaci, Keith Addis, Rod Holcomb; co-executive producer Jan Oxenberg; producers Richard Dreyfuss, Alysse Bezahler, Dianne Houston, Chris Nelson, Emile Lavisetti; writers Tom Garrigus, Sharon Lee Watson. Regency Television. CBS.
"Save The Country" written by David Yorkin; directed by Don Scardino.

Emergency: created by Jack Webb; executive producers Jack Webb, Robert Cinader; producers Gino Grimaldi, Edwin Self, Hannah Louise Shearer, William Stark. Mark VII Ltd. NBC.

Enterprise: created by Rick Berman & Brannon Braga, based upon Star Trek which was created by Gene Roddenberry; executive producers Rick Berman, Brannon Braga; supervising producers Merri D. Howard, Peter Lauritson; consulting producer Fred Dekker; producers Antoinette Stella, Dawn Velazquez, J.P. Farrell; co-producer Brad Yacobian. Paramount Network Television Prods. UPN.
"Fight or Flight" written by Rick Berman & Brannon Braga; directed by Allan Kroeker.

ER: created by Michael Crichton; executive producers Michael Crichton, John Wells, Lydia Woodward, Jack Orman; co-executive producers Carol Flint, R. Scott Gemmill, Mimi Leder, Robert Nathan, Walon Green; supervising producer Paul

Manning; producers Christopher Chulack, Christopher Misiano, Dee Johnson, Patrick Harbinson, Richard Thorpe, Jonathan Kaplan, Neal Baer; co-producers Lance Gentile, Wendy Spence. Constant C Prods. Amblin Entertainment. Warner Bros. NBC. "Be Still My Heart" written by Lydia Woodward; directed by Laura Innes. "Hell or High Water" written by Neal Bear; directed by Christopher Chulack. "Last Call" story by Samantha Howard Corbin & Carol Flint, teleplay by Samantha Howard Corbin; directed by Rod Holcomb. "The Storm, Pt. 1" written and directed by John Wells.

Falcon Crest: created by Earl Hamner & Earl Hamner, Jr.; executive producers Claire Whitaker, Earl Hamner, Earl Hamner, Jr., Michael Filerman, Rod Peterson, Jeff Freilich; supervising producers Ann Marcus, E.F. Wallengren, Greg Strangis, Howard Lakin, Robert L. McCullough; producers Rena Down, Barry Steinberg, John F. Perry, Malcolm L. Harding, Phil Parslow, Howard Stern; associate producers Victoria La Fortune, Myron Lee Nash. Lorimar. CBS.

Fame: based on the film; executive producers Debbie Allen, William Blinn, Patricia Jones; co-executive producers Harry Longstreet, Renee Longstreet, Donald Reiker; producers Ira Steven Behr, Michael McGreevey, Stan Rogow, producer Chris Seiter, Mel Swope; associate producers Parke Perine, Claylene Jones, Michael Hoey, Karina Friend Buck. MGM TV. NBC.

Family Law: created by Anne Kenney, Paul Haggis; executive producers David Shore, Fred Gerber, Stephen Nathan, Paul Haggis, Anne Kenney; producers Gary Law, Bill Chais, Christopher Ambrose, Gregg Gettas, Lawrence Kaplan, Linda McGibney, Scott

Cameron, Ashley Gable; co-producers Hilton Smith, Tommy Moran, Jan Nash. Paul Haggis Prods. CBS.

Felicity: created by J.J. Abrams, Matt Reeves; executive producers Brian Grazer, J.J. Abrams, Jennifer Levin, John Eisendrath, Laurie McCarthy, Matt Reeves, Ron Howard, Tony Krantz; producers Adam Horowitz, Edward Kitsis, Gerrit Van Der Meer, Josh Reims, Lawrence Trilling, Mychelle Deschamps, Sara Caplan. Imagine Television. Warner Bros.

The Fugitive: based on the original TV series from characters created by Roy Huggins; executive producers R.W. Goodwin, Roy Huggins, Arnold Kopelson, Anne Kopelson, John McNamara; co-executive producer Lisa Melamed; supervising producers Randi Anderson, Kim Newton; producers Valerie Mayhew, Vivian Mayhew, Vladimir Stefoff, David Ehrman. CBS TV, Warner Bros. (2000-2001 series).

Gilmore Girls: created by Amy Sherman-Palladino; executive producers Gavin Polone, Amy Sherman-Palladino; co-executive producer Michael Katleman; executive consultant Daniel Palladino; producers Jenji Konan, Mel Efros, Patricia Fass Palmer, Sheila Lawrence. Dorothy Parker Drank Here Prods, Hofflund/Polond. Warner Bros. "Double Date" written by Amy Sherman-Palladino; directed by Lev L. Spiro.

The Guardian: created by David Hollander; executive producers David Hollander, Mark Johnson, Michael Pressman; co-executive producers Vahan Moosekian;

supervising producers Sara Cooper, Michael R. Perry; producers Peter Parnell, Alfonso H. Moreno, Jimmy Miller. David Hollander Prods, Gran Via Prods. CBS.

Hill Street Blues: created by Michael Kozoll & Steven Bochco; supervising producer Gregory Hoblitz; producers David Anspaugh, Anthony Yerkovich. Bochco Prods. NBC.

Homicide: created by Paul Attanasio; executive producers Tom Fontana, Barry Levinson; co-executive producers Henry Bromell, Jim Finnerty, Paul Attanasio; supervising producers Julie Martin, James Yoshimura; producers Anya Epstein, David Simon; consulting producers Eric Overmyer, Gail Mutrux; associate producer Debbie Sarjeant. Baltimore Pictures, Fatima Prods. NBC. "The Documentary" written by Eric Overmyer, story by Eric Overmyer & Tom Fontana & James Yoshimura; directed by Barbara Kopple. "Stakeout" written by Tom Fontana & Noel Behn, teleplay by Noel Behn; directed by John McNaughton.

J.A.G.: created by Donald P. Bellisario; executive producer Donald P. Bellisario; co-executive producers Chas Floyd Johnson, Mark Horowitz, Stephen Zito; supervising producers Dana Coen, David Ehrman; consulting producer Tom Towler; producer Avery C. Drewe; co-producers Evan Katz, Julie B. Watson, David Belisarius, Nan Hagan, Mark Schilz. Bellisario Prods. CBS. "Capital Crime" written by Don McGill; directed by Richard Compton.

Judging Amy: created by Barbara Hall, Amy Brenneman, Bill D'Elia, Connie Tavel, John Tinker; executive producers Amy Brenneman, Barbara Hall, Connie Tavel, Hart Hanson, Joseph Stern; co-executive producers David Zucker, Thomas R. Moore, Daniel Sackheim. Barbara Hall/Joseph Stern Prods. CBS.

Knot's Landing: created by David Jacobs; executive producers David Jacobs, Lynn Marie Latham, Michael Filerman; producers Mary Catherine Harold, Bernard Lechowick, John Romano, Richard Winnie. Lorimar. CBS.

Kolchak: The Night Stalker: created by Jeff Rice; executive producers Cy Chermak, Darren McGavin, Paul Playdon; writers Rudolph Borchert, David Chase, Steve Fisher, Arthur Rowe, Robert Zemeckis, Bill Ballinger. Francy Prods., Universal TV. ABC.

L.A. Law: created by Steven Bochco & Terry Louise Fisher; executive producers Steven Bochco, Terry Louise Fisher; co-executive producers Mark Tinker, Elodie Keene; producers Paul Haggis, Denny Salvaryn, Anne Kenney, William M. Finkelstein, Peter Schneider, Julie Martin, Paul Manning. Bochco Prods. CBS.

Law & Order: created by Dick Wolf; executive producers Rene Balcer, Arthur Penn, Barry Schindel, Ed Sherin; co-executive producer Kathy McCormick, Peter Jankowski, William Finkelstein; supervising producer Arthur W. Forney, Gary Karr, William N. Fordes; consulting producer David Black; producers Jeffrey Hayes, Lewis H. Gould, Billy Fox, David Shore. Wolf

Prods. NBC.

"The Collar" written by Richard Sweren; directed by Matthew Penn.

"Ritual" written by Kathy McCormick & Richard Sweren; directed by Brian Mertes.

Law & Order: Criminal Intent: created by Dick Wolf, developed by Rene Balcer; executive producers Dick Wolf, Peter Jankowski, Rene Balcer; co-executive producers Arthur Forney, Fred Berner, Geoffrey Neigher; consulting producers Marlane Gomard Meyer, Theresa Rebeck; producers John L. Roman, Rox Weinman. Wolf Prods. NBC.

Law & Order: Special Victims Unit: created by Dick Wolf; executive producers Dick Wolf, Neal Baer, Peter Jankowski, Ted Kotcheff; supervising producer Jack Eckerle; consulting producers Eric Overmyer, Samantha Howard Corbin; producers David De Clerque, Dawn De Noon, Joe Lazarov, Lisa Marie Petersen, Roz Weinman. Wolf Prods. NBC.

Little House On The Prairie: developed for television by Blanche Hanalis, based upon the "Little House" series of books by Laura Ingalls Wilder; executive producer Michael Landon; producer Arthur Heinemann. NBC.

"Christmas At Plum Creek" written by Victor French; directed by Leo Penn.

Magnum P.I.: created by Donald Bellisario & Glen A. Larson; executive producers Donald Bellisario, Glen A. Larson, Tom Selleck; co-executive producer Chas Floyd Johnson; supervising producers Douglas Benton, John David, Joel Rogosin; producers Chris Abbott, Jay Huguely, Stephen Miller, Rick Weaver,

David Bellisario, Tom Green; co-producers Jill Donna, J. Rickley Dumm, Douglas Green. Belisarius Prods., Glen A. Larson Prods. CBS.

Matlock: created by Dean Hargrove; executive producers Andy Griffith, Dean Hargrove, Fred Silverman; supervising producer Joel Steiger; producers Ron Carr, Anne Collins, Jeff Peters, Robert Schlitt; associate producer William S. Kerr. Dean Hargrove Prods., The Matlock Co. NBC, then ABC.

Melrose Place: created by Darren Star; executive producers Darren Star, Aaron Spelling, Charles Pratt Jr., Frank South, E. Duke Vincent; co-executive producers James Kahn, Carol Mendelsohn; supervising producers Peter Dunne, Dee Johnson, Frederick Rappaport; producer Kimberly Costello; co-producers Heather Locklear, Allison Robbins, Antoinette Stella. Spelling TV. FOX.

Miami Vice: created by Anthony Yerkovich; executive producers Michael Mann, Anthony Yerkovich; producers Liam O'Brien, Richard Brams, John Nicolella, John Mankiewicz, Donald L. Gold, Patti Kent, Frederick Lyle, Ed Waters. Michael Mann Prods. NBC.

Moonlighting: created by Glen Gordon Caron; executive producer Jay Daniel; producers Christopher T. Welch, Barbara Hall, Ron Osborn, Jeff Reno, Artie Mandelberg. Glen Gordon Caron Prods. ABC.

"Between A Yuk And A Hard Place" written by Kerry Ehrin; directed by Dennis Dugan.

"Camille" written by Roger Director; directed by Peter Werner.

"The Dream Sequence Always Rings Twice" written by Debra Frank & Carl Sautter; directed by Peter Werner.
"It's A Wonderful Job" written by Debra Frank & Carl Sautter; directed by Ed Sherin.
"It's Maddie's Turn To Cry" written by Roger Director and Ron Osborn & Jeff Reno; directed by Allan Arkush.
"North By North Dipesto" written by Debra Frank & Carl Sautter; directed by Chris Hibler.
"A Womb With A View" written by Glenn Gordon Caron & Charles H. Eglee; directed by Jay Daniel.

Murder, She Wrote: created by Peter S. Fischer and Richard Levinson & William Link; executive producers Peter S. Fischer, Richard Levinson, William Link; producers Robert F. O'Neill, Robert E. Swanson. Corymore Prod., Universal TV. CBS.

My So-Called Life: created by Edward Zwick & Marshall Herskovitz; executive producers Edward Zwick, Marshall Herskovitz; co-executive producers Winnie Holzman, Scott Winant; coordinating producer Charles Carroll, consulting producer Jill Gordon; producers Brooke Kennedy, Alan Poul; co-producer Monica Wyatt. Bedford Falls. MTV.

La Femme Nikita: based on the film; executive producer Jay Firestone; supervising producer Peter M. Lenkov; producer Jamie Paul Rock; writers Robert Cochran, Peter Bellwood, David Ehrman, Lawrence Hertzog, Ed Horowitz, Naomi Janzen. Fireworks Entertainment. USA.

Northern Exposure: created by Joshua Brand & John Falsey; executive producers Joshua Brand, John Falsey, David Chase, Henry Bromell, Diane Frolov; co-executive producers Michael Fresco, Robin Green, Jeff Melvoin, Andrew Schneider, Michael Vittes; consulting producers Sam Egan, Barbara Hall; supervising producer Charles Rosin; producers Cheryl Bloch, Geoffrey Neigher, Matt Nodella, Robert T. Skodis, Robert C. Thompson; co-producers Martin Bruestle, Alan Brent Connell, Joe Lazarov. Universal TV. CBS.
"Birds of a Feather" written by Robin Green & Mitchell Burgess; directed by Mark Horowitz.

NYPD Blue: created by David Milch & Steven Bochco; executive producers David Milch, Steven Bochco, Mark Tinker, Burton Armus, Channing Gibson; co-executive producers Nicholas Wootton, Bob Doherty, Jody Worth; producers Bill Clark, David Mills, Gardner Stern, Leonard Gardner, Tedd Mann, Walon Green, Theresa Rebeck, Doug Palau, Jill Goldsmith, Alexandra Cunningham. Bochco Prods. NBC.
"Personal Foul" story by David Milch, teleplay by Burton Armos.

Once & Again: created by Marshall Herskovitz & Edward Zwick; executive producers Marshall Herskovitz, Edward Zwick; producers Liberty Godshall, Winnie Holzman, Dan Lerner, Jan Oxenberg, Daniel Paige, Sue Paige, Peter Schindler. Bedford Falls. ABC.
"Gardenia" written by Richard Kramer; directed by Edward Zwick.

Oz: created by Tom Fontana; executive producers Tom Fontana, Barry Levinson, Jim Finnerty; supervising producers Bridget Potter; producers Adam Bernstein, Sean Whitesell, co-producers Debbie Sarjeant; associate producers Mark A. Baker, Irene Burns. Rysher Entertainment, The Levinson/Fontana Co. HBO.

Pasadena: created by Mike White; executive producers Mike White, Bill Robinson, Brad Grey, Diane Keaton, Mark B. Perry, R.W. Goodwin; producer Dana Baratta; associate producers Crawford Hawkins, Geno Escarrega. Brad Grey TV. FOX.

Philly: created by Alison Cross & Steven Bochco; executive producers Steven Bochco, Rick Wallace, Kevin Hooks; co-executive producers Alison Cross, Jon Hiatt; producers Dayna Kalins Bochco; co-producers Keith Eisner, Tom Szentgyorgyi, Lisa Vinnecour; associate producers Jesse Bochco, Alex Shevchenko. Paramount Television. ABC.

The Ponderosa: based on characters created by David Dortort; developed by Beth Sullivan; executive producer David Dortort; producers Jan Bladier, David Lee. Sullivan Co, Paxton Entertainment. PAX TV.

The Practice: created by David E. Kelley; executive producers David E. Kelley, Bob Breech; co-executive producer John Tinker; supervising producer Christina Musrey; producers Gary M. Strangis, Pamela Wisne, Joseph Burger-Davis, Jeff Rake; co-producer Lynne E. Litt; associate producers Tammy Ann Casper,

Steven Lang. Twentieth Century Fox Television. ABC.

Providence: created by John Masius; executive producers John Masius, Robert DeLaurentis, Michael Fresco, Ann Hamilton; co-executive producers Tim Kring, Monica Wyatt; supervising producer Ken LaZebnik; producers Kevin Cremin, Robert Fresco, Art Rusis; co-producers Ellie Triedman, Carol Barbee, Karen Gaviola, John Patterson, Kristoffer Tabori, Ian Toynton, James Whitmore, Jr., Craig Zisk,; writers Nancy Won, Jennifer Johnson. NBC Studios. NBC.
"Syd in Wonderland" written by Tim King; directed by Randall Zisk. "Paradise Inn" written by Robert DeLaurentis; directed by Michael Fresco.

Quantum Leap: created by Donald P. Bellisario; executive producers Donald P. Bellisario, Chris Ruppenthal; producers Tommy Thompson, Scott Ejercito. Belisarius Prod., Universal TV. NBC. "A Little Miracle, December 24, 1962" written by Sandy Fries; directed by Michael Watkins.

Remington Steele: created by Robert Butler & Michael Gleason; executive producers Michael Gleason, Robert Butler; supervising producer Glenn Gordon Caron; producers Gareth Davies, Charles Rosin, Robert Bailey, Kevin Inch, Richard DeRoy, Jeff Melvoin, Jack Mongan, Carol Vitale, Lee David Zlotoff. MTM Entertainment. NBC.

Roswell: created by Jason Katims; executive producers Jason Katims, David Nutter, Jonathan Frakes, Kevin Kelly Brown,

Lisa J. Olin; co-executive producers Ronald Moore, Carol Trussell; producers Aaron Harberts, Fred Golan, Tracey D'Arcy, Gretchen J. Berg, Christopher Seitz, John Heath. Regency Television. UPN.

Six Feet Under: created by Alan Ball; executive producers Alan Ball, Robert Greenblatt, David Janeollier; co-executive producers Alan Poul, Christian Williams; co-producers Bruce Kaplan, Christian Taylor; producers Kate Robin, Laurence Andries, Rick Cleveland. Alan Ball Prods. HBO.

Smallville: created by Alfred Gough & Miles Millar; executive producers Alfred Gough, Brian Robbins, Miles Millar, Michael Tollin, Joe Davola; co-executive producers Michael Watkins, Alex Taub; supervising producer Mark Verheiden; producer Robert Petrovicz; co-producers Michael Green, Doris Egan, Greg Walker. Tollin/Robbins Prods. Warner Bros.

The Sopranos: created by David Chase; executive producers David Chase, Brad Grey; co-executive producers Mitchell Burgess, Robin Green, Frank Renzulli; producers Ilene Landress, Gregg Glickman. Chase Films, Brillstein-Grey Entertainment, Sopranos Prods. HBO.

Special Unit 2: created by Evan Katz; executive producers Evan Katz; producers John T. Kretchmer, Rose Sharon, Ron Binkowski; consulting producer Jack Bernstein, Martin Weiss; producer Keira Morrisette. Rego Park, Paramount TV. UPN.

Star Trek: created by Gene Roddenberry; executive producer Gene Roddenberry; producer Gene L. Coon; co-producers Robert H. Justman, John D.F. Black, Fred Freiberger. Desilu Prods. NBC.

St. Elsewhere: created by Joshua Brand & John Falsey; executive producer Bruce Paltrow; producers John Masius, Tom Fontana, John Falsey, Joshua Brand, Mark Tinker, Beth Hillshafer, Abby Singer. MTM Entertainment. NBC. "After Dark" written by Steve Lawson, story by Steve Lawson and John Masius & Tom Fontana; directed by Eric Laneuville. "After Life" written by John Tinker and John Masius & Tom Fontana. "Drama Center" written by John Tinker, story by John Masius & Tom Fontana; directed by David Anspaugh. "The Last One" written by Bruce Paltrow and Mark Tinker, story by Tom Fontana, John Tinker and Channing Gibson; directed by Mark Tinker. "Murder, She Rote" written by Tom Fontana and John Masius and Steve Bello. "A Pig Too Far" written by John Tinker and James Kahn; directed by Linda Day. "Sweet Dreams" written by John Masius & Tom Fontana; directed by Mark Tinker. "A Wing And A Prayer" written by Raymond DeLaurentis and Robert DeLaurentis; directed by Bruce Paltrow. "The Women" written by John Ford Noonan, story by John Masius & Tom Fontana; Bruce Paltrow.

Strong Medicine: developed by Whoopi Goldberg; created by Tammy Ader; executive producers Tammy Ader,

Whoopi Goldberg, Robert Lieberman; co-executive producer Jeremy R. Littman; supervising producer Rick Rosenthal; producers Rick Alexander, John Perrin Flynn, Allison Robbins; co-producer Joe DeOliveira. Lifetime TV, Columbia Tri-Star TV, Onetto Prods. Lifetime.

Third Watch: created by Ed Bernero & John Wells; executive producers John Wells, Christopher Chulack, Brooke Kennedy, Ed Bernero; producers Scott Williamson, Charles Carroll; co-producers Guy Norman Bee, Janine Sherman Barrois, Glenn Kershaw. John Wells Prods. NBC.
"Sex, Lies, & Videotapes" written by Janine Sherman Barrois; directed by Felix Enriquez Alcala.

Thirtysomething: created by Marshall Herskovitz & Edward Zwick; executive producers Marshall Herskovitz & Edward Zwick; producers Lindsley Parsons III, Richard Kramer, Ann Lewis Hamilton, Joseph Dougherty, Ellen S. Pressman, Scott Winant. Bedford Falls. ABC.
"Couples" written by Marshall Herskovitz & Edward Zwick; directed by Marshall Herskovitz.
"South By Southwest" written by Paul Haggis; directed by Dan Lerner.
"Whose Forest Is It Anyway" written by Richard Kramer, story by Kathleen Tolan; directed by Peter Horton.

Touched By An Angel: created by Martha Williamson, producers Brian Bird, Burt Pearl, Glenn Berenbeim, Jon Anderson, Jule Selbo, Ken La Zebnik, Marilyn Osborn, R.J. Colleary, Robert Visciglia,

Jr., Susan Cridland Wick. Moon Water Prods., Caroline Prods. CBS.

Twice in a Lifetime: created by Steve Sohmer; executive producers Alyssa Cartegena, Michael Prupas; producers Pamela K. Long, Barney Rosenzweig, Stephen Brackley, Marilyn Stonehouse; co-producers Paula Smith, Michael Maschio. Pebblehut Prods. Inc. PAX TV.

U.C.: Undercover: created by Don Winslow & Shane Salerno; executive producers Don Winslow, Shane Salerno, Danny DeVito, John Landgraf, Michael Shamberg, Stacey Sher, Thomas Carter; producer Joseph Patrick Finn. Jersey Films, Chasing Time Pictures, Regency Television. NBC.

Wagon Train: producers Howard Christie, Richard Lewis; writers John Dunkel, William Fay, Melone Halsey, Kathleen Hite, Jean Halloway, John McGreevy, Tony Paulson, Sutton Roley, Peggy Shaw, Lou Shaw. Revue Studios, Universal TV. NBC, then ABC.

West Wing: created by Aaron Sorkin; executive producers Aaron Sorkin, Thomas Schlamme, John Wells; co-executive producer Kevin Falls; producers Michael Hissrich, Lawrence O'Donnell, Llewellyn Wells; co-producer Patrick H. Caddell, Kristin Harms; producers Christopher Misiano, Alex Graves, Paul Redford, Neal Ahern. John Wells Prods. NBC.
"The Fall's Gonna Kill You" story by

Patrick H. Caddell, teleplay by Aaron Sorkin; directed by Christopher Misiano.
"In The Shadow of Two Gunmen, Pt. 1" written by Aaron Sorkin; directed by Thomas Schlamme.

Wiseguy: created by Stephen J. Cannell & Frank Lupo; executive producers Stephen J. Cannell, Frank Lupo; producers David J. Burke, Stephen Kronish. Stephen Cannell Prods. CBS.

The X-Files: created by Chris Carter; executive producers Chris Carter, Frank Spotnitz, Howard Gordon, R.W. Goodwin, Vince Gilligan, John Shiban; co-executive producers James Wong, Glen Morgan, Bernadette Caulfield, Daniel Sackheim, David Nutter, Harry V. Bring, Joseph Patrick Finn, Kim Manners, Paul Brown, Paul Rabwin, Rob Bowman, Michelle MacLaren. Ten Thirteen Productions. Fox.
"E.B.E." written by Glen Morgan & James Wong; directed by William Graham.
"The Host" written by Chris Carter; directed by Daniel Sackheim.
"The Field Where I Died" written by Glen Morgan & James Wong; directed Rob Bowman.
"Soft-Light" written by Vince Gilligan; directed by James A. Contner.

Filmography

It's A Wonderful Life: produced and directed by Frank Capra, story by Robert Riskin, screenplay by Frances Goodrich, Albert Hackett, and Frank Capra, additional scenes by Jo Swerling. RKO Pictures/Liberty Films.

Raiders of the Lost Ark: produced by Robert Watts, directed by Steven Speilberg, story by George Lucas, screenplay by Willard Huyck & Gloria Katz. Paramount Pictures.

NOTE: In all the above television series and feature films, there are so many more names credited on each that are not listed here. The contributions made by these talented people are just as noteworthy and important as the names listed above. They were only omitted due to the volume of names that would have to be included here. Thus, I have only listed the creators of the series and some of the series producers. Since TV producers change yearly, it was not possible to include every producer of a series that worked on a particular show during its lengthy run due to the volume of names. For specific episodes of a TV series that were cited, I have included the writer and director of that particular episode.

TV Teleplay Road Map

Title		Cast Type
Premise		Hook
Central Idea		Central (?) of Series

Central Question Avenue

Act One
Tow-Away

| 1ST |
| 2ND |
| 3RD |
| 4TH |
| 5TH |
| 6TH |
| 7TH |
| 8TH |
| 9TH |
| 10TH *Green Light – Go!* |

SPEED LIMIT 20

Act Two

| 11TH |
| 12TH |
| 13TH |
| 14TH |
| 15TH |
| 16TH |
| 17TH |
| 18TH |
| 19TH |
| 20TH *U-Turn* |

SPEED LIMIT 35

U-TURN

Act Three

| 21ST |
| 22ND |
| 23RD |
| 24TH |
| 25TH |
| 26TH |
| 27TH |
| 28TH |
| 29TH |
| 30TH *Road of No Return!* |

SPEED LIMIT 50

Act Four
Climax

| 31ST |
| 32ND |
| 33RD |
| 34TH |
| 35TH |
| 36TH |
| 37TH |
| 38TH |
| 39TH |
| 40TH *Cliffhanger (if applicable)* |

SPEED LIMIT 65

Resolution

| Themes | | TV Tunnel |

Driver		Villain
Goal		Goal
Need		Need
Arc

N

1. **GO** The driver is hurled a crisis and/or dilemma and often must make a choice.

2. Keeps the viewer guessing about story's outcome.

3. **DETOUR** It shifts the story down a new road.

4. **DANGER AHEAD** It makes the road more hazardous for the driver.

5. **NEXT EXIT** Next Act This Exit: It must speed the story into the next Act.

This map is designed to be enlarged on a photocopier at 130% on an 11" x 17" sheet

Appendix

Family Creede

by Marilyn Webber & Minda Webber

LOGLINE: It's Dallas meets West Wing. What if J.R. had become governor of Texas? Well, the Creedes aren't exactly the Ewings, more like the Kennedy clan of Texas politics, with even more power, greed, politics, sex, and family squabbling going on than the National Inquirer can keep up with. The Creedes and the Youngs are the modern day Hatfield and McCoys, only their feud's bigger and there's a whole lot more at stake than the family cow.

NOTE: This is the third draft of a television pilot my writing partner and sister, and I are developing on spec.

FAMILY CREEDE

an original TV pilot
created and written
by
Marilyn Webber
&
Minda Webber

© 2002 Marilyn Webber & Minda Webber

FAMILY CREEDE
"It's All in the Family"

TEASER

FADE IN:

EXT. AUSTIN: STATE CAPITOL BUILDING - MORNING

JACE YOUNG, 41, the governor's cousin and once poor relation, has
been Jackson's rival ever since they learned to crawl. Jace is
always trying to erase that invisible tag of being born
"illegitimate". From an advantageous spot, he watches as reporters
gather and smiles.

His wife, ISABELLA YOUNG, 39, descendent of a Spanish land grant
owner, is a proud, powerful, and stunning woman. She's also a cold,
manipulative bitch, especially to her family from whom she demands
absolute perfection. She joins her husband.

                    ISABELLA
          Don't ever summon me as if I were the
          maid -

                    JACE
          - Sit down, querida.

His grin is as wide as the Cheshire cat's. Curious, she sits.

                    ISABELLA
          This better be worth my time.

                    JACE
          I got a worm who's about to squirm on
          the hook.

Isabella follows his gaze towards the Governor's Mansion - now she's
interested.

INT. GOVERNOR'S LIMO - MORNING

GOVERNOR JACKSON CREEDE, 42, reads over a speech. A true Texas
political blue-blood, Jackson's got a smile that could charm the skin
right off a rattlesnake. He's shrewd, loyal, and competitive. Like
most politicians, he lives his world in shades of gray.

                    JACKSON
          I'm speaking to a bunch of farmers, for
          heaven's sake; they don't care what
          some dead Greek poet said almost two
          thousand years ago. Stop showing off
          your Harvard education, Darla, and
          write me a speech farm folk can
          understand.

He hands the speech back to his speechwriter, DARLA, 27, who nods,
disappointed her speech didn't go over better. Darla's pretty, but
down plays it, dressing conservatively for the job.

                    DARLA
          Yes, Governor.

Jackson's aide, RAN CALDER, 30, knows where all the bodies are
buried, so to speak, and someday that knowledge will take him places
he wants to go. For now, he's content with making sure the Governor
stays top dog.

                    RAN
          You have a lunch with Senator Beecher
          and Senator Cavazos to discuss the
          Bilingual Bill-

                    JACKSON
          -That's not a popular bill with the
          majority; it's a waste of time.

                    RAN
          In three years, Governor, we're not
          going to be the majority. By two
          thousand and five, the Hispanic
          population in this state will outnumber
          the Caucasians. A large percentage of
          whom will speak Spanish as their first
          language.

                    JACKSON
          You know Senator Creede's view on this,
          and what he says goes in the Senate -

                    RAN
          - With all due respect, Governor, your
          daddy's view is outdated.

                JACKSON
      - He's my daddy after business hours,
      Ran. From eight to six, he's Senator
      Creede.

                RAN
      Yessir.

Jackson gets out of the limo with his ENTOURAGE as Ran and Darla
exchange a look.

EXT. AUSTIN: STATE CAPITOL BUILDING - MORNING

As Jackson starts up the steps to the building, REPORTERS swarm him,
although his SECURITY MEN keep them at a distance.

REPORTER LIEN NUYEN (pronounced "Lee-in Win") 24, a pretty Vietnamese
woman, takes the front lines as she sticks the microphone in his face
-

                LIEN
      Governor Creede, do you deny the rumors
      that in 1992 you won your mayoral race
      by defrauding the public?

                JACKSON
What?!

Jackson shoots Ran a quick look - how'd he get ambushed?!

In the GATHERING CROWD, Jace glances superiorly at his wife who is
interested now -

From the steps, Lien continues the barrage of questions -

                LIEN
      Your biographer, Nash Fields, is
      claiming that during the 1992 mayoral
      race you falsified votes by using names
      off the tombstones in Brazos county.
      Is this true?

                JACKSON
      - That's the most ludicrous thing I
      ever heard -

                REPORTER
      - So you deny the accusations,
      Governor?

Turning to look into the camera with the sincerity of Gandhi -

                    JACKSON
          My fellow Texans know that I would
          never cheat the decent citizens of this
          great state, and rob them of their
          chosen candidate. Now if you'll excuse
          me, I'm late for a meeting on the
          Breakfast Bill, which as you know, will
          ensure that every child in the state of
          Texas will start school with a healthy
          breakfast and a full stomach.

Jackson nods for his security men to push forward and he hurries up
the steps as Lien still tries to pursue him -

                    LIEN
          What about your biographer's statement
          that he has proof documenting these
          allegations-

Ran blocks her -

                    RAN
          - Governor Jackson has no further
          comment at this time except to say that
          he is completely innocent of these
          dreadful and false rumors.

Ran hurries after the governor -

                    LIEN
          Do you deny that Nash Fields has been
          recently fired for exposing this story?

Lien frowns, frustrated as the Governor's about to disappear inside
the building.

Jackson turns to smile and wave into the cameras of the pursuing
reporters, before he's encircled by his security people.

INT. AUSTIN: STATE CAPITOL BUILDING - MORNING

Jackson hurries inside the building as Ran and Darla catch up with
him -

                    DARLA
          Governor, you might not want to appear
          so cavalier about these allegations -

                    JACKSON
          My daddy always told me, "When they're
          running you out of town, put on a
          smile, and people'll think you're
          leading a parade."

Off Ran and Darla's exchanged look -

FADE OUT

                    <u>END OF TEASER</u>

FADE IN:

EXT. AUSTIN: STATE CAPITOL BUILDING - MORNING

Jace turns to his wife for approval -

> ISABELLA
> I wouldn't look so cocky. He's not
> impeached yet.

Before Jace can reply, Lien catches sight of them and rushes over
with her CAMERAMAN.

> LIEN
> Mr. Young? What do you have to say
> about the allegations against your
> cousin, Governor Creede?

Jace starts to answer, but Isabella, as always, steals focus as she
puts her arm around Jace -

> ISABELLA
> My husband and I stand by Jackson. We
> know what kind of man the governor
> truly is, and we are confident that
> once this scandal is investigated, the
> rest of Texas will know him as his
> family does.

She smiles convincingly as Jace gives his wife a squeeze -

> JACE
> That's right, and I personally
> challenge anyone to try and prove that
> my cousin committed voter fraud.

Lien turns to the cameraman as Jace and Isabella put on their best
sympathetic faces in the background.

> LIEN
> Thank you, Mr. and Mrs. Young. As you
> can see, a very shocked Governor Creede
> and family are denying all charges of
> fraud in the 1992 mayoral polls. We
> promise to stay on this story. This is
> Lien Nguyen for KACB.

INT. GOVERNOR'S OFFICE - MOMENTS LATER

The governor watches Jace's interview on the television before clicking it off and hurling the remote into the couch.

                    JACKSON
          Damn them! They just attached scandal
          to this as well as set in motion every
          journalist and amateur detective to
          prove that I cheated - why didn't I
          know about this press blitz before -

                    RAN
          - Because I didn't know.

                    JACKSON
          I pay you to know.

The two men glare at each other for a moment, then Ran summons his courage -

                    RAN
          The mayoral race was before my time
          here. Are these allegations true?

Before Jackson can reply, his father, SENATOR ROYAL CREEDE, 66, barges into the room. Rambunctious, extremely wealthy, and larger than life, he turns to holler at the secretary -

                    ROYAL
          No calls or interruptions, Lenore!

He SLAMS the door -

                    ROYAL (CONT'D)
          How the hell did that little
          peckerwood, Fields, find that out?!

                    RAN
          Then you did -

                    JACKSON
          - Yes, I inspire dead people. At least
          you can count on them to vote.

                    RAN
          This is not a joke, governor. This
          could get you impeached -

                    JACKSON
I wasn't going to let that sniveling
Dixon run my city, and no one's going
to impeach me. Hell, LBJ did it, and
look where he ended up.

                    RAN
Yeah, well, before you start running
for president, can anyone prove that
you personally knew about the fraud?

                    ROYAL
Absolutely not. It was handled very
discreetly.

                    RAN
Obviously not that discreetly.

                    JACKSON
I want you to find that little snake in
the grass, Nash, and get him in my
office today! I want to know who he's
working for.

                    RAN
You think someone set you up?

                    ROYAL
This reeks of one of our enemies.
Start with that sore-loser, Dixon.

                    JACKSON
Get on the polls. Find out how bad
this is hurting me.

                    RAN
We need some quick damage control.
Something to shift the spotlight off
the fraud. You'll also need a fall guy
should this thing go sour.

                    ROYAL
I'll handle that. In the meantime,
everyone continues to deny everything.

                    JACKSON
The farmers in Mexico, they still
damming up the Rio Grande?

                    RAN
          Yeah, but I don't think now's the time
          for an international incident. It
          could blow up in your face.

                    JACKSON
          Duarte owes me. Have the farmers in
          the valley start something, and I'll
          finish it. That ought to shift the
          spotlight. Have Darla start working on
          a press release.

Royal and Ran nod.

                    JACKSON (CONT'D)
          Let's just make sure none of us get
          caught with our cigars where they
          shouldn't be.

Off their nods -

EXT. AUSTIN HIGH RISE OFFICE BUILDING - DAY

To establish the affluent building and area overlooking the Guadalupe
River.

INT. ISABELLA'S OFFICE - DAY

The office is posh and classy. Isabella reads contracts as Jace
nibbles on her neck from behind her.

                    JACE
          Let's see him weasel out of this one.

                    ISABELLA
          You're positively orgasmic over this,
          aren't you?

He slips his arms around her.

                    JACE
          Not quite, but I could get there.

He starts kissing her neck. She indulges him for a moment.

                    ISABELLA
          You're celebrating far too quickly, mi
          amorcito. We don't even know if the
          accusation is true…Or do we?

She rises, and turns around to kiss him seductively. From his reaction, it's obvious, Isabella isn't always kissing him like that.

> JACE
> Let's just say this time, Jackson's finally going to be exposed for the bastard he is.

He moves his kisses lower towards her breast -

> ISABELLA
> I thought that family title belonged to you?

Jace pushes her away, glaring at her.

> JACE
> You're like a scorpion; you just can't help yourself, can you?

She goes to him all contrite.

> ISABELLA
> Lo siento, mi querido. I like it when you go after what you want.

> JACE
> You like it when I go after Jackson.

She smiles seductively, slipping back into his arms.

> ISABELLA
> Let's not haggle over semantics when we both want the same thing.

She kisses him and he kisses her back. They skyrocket past foreplay and get to it -

EXT. PARK AREA NEAR WATER FOUNTAIN - LATE AFTERNOON

Ran starts to use his cell phone, but glances around the park cautiously. He then steps nearer to the water fountain and dials.

> RAN
> Hey, it's me. I hear you fellas are
> having some trouble down your way…On
> the contrary, the governor's very
> sympathetic to your cause…Of course,
> the governor likes to help those who
> help themselves…Interested?…Good.
> Here's what you need to do…

INT. GOVERNOR'S OFFICE -DAY

Jackson grabs his suit jacket as his secretary, LENORE, takes
shorthand. At age sixty and a capitol hill life-timer, she's pretty
much seen it all. Nothing shocks or impresses her, least of all
Jackson.

> JACKSON
> You can reach me at the mansion. Oh,
> ah -

He goes to close the door, then turns, lowering his voice -

> JACKSON (CONT'D)
> - if you could make those reservations
> we discussed earlier.

> LENORE
> I didn't hear you?

He goes over to her, leaning down with his best grin -

> JACKSON
> Make the reservations, Lenore. And
> don't mention them to anyone.
> Especially not to Mrs. Creede.

> LENORE
> I presume you want me to hold all your
> calls that night?

> JACKSON
> You presume right.

He starts out the office door, muttering to himself -

> JACKSON (CONT'D)
> One of these days I'm gonna make you
> like me.

                              LENORE
                    Not in this millennium.

Jackson shoots her a look -

                              JACKSON
                    You know, Lenore, if it wasn't for the
                    fact that my father owed your husband a
                    favor, you'd have a gold retirement
                    watch right now.

He exits as she smiles, secure in the favor that binds him.

EXT. GOVERNOR'S MANSION - NIGHT

The near hundred and fifty year-old Greek Rival mansion majestically
overlooks the Texas Capitol in its background.

INT. GOVERNOR'S MANSION: FAMILY DEN - NIGHT

SAWYER CREEDE, 17, with bleached blond hair cropped short and wearing
an earring, sits on the couch eating a piece of pizza with his
sister, SUTTON.

SUTTON CREEDE, 14, a tomboy who doesn't quite have her father's
charm, but she can bullshit with the best of them, is glued to the
television as they watch the news about their father. At present,
their grandfather is shown -

                              ROYAL (V.O.)
                    Nash Fields is a disreputable and
                    obviously disturbed young man who's
                    trying to garner his fifteen minutes of
                    fame by attempting to sully the Creede
                    family name.

                              SAWYER
                    You tell 'em, grandpa.

                              SUTTON
                    You think daddy'll be indicted?

                              SAWYER
                    Don't worry. He's like a cat with nine
                    lives.

                              SUTTON
                    Yeah, but he's bound to be on the tenth
                    life by now.

Sawyer LAUGHS as his father enters. Sutton mutes the TV.

                    SUTTON (CONT'D)
          Hey, daddy!

She hops up to give him a big hug.

                    JACKSON
          Oh, I needed that, Sutton.

Sawyer remains on the couch, eating his pizza.

                    JACKSON (CONT'D)
          Sawyer, what are you doing home?

                    SAWYER
          Don't panic, I haven't dropped out of
          UT. Or maybe you'd prefer that?

                    SUTTON
          Sawyer brought some pizza. Want some?

                    JACKSON
          In a little bit. Son, did you know you
          left your pizza delivery light on?
          Your car battery'll run down.

                    SAWYER
          I'm just taking a break. I still got a
          couple pizzas to deliver.

                    JACKSON
          Then what the hell are you doing here
          watching TV?

                    SAWYER
          It's for the Barker's down the road.
          The pizzas will keep -

          - I swear, Sawyer, do you take anything
                    JACKSON
          seriously? How do you expect to become
          a responsible adult when you shrug off
          every responsibility? You better hope
          they don't catch you sitting here on
          your duff eating their pizzas -

Sawyer tosses down his plate and leaps up to face his father.

                    SAWYER
          - Oh, that's classic, you lecturing me
          about integrity? I'm not the one who
          defrauded the public at the polls.
          Thanks for letting us know our whole
          life is a charade.

Sutton shrinks back as she sees her daddy's temper flare.

                    JACKSON
          Be thankful, boy, there's a couch
          between us right now.

                    SAWYER
               (to his sister)
          - Tell mom I'll call her later.

                    JACKSON
          I'm not finished with this
          conversation!

                    SAWYER
          And I'm not one of your political
          lackeys that you can order about. I
          pay my own way now, so stay the hell
          out of my life!

Sawyer SLAMS the door. A beat. TIRES SQUEAL out of the driveway.
Jackson frowns - could this day get any worse?

                    SUTTON
          Daddy?

It takes Jackson a moment, but he tries to dissipate his anger, for
his daughter's sake.

                    JACKSON
          What is it, sweetheart?

                    SUTTON
          Is this thing really serious?

Jackson goes over to his daughter and hugs her.

                    JACKSON
          Everything's going to be fine; don't
          you worry your pretty little head over
          it. It'll all blow over soon enough.

Jackson turns off the television.

                    SUTTON
          Well, just in case, in your name, I
          donated twenty-five thousand dollars to
          the "Save-A-Bat" Fund.

                    JACKSON
          Now, what'd I tell you about forging my
          name on checks?

                    SUTTON
          Daddy, sixty-two percent of Texans are
          environmentally conscious. Thirty-six
          percent believe in preserving the bats
          as an Austin icon. Do you really want
          to isolate half your voters, especially
          with all this dead voter stuff?

Sutton looks up at her father and gives him her best smile; she's
definitely daddy's girl. He ruffles her hair.

                    JACKSON
          Remind me to raise your allowance.

INT. GOVERNOR'S MANSION: THE NURSERY - NIGHT

CLEMENTINE CREEDE, 39, affectionately known as Clem, is a Texas
beauty. While she's very much a lady, she can claw like the best of
them when challenged. In her wheelchair, Clem nurses her ten month-
old baby son, SCHOLAR.

Jackson steps into the doorway and takes a moment to appreciate his
wife and son.

                    CLEMENTINE
          You have as big an appetite for things
          as your daddy.

He enters, going over to the bed next to her.

                    JACKSON
          Everywhere I go today, people are
          spreading rumors about me.

                    CLEMENTINE
That's because powerful and sexy men are always talked about.

He kisses his wife before collapsing on the bed.

                    JACKSON
          God, it's good to be home.

                    CLEMENTINE
          Ran's already briefed me on the
          official response. Off the record,
          should I be worried?

Jackson sits back up, staring at her.

                    JACKSON
          Only about that son of yours.

Clem looks back down lovingly at Scholar.

                    CLEMENTINE
          He looks perfect to me.

                    JACKSON
          That's because he hasn't grown up yet,
          and turned into the spawn of Hell.

                    CLEMENTINE
          Did you chase Sawyer out of here again?

                    JACKSON
          He started it!

                    CLEMENTINE
          I swear, you're more childish than he
          is.

                    JACKSON
          I'm not the one who broke my daddy's
          heart by enrolling in that hippie rock
          school.

                    CLEMENTINE
          The University of Texas is not a rock
          school. It's an esteemed university.

                    JACKSON
          Then how's he taking the History of
          Rock -n- Roll 101?

She buttons back her blouse.

                    CLEMENTINE
          He's never going to be an Aggie like
          you were, so deal with it.

Jackson picks up Scholar from her and holds his son.

                    JACKSON
          Well, this one's going to be an Aggie,
          aren't you, Scholar?

Clem shakes her head, her husband's hopeless.

                    CLEMENTINE
          Just tell him a story and put him to
          bed while I see if there's any pizza
          left for us.

Jackson holds his son as his wife wheels out of the room.

                    JACKSON
          Once upon a time, there was an evil
          ogre who tried to overthrow the good
          king's palace.

The baby stares up at him fascinated.

                    JACKSON (CONT'D)
          But the good king was very cunning, and
          he sent his knights out to find this
          evil ogre so they could behead the ogre
          for his betrayal.

Off Jackson's determined look -

FADE OUT
                    END OF ACT ONE

<u>ACT TWO</u>

FADE IN:

INT. SQUAD CAR - DAY

RANGER MONROE CREEDE, 36, a curvaceous blond with a wholesome
quality, drives along a Texas highway. She wears a Texas Ranger
badge and has a hard time talking on the cell phone as her lights are
FLASHING and SIREN BLASTING.

                    MONROE
          Yeah, well, I thought when I married
          you it was to be happily ever after -

                    LANNY (V.O.)
          - I know, I screwed up -

                    MONROE
          - Yeah, you did. How do you think
          Rylee felt sitting at the father-
          daughter luncheon minus her father?

                    LANNY (V.O.)
          I'll make it up to her.

                    MONROE
          You can't make it up to her!

                    LANNY (V.O.)
          I'm sorry -

                    MONROE
           - Look Lanny, I can't talk right now.
          Bye.

Monroe hangs up as she pulls up to the riot scene. She says a quick
prayer before getting out of the car.

EXT. MEXICAN BORDER - DAY

The border is blocked by dozens of TEXAS FARMERS and their tractors,
preventing any MEXICAN TRUCKERS from entering the state. Tempers on
both sides flare hotter than the sunny Texas day. Monroe joins the
LEAD HIGHWAY PATROLMAN.

                    MONROE
          What's going on?

                    HIGHWAY PATROLMAN
          Damn wetbacks are getting a taste of
          their own medicine.

Monroe stares hard at the officer.

                    MONROE
          Try it again, Officer Allen, without
          the racial slurs. And it's Ranger
          Creede.

He glares at her, but respects her position.

                    HIGHWAY PATROLMAN
          Ranger Creede. Some of the Mexican
          farmers have been damming up water from
          the Rio Grande, hoarding it. Our
          farmers in the valleys are losing their
          crops so they finally decided to return
          the favor and block trade from Mexico.

Monroe looks back at the two groups who are SHOUTING HOSTILITIES at
each other as the tension is escalating.

                    MONROE
          And what are you doing about it?

                    HIGHWAY PATROLMAN
          They have a right to demonstrate
          peaceably.

                    MONROE
          And how long do you think "peaceably"'s
          going to last before they start bashing
          heads?

She grabs his electronic megaphone away from him and goes toward the
angry farmers -

                    MONROE (CONT'D)
          Everyone, listen up! This is Ranger
          Creede. This demonstration is over. I
          want you to disperse immediately and
          quietly and let these truckers through.

The Mexican Truckers CHEER as the Texas Farmers BOO. Already the
PRESS arrives to make the chaos even worse. From all the shouting,
Monroe makes out a few lines from the noise -

                         JOURNALIST
          They have a right to be here, Ranger -

                      MEXICAN TRUCKER
          - Move your tractor, or I'll drive over
          your gringo-ass!

                        LEAD FARMER
          Not until your farmers give us back our
          water!

The FARMERS begin chanting as the truckers start revving their
engines. The farmers start their large tractors, but one farmer
reaches for a concealed gun. Monroe leaps at him-

                          MONROE
                Hey!

The bullet shatters into the trucker's tire as Monroe disarms the
farmer. The HIGHWAY PATROL OFFICERS swarm the group. Off the melee -

INT. GOVERNOR'S OFFICE - LATER THAT DAY

Ran and Jackson watch the news report on him: TOMAS VALLE, 37, a
handsome Hispanic DA with piercing eyes and an easy manner, talks on
screen to a reporter -

                       TOMAS (V.O.)
          Our office is investigating the 1992
          mayoral election, and the voters may
          rest assured that the District
          Attorney's Office will prosecute this
          case should these allegations prove to
          be true.

                        JACKSON
          That's all we need is another DA
          looking to make his name by ruining
          mine.

                      REPORTER (V.O.)
          Thank you, DA Valle. Well, it looks
          like the governor continues to be in
          the hot seat while police are still
          looking for Nash Fields, the person who
          came forth with these allegations - Oh,
          hold on. I've just been told we have
          some breaking news -

                          RAN
          Let's hope this works.

                    ANOTHER REPORTER (V.O.)
          Shots were fired along the Texas-
          Mexican border today as angry farmers
          gathered to protest the violation of
          the Water Treaty of 1964.

On TV, Monroe Creede is shown arresting the farmer in all the chaos -

                    JACKSON
          Is that my little sister?!

                    REPORTER (V.O.)
          Using their tractors, the Texas farmers
          blocked the border in retaliation
          against Mexican farmers who have
          reportedly dammed up parts of the Rio
          Grande for their own crops.

                    RAN
          Yessir.

Jackson stares at the news clip in disbelief -

                    REPORTER (V.O.)
          One Mexican Trucker was injured in the
          brawl by shattering glass -

Ran CLICKS OFF the television as Jackson takes out some Alka-Seltzer
and plops them in his water. He drinks it.

                    JACKSON
          What the hell is she doing down there,
          getting herself shot at?! She's a
          single mom, for heaven's sake. I
          didn't tell you to involve my sister.

                    RAN
          Having her there, is good press for
          you.

                    JACKSON
          Don't ever put my sister in danger
          again -

                    RAN
          - She was never in any danger,
          Governor. I made sure that was clear.

Jackson thinks about the situation. A beat.

                    JACKSON
          I don't want her participating in
          another re-enactment of the Alamo, is
          that clear?

                    RAN
          Yessir.

                    JACKSON
                (on speaker phone)
          Lenore! Get President Duarte on the
          phone. As in the President of Mexico.

                    RAN
          By the evening news, all they'll be
          talking about is how you saved the
          farmers in the valley and averted a
          major international crisis.

                    JACKSON
          I hope I'm paying you enough.

                    RAN
          No, sir. But one day, you will.

Jackson LAUGHS at the near threat. The two men exchange a look of
mutual trust and ambition.

                    LENORE (V.O.)
          President Duarte, of Mexico, on line
          one.

Jackson snatches the phone.

                    JACKSON
                (into phone)
          Presidente Duarte, buenos tardes -

Ran looks on, pleased their plan is working so well.

INT. CITY HIGH RISE - LATER THAT DAY

Isabella sits behind her desk, shouting into the phone.

                    ISABELLA
          I don't care if he wants to sell his
          land or not! Get me the deed.

DENNY MILLER, 43, a tired and nearly life-beaten man, enters the room
hesitantly. Denny dabs the sweat from his forehead with a
handkerchief. Isabella hangs up the phone.

                    ISABELLA (CONT'D)
          What are you doing here, Denny?

                    DENNY
          All this attention on the governor,
          they're gonna find out -

Isabella rises and goes around the desk -

                    ISABELLA
          - Denny, do I look worried?

He shakes his head and dabs some more.

                    ISABELLA (CONT'D)
          If you bring this out in the open, it
          will destroy the governor. Especially
          now.

                    DENNY
          But the governor knew nothing about it.
          Only, with all this mess going on about
          the polls, I know they'll blame him. I
          can't let that happen. This is all my
          fault.

She moves intimidatingly close to him -

                    ISABELLA
          Denny, you know the press. They don't
          care about the truth. They just want a
          scandal. Who's going to believe you?
          A man whose company was nearly bankrupt
          before getting this city contract? A
          man who went to school with the
          governor. You don't want to cost
          Jackson his career, not after all he's
          done for you and your dying son. You
          came to me to help you and to help
          protect the governor, isn't that right?

Denny nods his head slightly.

                    ISABELLA (CONT'D)
          Then trust me to take care of this.
          Everything's going to work out. Now go
          on home and keep your mouth shut.

INT. GOVERNOR'S OFFICE - AFTERNOON

Jackson's on the phone to his wife, but glares at Ran -

                    CLEMENTINE (V.O.)
          Don't forget to be home in time to
          drive with us to the pageant.

                    JACKSON
          I told you we should have never let her
          enter that pageant when she was three.
                    (whispering to Ran)
          Where is he?!

                    RAN
                    (whispering back)
          The police can't even find him.

                    JACKSON
                    (whispering to Ran)
          I don't want to hear excuses! Find
          him!

Ran nods, but waits for Jackson to get off the phone -

                    CLEMENTINE (V.O.)
          You were the one who caved in on that
          tantrum.

                    LENORE (V.O)
          Mr. Creede, you can't go in there -

Jackson looks up to see his older brother, MCKINLEY CREEDE, 48,
rushes into the room, followed by a frustrated Lenore.

A Vietnam Vet, Uncle Mac sometimes experiences Post Traumatic Stress,
and his bipolar disease occasionally tosses in some paranoia which
fuels his conspiracy theories.

                    UNCLE MAC
          Jackson, you've gotta listen to me!

                    JACKSON
          It's alright, Lenore.

Lenore shoots McKinley a look, but closes the door. Jackson motions
for McKinley to hold on.

                    UNCLE MAC
          Jackson, you have to stop them! They'll
          kill us all.

                    JACKSON
          Darlin', I've got to go; I'll see you
          tonight.

                    RAN
          Hello, McKinley.

McKinley looks at Ran - does he know him? Yes, Jackson's aide. He
stares suspiciously at Ran.

                    JACKSON
          Mac, just slow down -

                    UNCLE MAC
          - Listen to me, little brother. This
          city is in danger!

                    JACKSON
          Did you take your medicine today, Mac?

                    UNCLE MAC
          What has that got to do with anything?!
          You're not hearing me -

                    JACKSON
          - Take it now, Mac. And I'll listen.
          To every word.

Mac hesitates; reluctantly he takes out his pills and swallows one.

                    UNCLE MAC
          The bats. They want to remove them
          from the caves so they can inject them
          with rabies -

                    JACKSON
          - Nobody wants to do that, Mac -

                    UNCLE MAC
          - They'll turn them loose on the whole
          city. It's brilliant. I don't know
          why they haven't done it before.

Jackson and Ran exchange a look. Jackson goes over to his brother -

                    JACKSON
          They have to move some of the bats
          because of population control -

                    UNCLE MAC
          - That's just what they're saying.
          Everyone will get sick and no one will
          know why. Just like those test
          patterns the government does off the
          San Francisco Bridge where they spread
          the flu virus to study wind patterns in
          case of a biochemical war - You have to
          stop them before we're all rabid.

                    JACKSON
          - Okay, Mac, okay.

McKinley stares at Jackson serious.

                    JACKSON (CONT'D)
          I'll take care of this, I promise.

McKinley looks at his younger brother, and relaxes slightly.
Suddenly, the lack of sleep hits him. He rubs his head.

                    UNCLE MAC
          Okay…I'm tired.

                    JACKSON
          Why don't you let me take you home?

Jackson shoots a look at Ran.

                    RAN
          I'll send for the car. We'll go out
          the south entrance, reporters have been
          moved from there for security reasons.

Jackson starts leading McKinley out of his office -

INT. GOVERNOR'S OFFICE: RECEPTON AREA - AFTERNOON

They walk through -

                    JACKSON
          Lenore, cancel my afternoon.

She gives him an annoyed look, but starts dialing the phone -

                    UNCLE MAC
                 (whispering to Jackson)
          I wouldn't trust her -

Jackson smiles as they exit.

INT. AUSTIN: STATE CAPITOL BUILDING - A FEW MINUTES LATER

The governor steps out of the elevator with Mac and his security men as a distraught mother, JOANNE CLARK, 34, rushes towards the governor.

                    JOANNE CLARK
          Governor Jackson!

His SECRET SERVICE swarm the woman.

                    JOANNE CLARK (CONT'D)
          Please, I have to speak with the
          Governor!

                    JACKSON
          I'm sorry, if you'll make an
          appointment -

                    JOANNE CLARK
          - Please, my name's Joanne Clark. My
          daughter, she was kidnapped six years
          ago along I-90.

                    SECURITY GUARD
          Ma'am, you're going to have to step
          back -

                    UNCLE MAC
          You have to help her, Jackson.

The governor can't say no to his brother -

                    JACKSON
          It's alright, let her speak.

The security men back off slightly, but watch her -

                    JOANNE CLARK
          The police never found her. They just
          gave up on her. Then all those other
          girls. They don't stop him. Another
          girl was taken six months ago.

The mother takes out a picture and the governor motions for his security to relax - it's just a photograph.

                    JOANNE CLARK (CONT'D)
          This is my Lindsey. She had just
          turned nine…She'd be fifteen today.

She CRIES as Jackson stares down at the photograph thinking of his
own daughter.

>   UNCLE MAC
>   My brother's a powerful man. He'll
>   find your daughter, won't you, Jackson?

Jackson looks like a deer caught in headlights -

>   JACKSON
> Mrs. Clark, give your number to my aide, and I'll make sure someone
> is personally appointed to your daughter's case. We'll bring your
> daughter home.

>   JOANNE CLARK
>   God bless you, Governor Creede.

She hastily hands Ran her card, and he gives her a smile of
encouragement before hurrying McKinley out to the limo -

>   RAN
>   Governor, do you think that was wise?
>   To promise her that?

>   JACKSON
>   (quietly to Ran)
>   She knows her daughter's dead, Ran.
>   The least we can do is give her the
>   body to bury.

McKinley gets in as Jackson orders the chauffeur -

>   JACKSON
>   To my brother's home.

The CHAUFFEUR nods, but waits as Jackson turns to Ran -

>   JACKSON (CONT'D)
>   Call Woffard over at the Attorney
>   General's Office. I want to know why
>   we have fifty-six missing girls along
>   I-90, and no one sitting on death row
>   for it. And put that Tomas Valle on
>   it, give him something else to do
>   besides witch-hunt me.

>   RAN
>   Yes, Governor.

>   JACKSON
>   Oh, and get Monroe on it too.

                    RAN
          Your sister's not going to like that,
          Gov.

                    JACKSON
          I know, but that's what makes being
          governor so much fun.

INT. GOVERNOR'S LIMO - AFTERNOON

He grins as he gets into the car and Ran shuts the door. The
chauffeur drives away. A beat.

                    UNCLE MAC
          You know, momma would be proud of you,
          helping that woman -

                    JACKSON
          - Momma'd be proud of both of us.

                    UNCLE MAC
          I haven't done anything -

                    JACKSON
          - You fought for this country -

                    UNCLE MAC
          -Yeah, and look at me now.

                    JACKSON
          You risked your life in the name of
          freedom, and came home from Nam with a
          chest full of medals. Nothing I'll
          ever do, big brother, will compare to
          that.

The brothers exchange a look. McKinley needed to hear that.

                    JACKSON (CONT'D)
          Why don't you come to the pageant
          tonight; I know Starla would like that.

                    UNCLE MAC
          I can't. Too many people. Too many of
          their thoughts get all tangled up in my
          head.

                    JACKSON
          Well, then the barbecue. You haven't
          seen Scholar in awhile. Mostly, it'll
          just be the family.

                    UNCLE MAC
          I'll think about it. You believe me,
          about the bats?

Jackson nods quietly, and McKinley leans back against the seat,
comforted. Jackson stares out the window.

                                        DISSOLVE TO:

EXT. AUSTIN AUDITORIUM - NIGHT

To establish -

INT. AUDITORIUM - NIGHT

The Creede family eagerly waits for Starla to perform as MISS
ROUNDROCK sings New York, New York. Jackson looks at his watch, then
glances at Sawyer who glares at his father. Fortunately, Sutton
seats between her dad and her brother.

The senator, Royal Creede, has a twenty-four year old REDHEAD BIMBO
who's nicely stacked, on his arm as his date for the event. She
takes out her compact and reapplies her lipstick as Royal leans over
Clem to complain-

                    ROYAL
          What the hell is she singing about New
          York for? This is Texas!

                    CLEMENTINE
          Shhhh, Dad. Starla's up next.

He frowns and leans back in his seat. Jackson peeks over his wife to
see his father's date, then whispers to Clem -

                    JACKSON
          So who's the whore-du-jour with daddy?

                    CLEMENTINE
               (whispering back)
          Some twenty-four year old waitress he
          picked up.

                    JACKSON
          Obviously, from Hooters.

Clem gives him a stern look. Jackson shifts restlessly in his chair and glances at his watch again.

                    CLEMENTINE
          Why are you checking your watch every
          two minutes?

                    JACKSON
          Shhhh. Starla's up.

The audience CLAPS.

                    ANNOUNCER
          And now, Miss Austin, our own
          governor's daughter, Starla Creede
          twirling her fire batons to the Yellow
          Rose of Texas!

                    ROYAL
          That's my granddaughter! At least she
          picked a decent song.

                    JACKSON
          Heaven help us, here she goes.

Clem whacks him in the arm, and he mouths "Ow!"

Their eldest daughter, STARLA CREEDE, a stunning nineteen year-old who probably inspired all the dumb blond jokes, walks out onto the stage.

The MUSIC STARTS and Starla twirls two flaming batons. All goes well until she tosses them into the air and spins around to catch them: only one baton comes down, the other catches in the catwalk. The backstage curtains ignite.

Starla, in true pageant style, finishes her routine with one baton as a STAGE CREW HAND rushes above her on the catwalk to extinguish the fire. The foam snows down on her; she slips, but recovers by turning her slip into splits.

                    SAWYER
          Oh, that's gotta hurt.

Sawyer and Sutton burst out LAUGHING as Jackson buries his face in his hand. Clem APPLAUDS, shooting her kids a glare that says stop laughing. Jackson CLAPS weakly.

EXT. AUSTIN AUDITORIUM - A SHORT WHILE LATER THAT NIGHT

The family piles into the limo as Jackson hangs back, whispering to one of the PAGEANT JUDGES.

>   STARLA
>   I can't believe they gave it to that
>   bitch Patty.

>   ROYAL
>   You're still the most beautiful
>   contestant to us.
>   Sutton rolls her eyes as she climbs
>   into the car.

INT. LIMO - NIGHT

Starla sits across from the bimbo who sits next to Royal. Sawyer and Sutton sit on the other side of Starla.

>   REDHEAD
>   Your evening gown was amazing. It
>   really showed off your boobs.

Starla beams.

>   ROYAL
>   You should know about that, honey!

Royal and the Redhead LAUGH as he kisses her. Sutton whispers to her brother, Sawyer.

>   SUTTON
>   Okay, now I'm officially nauseous.

EXT. LIMO - NIGHT

Clem watches her husband who talks with one of the judges several yards away as the chauffeur opens her door -

>   JACKSON
>   I thought I gave your favorite charity
>   fifteen thousand good reasons why my
>   daughter should be crowned Miss Travis
>   County tonight?

>   JUDGE
>   I'm sorry, Governor, but I have to at
>   least give the appearance that these
>   things are legit. I couldn't very well
>   give her the crown after she nearly
>   burned down the place.

                              JACKSON
                 You owe me. Big.

A REPORTER catches sight of Jackson -

                              REPORTER
                 Governor Creede! Do you have any
                 comment on the investigation of your
                 mayoral race -

                              JACKSON
                          (to his security men)
                 - Get that reporter out of here.
                          (to the reporter)
                 This is my daughter's night. All I
                 have to say is that I am innocent, and
                 the evidence will prove that.

                              REPORTER
                 Governor, do you -

A SECURITY GUARD blocks the reporter. The pageant judge watches
Jackson go over to his wife who waits in the car with the door open
as the chauffeur puts away her wheelchair.

                              JACKSON
                 I'll see you later.

                              CLEMENTINE
                 Where are you going? It's nearly
                 midnight.

                              JACKSON
                 I have to take care of something. I'll
                 see you at home.

He kisses her on the cheek, and shuts the door. Worried, she stares
at him suspiciously as the car drives off -

EXT. POOR NEIGHBORHOOD ALONG EDGE OF CITY - NIGHT

A dump truck pulls into an empty field. Its headlights remain off as
the driver uses only the moonlight and the few streetlights to see
by. The truck dumps the load of dirt.

INT. MRS. GONZALES'S HOUSE - NIGHT

MRS. GONZALES, an elderly woman, peers suspiciously out her window
blinds. The many years of life have been indelibly etched into her
face. She talks on the phone -

                    MRS. GONZALES
          They're out here again! I've been
          calling for months, when are you people
          gonna come out and see about all this
          dirt?

EXT. CONSTRUCTION AREA ON OUTSKIRTS OF CITY - NIGHT

NASH FIELDS, 30, looks about the isolated area, becoming more
nervous. A car drives up. Its headlights go out. A man emerges
from the car, and starts walking towards him. Nash sees it's the
governor.

                    JACKSON
          And they say you writers have no balls.

                    NASH
          What do you want, Governor?

                    JACKSON
Your retraction in tomorrow's headlines.

                    NASH
          You used names off tombstones to win a
          political office.

                    JACKSON
          That's just a technicality. You have
          to look at the big picture.

                    NASH
          And that is?

                    JACKSON
          A bright, intelligent writer such as
          yourself, you could have anything you
          want.

                    NASH
          I have what I want. I have you by the
          balls.

Jackson LAUGHS, but steps intimidatingly closer to Nash -

                    JACKSON
          I can squash you like a bug. I have
          many powerful friends who want to make
          sure I stay governor. You see, my
          balls are fine; you just haven't
          realized it yet.

                    NASH
          What are you offering?

                    JACKSON
          For your retraction and hasty departure
          from this country, an all expense-paid
          trip to anywhere you want to go outside
          the United States. Free room and
          board. You could work on that novel
          you were always talking about.

                    NASH
          Europe would be nice.

                    JACKSON
          Fine. As long as you stay out of the
          country, keep your mouth shut, and of
          course, hand over all evidence you've
          collected in regard to this matter.

                    NASH
          How do you know I won't make copies of
          what I have?

                    JACKSON
          Because you're smart, Son. And you
          know it's more advantageous to have me
          as a friend than an enemy.

Nash debates, then offers his hand. They shake on it.

                    JACKSON (CONT'D)
          Oh, there is one more thing. I want to
          know who put you up to this?

Off Nash's hesitation -

FADE OUT

                    END OF ACT TWO

<u>ACT THREE</u>

FADE IN:

EXT. STREET INTERVIEWS - DAY

QUICK CUT the various interviews with PEOPLE ON THE STREET:

>   ELDERY WOMAN (V.O.)
>   My James would have voted for Governor
>   Creede whether he was dead or not. I
>   don't see what all the fuss was about.

>   YUPPIE MAN (V.O.)
>   I'm glad to know that our governor
>   didn't commit voter-fraud. I didn't
>   vote for Governor Creede, but I think
>   he's handled this scandal graciously,
>   and I will vote for him next year.

>   REPORTER(V.O.)
>   These reactions coming after the
>   retraction by Nash Fields, the
>   Governor's biographer, that the
>   allegations of voter-fraud were just a
>   publicity stunt for the biography.
>   While the DA's office says they are
>   still investigating, it appears most of
>   the records relevant to the case were
>   destroyed in the Flood of 1993. Polls
>   show that fifty-eight percent of voters
>   support the governor -

INT. ISABELLA'S OFFICE - DAY

Jace and Isabella watch the news on television.

>   ISABELLA
>   (sarcastically)
>   I see your plan worked brilliantly.

Jace kicks the television, SMASHING IT.

>   JACE
>   I can't believe this! Hell, he even
>   controls the weather. What's it take,
>   short of murder, to destroy those damn
>   Creede's?!

Jace glares at his wife. Off Isabella's thoughtful reaction -

INT. TEXAS RANGERS HEADQUARTERS - DAY

Monroe enters. Several RANGERS applaud her.

> TEXAS RANGER
> There's the woman who keeps our slogan
> alive - "One Ranger, One Riot."

> TEXAS RANGER #2
> Hey, don't mess with her. She's with
> the Tractor Brigade -

CHUCKLES scatter around the room.

> MONROE
> Ya'll should work on your comedy act
> before you take it on the road -

> CHIEF
> - Ranger Creede!

Monroe turns to see her CHIEF motioning her from his office. As she
passes a third Ranger, he whispers -

> TEXAS RANGER
> You're supposed to shoot the bad guys,
> not stop the good guys.

She gives him a piercing glance on her way into -

INT. TEXAS RANGERS HEADQUARTERS: CHIEF'S OFFICE - DAY

Her CHIEF, 53, sits back behind his desk scowling -

> CHIEF
> I guess you know the phones have been
> ringing off the hook since yesterday.
> Some folks want to give you a medal,
> and some, mostly those from the valley,
> want to hang you.

> MONROE
> I was just doing my job.

> CHIEF
> You're being transferred to the Cold
> Case Division -

                    MONROE
          - But I've only been a Ranger for eight
          months, Sir. I thought that division
          was for more seasoned officers?

                    CHIEF
          You'll be working on the I-90 murders.

                    MONROE
          Isn't that an ongoing investigation?

                    CHIEF
          Yes, but there's fifty-six cases. Half
          of which are over four years old.
          Specifically, you'll be working on the
          Lindsey Clark case.

                    MONROE
          Sir, I don't understand why I'm
          suddenly being promoted -

                    CHIEF
          - You don't?

She looks at him puzzled, what's with his attitude?

                    MONROE
          No, I don't.

                    CHIEF
          Well, then maybe you should ask your
          brother, the governor.

Monroe's face flushes red.

                    MONROE
          I don't want any special treatment. I
          can earn my own promotions -

                    CHIEF
          The governor wants you transferred to
          the Cold Case Division. You have a
          problem with that, Ranger Creede, take
          it up with your brother.

Monroe nods curtly before leaving and SLAMMING the door.

INT. GOVERNOR'S OFFICE - DAY

Ran, Darla, and Jackson watch the end of his press release-

                    JACKSON (V.O.)
          I want to thank the wonderful folks of
          this city and this state for standing
          by me through these ridiculous and
          fraudulent rumors. Truth is the
          backbone of justice, and justice was on
          my side.

Ran turns off the news as Jackson sits back on his couch, pleased
with himself.

                    JACKSON (CONT'D)
          Thank God, for Mother Nature.

                    RAN
          Don't get too cocky, this could come
          back to haunt us. You really believe
          Nash when he says he was working alone?

                    JACKSON
          No, but I've got a scapegoat for this
          whole mess if I ever need one. Always
          keep an ace up your sleeve.

                    RAN
          Well, just try and behave yourself from
          here on out. Next year's going to be a
          tough election. You can't afford any
          more scandals.

                    JACKSON
          I'll be a perfect gentleman and
          politician. Scout's honor.

He holds up the Boy Scout sign as Ran looks on doubtful. Jackson
starts out of the office -

                    JACKSON (CONT'D)
          Now, if you'll excuse me, I'm leaving
          early today.

                    RAN
                    (worried)
          Where you off to now?

                    JACKSON
          To enjoy a little R&R.

As Jackson exits the room -

                              RAN
                    Just don't forget that a Texas Monthly
                    photographer is going to be at the
                    barbecue tomorrow.

Ran hopes the governor's not going to get into more trouble.

EXT. POOR NEIGHBORHOOD - DAY

The houses look as worn and battered as their RESIDENTS. In a field
behind them, piles of dirt have been dumped. Mrs. Gonzales frowns
suspiciously as Lien scribbles notes.

                         MRS. GONZALES
                    It's about time you people came around.
                    I been calling for months.

                              LIEN
                    When did the dumping begin?

                         MRS. GONZALES
                    About October or so. They only come at
                    night, dump their stuff, then leave.

                              LIEN
                    And you've never seen any markings on
                    the truck, a license plate, a company
                    logo?

                         MRS. GONZALES
                    It's too dark. You tell me, who goes
                    dumping dirt in the middle of the
                    night?

                              LIEN
                    I don't know. I'll have to get back to
                    you on that one.

Lien walks into the vacant field as Mrs. Gonzales watches. Lien
kneels to scoop up a dirt sample, putting it in a baggy.

EXT. QUIET MIDDLE CLASS NEIGHBORHOOD - NIGHT

It's a summer night.

INT. UNCLE MAC'S HOME - NIGHT

Uncle Mac watches TV as Sawyer opens his uncle's refrigerator. It's
empty. Sawyer puts the groceries in it.

                    SAWYER
                (continuing the story)
            The stagehand was putting out the fire
            with that foam spray, and it was, like,
            snowing on Starla, and she slipped, but
            she covered well by turning it into the
            splits.

                    UNCLE MAC
            That must have been something to see.

                    SAWYER
            Yeah, you should have come, Uncle Mac.

Sawyer shuts the refrigerator.

                    UNCLE MAC
            You didn't have to bring all that. I
            was going to the store tomorrow.

Sawyer looks at his uncle and smiles.

                    SAWYER
            You want me to make something for
            supper?

                    UNCLE MAC
            I ordered from that Chinese place you
            like. They should be here.

McKinley peers out the window, but doesn't see anyone.

                    UNCLE MAC (CONT'D)
            Why don't you play something on that
            guitar of yours. Let me see what
            you're learning at that fancy
            university.

                    SAWYER
            Yeah? Okay. I've been working on that
            song you told me about.

Sawyer gets out his bass guitar, hooks it up to the amp, and starts
PLAYING A SIXTIES TUNE. The music's so loud they don't hear the
DOORBELL. Uncle Mac closes his eyes, transported back in time.

CLOSE ON: the glass doors as the CHINESE FOOD DELIVERY BOY brushes
aside the shrubbery to knock on the glass -

                                                              SMASH CUT TO:

EXT. VIETNAM - NIGHT (FLASHBACK)

A young, 18 year old McKinley, clenches his Marine infantry rifle as
a patrol of VIET CONG appear almost magically from the woods -
Someone YELLS and bullets roar past, lighting up the night like an
infestation of fireflies.

                                                              SMASH CUT TO:

INT. UNCLE MAC'S HOME - NIGHT

Mac dives to the floor, searching for a weapon as he knocks Sawyer
down -

                         UNCLE MAC
                Viet Cong!

As the Chinese delivery guy emerges from the leafy shrubs and bamboo
rods around the back porch to knock on the back door,

Sawyer looks up to realize -

                    CHINESE DELIVERY BOY
                No one answer front door -

                         UNCLE MAC
                - I'll kill you murdering sons-of-a-
                bitches -

The Chinese Delivery Boy jumps back as Mac lunges up at him with a
butter knife. Sawyer leaps on his uncle, knocking him off balance
and the two tumble back onto the floor -

                         SAWYER
                Uncle Mac! It's okay! It's just Wong
                from China Express.

                         UNCLE MAC
                We have to kill them -

                         SAWYER
                - No! He's not Viet Cong. Look at me,
                Uncle Mac! It's Sawyer. He's Chinese.
                You're home in Texas. You're safe.
                It's me, Sawyer.

Uncle Mac stares at his nephew confused and terrified as he gets a
grip on reality. He lets Sawyer take the butter knife. The Chinese
Delivery Boy throws down the food -

                    CHINESE DELIVERY BOY
          I no deliver here no more! He should
          be in looney house!

The Chinese Delivery Boy grabs the twenty off the table.

                    CHINESE DELIVERY BOY
                    (CONT'D)
          And I keeping change!

He exits as Mac sits up, leaning against his cabinet and trying to
stop shaking. He pops a pill, embarrassed.

                    SAWYER
          You okay?

                    UNCLE MAC
          Bet you wished you'd stayed at the
          dorm, huh?

                    SAWYER
          What, are you kidding? This is far
          superior to any dorm party.

                    UNCLE MAC
          You won't say anything to your dad,
          about this -

                    SAWYER
          - What's to tell? We just hung out and
          had some Chinese food.

                    UNCLE MAC
          I wish I had a son like you.

He looks at Sawyer who wishes his father could look at him with the
same acceptance his Uncle Mac does. Sawyer rises and offers a hand
to his uncle.

                    SAWYER
          Come on, let's eat, I'm starving.

They start opening the cartons of food.

                    UNCLE MAC
          Yeah, well, you better enjoy it. We
          won't be getting Moo Shu Pork from
          these guys again.

Off their grins -

EXT. LAKE TRAVIS RESORT - LATER THAT NIGHT

Moonlight glistens across Lake Travis. The resort is secluded in a grove of mesquite and pine trees. Rows of private cabins speckle the ridge. Lien hurries out of her car and rushes over to NICK, the cameraman.

                    LIEN
          Did I miss him go in?

                    NICK
          Only thing you've missed is being a
          midnight snack for mosquitoes. Think
          our insurance covers West Nile Virus?

Nick slaps at a mosquito.

                    LIEN
          Just be ready.

                    NICK
          You know, I'm beginning to get the
          feeling you have it in for the gov.

                    LIEN
          Shhhh. Here comes some headlights. Be
          sure to wait until he opens her door.
          We want to get them both.

A pickup with tinted windows pulls up. Lien can't see the woman, but sees Jackson get out of the driver's seat.

                    LIEN (CONT'D)
               (whispering)
          "Mr. Squeaky Clean" is about to be
          caught in a lover's nest. The voters
          can't forgive him for this.

                    NICK
          I knew it; it is personal.

Lien ignores him as she watches Jackson opening the lady's door. Suddenly, bright lights assault him as Nick turns on the camera lights. Lien steps from behind the shrubs -

                    LIEN
          Governor Jackson! Can you tell us who
          your lady companion is? Does your wife
          know about your affair -

Jackson spins around, caught. Off his fury -

FADE OUT

                    <u>END OF ACT THREE</u>

ACT FOUR

FADE IN:

EXT. RESORT CABIN - NIGHT

Jackson, blinded by the flashes, reacts furiously -

> JACKSON
> I swear you press are lower than snake
> spit!

> LIEN
> Governor, who's the woman?

Jackson throws his hands up as if being arrest.

> JACKSON
> Alright, you caught me red-handed.

He reaches in and lifts the woman into his arms, swinging her around
for the camera -

> JACKSON (CONT'D)
> I believe you've met my wife.

Jackson glares at them as Clementine tries not to laugh. The camera
lights fade -

> LIEN
> Sorry, Governor Jackson, we -

Jackson carries his wife towards the cabin in a huff as Lien stands
with the proverbial egg on her face.

INT. RESORT CABIN - NIGHT

Jackson kicks the door shut, then tosses his wife onto the bed,
falling beside her as she LAUGHS.

> CLEMENTINE
> - If you could have seen your face.

> JACKSON
> Can't a man sneak off with his wife for
> a lustful weekend without it having to
> make statewide news? Talk about
> performance anxiety…

Clem LAUGHS.

                    CLEMENTINE
          I don't think it's going to be a
          problem, Governor.

She kisses him and he nestles closer, but then falls back as he
stares up at the ceiling.

                    JACKSON
          I bet that dinosaur, Lenore, told them
          about this -

                    CLEMENTINE
          - Jackson.

                    JACKSON
          What? Oh, sorry, where was I?

He slides on top of her, giving her a long, passionate kiss. She
doesn't respond and he looks at her - what is it? A beat.

                    CLEMENTINE
          Maybe you should be sneaking off with
          someone who isn't crippled.

He stares down at her. She explores his eyes -

                    JACKSON
          I told you, last night was state
          business. The vows say for better or
          worse. And if this is the worst, then
          I'm a very fortunate man.

They exchange a smile, decades of shared joy and sorrow in their
expressions. Off their passionate and tender kiss -

                                        DISSOLVE TO:

EXT. FAMILY RANCH - AFTERNOON

A beautiful ranch happily situated in the Texas Hill Country. A
rustic mansion stands formidable in the center of the land. Picnic
tables take shelter under mesquite trees and catering tents dot the
lawn. Cattle graze along the slopes.

Around the grand pool shaped, like a boot, GUESTS mingle. Wearing a
very sexy bikini, Isabella stretches in a lounge chair looking over
to Jackson who walks across the deck.

                    ISABELLA
          I'll take that beer.

Jackson steps over to her, and can't help but notice her curvaceous
figure as he stares down upon her.

                    JACKSON
          Isabella. Since when do you drink
          beer? I'll get you a glass of wine.

She grabs his arm, and runs her finger down his arm.

                    ISABELLA
          I just wanted you to see a little
          preview of what you're missing. In
          case you've forgotten.

                    JACKSON
          Now, what would your husband say if he
          heard you talking like that?

                    ISABELLA
          Probably the same thing your wife would
          say.

Isabella glances behind him where Clem rolls across the patio,
shooting Jackson a warning glance.

                    JACKSON
          You just love getting me in trouble,
          don't you?

Isabella brushes against him as she rises from the chair.

                    ISABELLA
          Oh, I don't think we've even explored
          trouble yet.

Her seductive smile holds his attention a moment longer before he
hands her the beer and walks away.

Isabella stares after him as her husband joins her, sipping a cold
beer. He follows her gaze, watching across the lawn at Jackson in
his element.

                    ISABELLA (CONT'D)
          Smile, mi amorcito, your green-eyes are
          showing.

                    JACE
          Not half as much as yours. You might
          as well give him up. He'll never leave
          her now that she's in that chair.

                    ISABELLA
          I don't accept defeat as easily as you
          do.

                    JACE
          Don't you ever get tired, Isabella, of
          wanting what you can't have?

                    ISABELLA
          You forget I've already had him.

Jace pushes his wife into the pool and takes another sip. Isabella
pops up from the water, fuming at her husband.

                    JACE
          You looked a little too hot, mi amor.
          Why don't you stay in the pool and cool
          off.

Jace walks off as Isabella angrily tosses her hair back. She starts
out of the pool, nowhere near being cooled off.

CAMERA PANS TO Jackson who hands his wife a plate of ribs.

                    CLEMENTINE
          So what were you talking about so
          cozily with Isabella?

                    JACKSON
          Talking with Isabella is never cozy.
          She's about as cuddly as a porcupine.
                    (kissing her passionately)
          She's not even in your league, darlin'.

On another part of the lawn, Starla twirls a fire baton, entertaining
her grandfather. Attached to his arm, is the redheaded bimbo who is
dressed to reveal her assets. Sawyer stands near them.

                    CLEMENTINE
          Go say hello to your son.

                    JACKSON
          He can come say hello to me.

She gives him a look -

                    JACKSON (CONT'D)
          Alright, I'll go wish him a happy life
          as a rock star.

Jackson wanders over to his son, offering him a soda. Sawyer looks
at his dad cautiously, but takes it. A long beat.

                    SAWYER
          So I'm glad they cleared you of that
          thing.

                    JACKSON
          Yeah, me too.

Jackson smiles at his son, but then notices Sawyer's wearing an
earring. He taps his son's ear.

                    JACKSON (CONT'D)
          What's with the earring? Don't tell me
          you're becoming like cousin Bo?

                    SAWYER
          Dad, wearing an earring doesn't mean
          you're gay. It's just part of my image
          with the band. It's hip.

                    JACKSON
               (a beat)
          Have you spoken with your Uncle Mac
          lately?

                    SAWYER
          Yeah, I saw him last night. He was
          fine.

                    JACKSON
          He's on some tear about the bats, so
          watch out. Did you make sure he had
          some food in the refrigerator?

Sawyer nods as they sip their drinks.

In another part of the lawn, Monroe scans the CROWD for her brother.
She spots him, but before she can reach her brother, her attention's
diverted -

                    TOMAS
          Ranger Creede!

Monroe turns to see the handsome Latino calling her name.

                    TOMAS (CONT'D)
          I'm Tomas Valle. With the DA's Office.
          I hear we're going to be working
          closely together - on the Lindsey Clark
          case.

                    MONROE
          Oh, yes. Hello.
          Monroe stares over at her older
          brother, Jackson. He catches her
          glance and grins as he waves.

                    MONROE (CONT'D)
          I'm sorry…Tomas, is it? If you'll
          excuse me for a minute -

Monroe storms across the lawn towards Jackson.

                    SAWYER
          Aunt Monroe doesn't look too happy.

                    JACKSON
          Son, would you go make sure the ribs
          aren't burning.

Sawyer SIGHS, and goes over towards the grill -

                    MONROE
          - Jackson Andrew Creede!

                    JACKSON
          Now before you go and get all pissy on
          me -

                    MONROE
          - How dare you use your influence to
          orchestrate my life. If I want to be
          on the Cold Case Division, I can get
          there on my own merit -

                    JACKSON
          - I know you can.

                    MONROE
          I am not some puppet you can play
          with -

                    JACKSON
          - This isn't about you, Monroe. If
          you'll just give me a moment to
          explain.

She shuts up, staring at him expectantly. His explanation better be
good.

                    JACKSON (CONT'D)
          Lindsey Clark's mother came to see me
          yesterday. Her daughter would have
          been Rylee's age.

Monroe's anger begins to subside as she glances over to where her
daughter hangs out by the pool.

                    JACKSON (CONT'D)
          We've found enough of these missing
          girls along I-90 to know what's
          happened to her. For six years, Joanne
          Clark's waited to bury her daughter. I
          promised her we'd find her daughter. I
          need someone I know can keep my
          promise. I need the best.

                    MONROE
          You almost had me.

                    JACKSON
          "The best" bit, overdo it?

                    MONROE
          Just a tad.

                    JACKSON
          I'm serious, little sister. I need you
          on this one.

His sincerity touches her and she relents.

                    MONROE
          Alright, but no more meddling in my
          affairs.

                    JACKSON
          I didn't know you had any affairs to
          meddle in. What have you been keeping
          from me, sister dear?

Monroe LAUGHS, and Jackson knows he's been forgiven.

CADEN YOUNG, better known as CADE, 22, emerges from around the ranch house, looking very handsome in his naval uniform.

Cade walks across the patio by the pool where his cousins, RYLEE and Sutton, now hang out with a couple of their sophomore FRIENDS.

> CADE
> Hey, keep it down. Some of the guests
> are already working on a hangover.

RYLEE, 15, a cheerleader and responsible teen, SQUEALS with delight and rushes out of the pool. She epitomizes the girl-next-door. She hugs her cousin, getting his uniform soaked.

> RYLEE
> Cade!

> CADE
> Careful, you're soaking the uniform.

He hugs her back before pushing her away slightly to notice -

> CADE (CONT'D)
> Wow. I see we've grown up over the
> last year.

Rylee blushes, punching him in the arm as Sutton grabs a towel and goes to join them -

> SUTTON
> Hi, cousin!

> CADE
> Hey, Sutton. You two just get prettier
> and prettier. I'm going to have to
> stay around just to make sure the boys
> behave themselves.

They LAUGH SHYLY.

> CADE (CONT'D)
> Where's your brother?

> SUTTON
> Skulking about somewhere. Look
> wherever dad isn't.

CAMERA PANS TO one of the catering tents where Monroe and Tomas topple food onto their plates. A C&W BAND SINGS in the background.

                    TOMAS
          - So you must have been named after the
          sexy and beautiful Marilyn Monroe.

She gives him a glance; he's not impressing her.

                    TOMAS (CONT'D)
          - Sorry, lame line, I know. It's a
          curse we Latino men have. We see a
          beautiful woman, and we can't help but
          pursue her. It's in our blood, to be
          lovers.

Monroe blushes. He offers her a small slice of watermelon, holding
it to her lips. She hesitates, then takes a bite. Its juice
dribbles down her chin, and she wipes it, smiling.

                    MONROE
          I was named after James Monroe, fifth
          president of the United States. My
          father named each of us after one of
          his favorite presidents.

Nearby, the Senator spots his daughter as if on cue, and holds up his
drink; he's completely smashed from the booze -

                    ROYAL
          There's my darlin' daughter! The Texas
          Ranger who single-handedly rescued our
          border. Remember, the Alamo!

The GUESTS nearby CLAP as the Redhead hangs on Royal's arm. Monroe
blushes.

                    ROYAL (CONT'D)
                  (slurring slightly)
          We can take those bastards this time!

                    MONROE
          If you'll excuse me, I think I better
          go wrangle my dad.

Tomas smiles, watching her go over to the senator as Jace walks past.
CAMERA FOLLOWS JACE who joins Jackson as he bastes a goat with BBQ
sauce as it roasts over a spit fire.

                    JACE
          Ironic isn't it? At the beginning of
          the week, it was your career in flames.
          Now, it's just one of your goats.

                    JACKSON
          Well, when I find out who was
          responsible for spreading such slander,
          I'll be roasting him too.

Jace smiles and Jackson becomes suspicious, but before he can
interrogate Jace, BO YOUNG, Jace's brother, hurries over. At 34, Bo
is a handsome gay guy who's always trying to find the next get-rich
scheme, a true idealistic dreamer.

                    BO
          Jackson! Have I got an investment for
          you.

                    JACKSON
          Not now, Bo.

                    BO
          I'm telling you, we'd make a fortune.
          We could put about a hundred ostriches
          here. You've got the land and the
          capital, I'd handle the daily business.

                    JACKSON
          I'm not turning my ranch into some bird
          farm. Now, your brother and I-

                    BO
          - But you can sell everything about
          them. Their feathers for pillows and
          fashion, their meat is low in
          cholesterol and get this, their poop is
          odorless.

Jackson just stares at his crazy cousin, not following -

                    BO (CONT'D)
          Odorless fertilizer - we'll make a
          fortune!

                    JACKSON
          I'm not investing in any fairy food or
          fairy fertilizer.

                    JACE
          Don't you call my brother a fairy!

                    BO
          Settle down, the photographer's here.

                JACKSON
      You made up those accusations and got
      Nash to do your dirty work!

                JACE
      You're the one who paid him to retract
      the truth!

Jackson slams his fist into Jace's jaw, and they go at it like two
dogs fighting over a bone. Bo leaps back, not wanting to get hit.

Behind them, LUCIANO YOUNG, 17, the quintessential All-American
athlete (Jace and Isabella's youngest son) tosses around the football
with Cade and Sawyer.

                SAWYER
      Well, there they go. One twenty
      minutes of togetherness. That's got to
      be a new family record.

                LUCIANO
      Who? Hey!

Luciano runs over to where his father fights, trying to pull his
uncle away from his dad as Sawyer and Cade watch.

                CADE
      I hear you got a music scholarship to
      the University of Texas. That's great.

                SAWYER
      Yeah, well, tell my dad. He thinks
      I've betrayed him.

                CADE
      Ah, he isn't so bad.

                SAWYER
      You can say that because he isn't your
      father.

                CADE
      Yeah, well, I'll trade you my mom for
      your dad any day.

They exchange a sympathetic grin.

                    SAWYER
          Come on, we better go help Luciano
          before he gets sidelined by one of our
          dads.

They hurry over as Clem wheels to the left to avoid collision as Jace
lunges at Jackson, knocking them both to the ground.

                    CLEMENTINE
          Jackson! Jace! Behave yourselves!

                    LUCIANO
          Dad, let go!

They roll around as Luciano tries to pull his father away. Monroe
also rushes into the melee -

                    MONROE
          Jackson Creede, Jace Young! Get up
          right now!

They do so, but continue to throw punches at one another, Luciano and
Cade dodge to avoid being hit as Sawyer jumps back too.

Monroe FIRES a gun, aiming over their heads. They stop fighting and
turn to look at her, stunned.

                    MONROE (CONT'D)
          It's time for the family photo.

The PORTRAIT PHOTOGRAPHER, who stands anxiously behind Monroe,
attempts a smile.

                    PHOTOGRAPHER
          Ah, yes, Governor, I'm with Texas
          Monthly? I was sent out here to get a
          portrait of the family. If I could
          just get a quick picture of the whole
          Creede clan, the Young family, too,
          then you can get back to your…barbecue.

Jackson plasters a smile on his face as he notices Sawyer standing
nearby with the football.

                    JACKSON
          Absolutely, we were just playing some
          touch football and things got a little
          heated, you know how it is.

Isabella pushes past her husband, whispering -

                    ISABELLA
          Be sure to stand on the photographer's
          left side so our names will be
          mentioned first.

Jace shoots his wife a look. Clem "accidentally" rams into Isabella
with her wheelchair, cutting her off from standing next to Jackson.
Clem smiles sweetly as she take her husband's arm.

                    CLEMENTINE
          Oh, excuse me, Isabella.

Isabella gives her a bitchy look as the group gathers for the photo.
Jackson playfully puts his arm around his cousin, Jace, but it's
really more a choke-hold.

                    JACKSON
                 (whispering)
          This isn't over.

                    JACE
          Damn right, it isn't.

Starla applies lip gloss, turning to her younger sister -

                    STARLA
          Sutton, do I have lipstick on my teeth?

                    SUTTON
          Did you apply lipstick to your teeth?

Sawyer CHUCKLES. Cade and Luciano stand next to Rylee and Monroe as
the senator stumbles slightly as he gets into the photograph with the
Redhead on his arm.

                    REDHEAD
          Oh, this is so exciting.

Jackson sees the money-chasing redhead next to his father -

                    JACKSON
          Honey, this is family portrait.

                    ROYAL
          Ah, hell, she's gonna be family soon
          enough, aren't ya, darlin'?
          The Redhead GIGGLES at the secret.
          The rest of the family looks stunned by
          the news - The photographer is ready -

                    ROYAL (CONT'D)
              Everybody say Creede!

The family forces their smiles. If a picture says a thousand words,
oh boy -

INT. SCIENCE LAB - DUSK

A LAB TECHNICIAN puts a slide under the microscope. Lien peers
through the scope -

                    LIEN
              What am I looking at?

                    LAB TECHNICIAN
              Mercury, PCB's, chlorides, arsenic -

She looks at him, excited - she's got a story -

                    LIEN
              - It's toxic?

                    LAB TECHNICIAN
              As a waste dump. Somebody's got a
              dirty, little secret.

EXT. FAMILY RANCH - THAT NIGHT

The BBQ is over. Jackson hands her a roll of bills. The DRIVER
waits, holding the door open. She's a little tipsy.

                    REDHEAD
              You heard what your daddy said, we're
              practically engaged -

                    JACKSON
              Not yet, honey. Here's some cash. I
              don't want you to see the senator
              again.

                    REDHEAD
                   (throws money at him)
              I don't want your money.

                    JACKSON
              Just my daddy's.

She slaps him, then almost loses her balance, being tipsy.

                    REDHEAD
          I'm going to marry your father, so get
          used to it.

She gets into the car, SLAMMING THE DOOR before the driver can shut
it. Jackson looks at the driver.

                    JACKSON
          Take care of her.

Jackson stares at them as they drive off.

INT. FAMILY RANCH BEDROOM - NIGHT

Royal struggles with putting his arm in his pajama top. Jackson goes
to help his dad.

                         ROYAL
              How can we take a family photo without
              McKinley? He should have been here…I
              should have never named your brother
              after a dead president.

                         JACKSON
              You named us all after dead presidents.

                         ROYAL
              I mean, one who was assassinated. It
              brought him bad luck.

His dad falls back against the pillow -

                         ROYAL (CONT'D)
              If that damn commie hadn't shot
              McKinley…

Royal drifts off, SNORING LOUDLY. Jackson shakes his head and closes
the door. He goes into the nursery.

INT. FAMILY RANCH: NURSERY - NIGHT

Jackson stares down at Scholar who looks up from the crib.

                    JACKSON
          Hi, little one. You couldn't sleep
          either, huh?

He picks up his baby boy.

                    JACKSON (CONT'D)
          Between you and me, you're the last
          hope of this bunch.

Scholar coos, melting Jackson's heart even more.

                    JACKSON (CONT'D)
          Your sister, Starla, nearly burnt down
          the Civic Center, and your other
          sister, Sutton, is bankrupting me with
          her charities. Then there's your
          brother, Sawyer, and that earring of
          his, and your uncle Jace, well, let's
          not even get started about him…

Scholar grins up at his father, seeming to understand every word.
The baby yawns.

                    JACKSON (CONT'D)
          You're ready for your bedtime story,
          aren't you?

Jackson sits down to rock his son.

                    JACKSON (CONT'D)
          Let's see, ah…Once upon a time, there
          was a beautiful princess …who was
          really a bimbo in disguise. The bimbo
          princess used her magical, silicon
          hooters to get her claws into your
          granddaddy Creede's fortune…

INT. FAMILY RANCH: MASTER BEDROOM - NIGHT

Clem sits in bed, listening to Jackson over the baby monitor. She
smiles.

                    JACKSON (V.O.)
               (on the monitor)
          …But the king was on to the sleazy
          princess. That's because he had
          married wisely, for the queen was the
          most amazing lady in all the land. She
          supported the king, and forgave him
          when he punched out the black knight
          named Jace…

Clem stands up and stretches her back. She walks over to the window,
revealing that she really can walk, and stares out into the night,
lost in thought. The moon shines brightly.

DISSOLVE TO:

EXT. WOODS IN THE HILL COUNTRY - NIGHT

CAMERA PANS DOWN FROM MOON to a river, following a leaf which floats downstream until it's blocked. CAMERA WIDENS TO reveal the body of the redhead. Her face is half in the water, but her gaze is that of cold horror. Off her lifeless stare -

To be continued…

FADE OUT

END OF ACT FOUR

Gardner's Guide to Television Scriptwriting: The Writer's Road Map

Index